"Elena Aguilar brings to *The PD Book* a wealth of know[ledge...]
delivering high-quality learning experiences for teache[rs... Educators]
who design and deliver PD will gain unique, interesting, and pertinent insights
from Aguilar's ideas, her research, and the tools she offers for making PD joyful,
meaningful and equitable."
    —Robert Ryshke, Executive Director of the Center for Teaching,
    Westminster School, Atlanta, GA

"Grounded in research on adult learning and drawing from many years of experience, Elena Aguilar and Lori Cohen take readers on a journey into creating
transformative professional development. They share strategies for building
community and creating spaces that are antiracist and welcoming for participants
of all backgrounds. Chapters show presenters how to engage emotions, effectively
counter resistance, and navigate power. This book is a must-have for new as well
as seasoned professional developers, invigorating all with the courage to provide
bold, motivating, and magical sessions."
    —Becki Cohn-Vargas, Ed.D. Author of *Identity Safe Classrooms,*
    Places to Belong and Learn

"Ever wonder how to craft the kind of PD that changes hearts, minds, and behaviors? Mystery solved. Elena and Lori provide us with the concrete knowledge,
tools, and skills to create inspirational PD that ultimately transforms schools."
    —Jenn David-Lang, Editor, THE MAIN IDEA

"In this book, Elena invites educators to level up their ability to humanize learning for adults. These are the key skills we need today if we are serious about
reimagining what teaching and learning look like for equity-minded coaches and
teacher-leaders who are in charge of professional learning."
    —Zaretta Hammond, teacher educator and author of *Culturally Responsive*
    Teaching and the Brain

"Today's students need their teachers to be engaged in professional learning that
helps these educators develop new relationships to learning and to each
other. Aguilar's latest book shares key guideposts, facilitation moves and reflective
questions that will help novice and experienced PD leaders alike to change how
educators are thinking and feeling about professional learning so that it truly
transforms their teaching."
    —Jill Harrison Berg, Ed.D. Author of *Uprooting Instructional Inequity:*
    The Power of Inquiry-Based Professional Learning

"Elena and Lori's approach to professional learning is truly transformational. The tools and insights transcend any sector and prepare readers to facilitate professional development that pushes leaders and learners further down path toward justice."
—Sherene Judeh, Chief Program Officer of Ampact

"Aguilar and Cohen have written the quintessential book on adult learning. With a keen eye to equity, *The PD Book* provides the perfect blend of anecdotes, tools, and practical guidance for anyone wishing to design and deliver transformative professional development in the education space.
—Ben Owens, Co-Founder of Open Way Learning

"Elena has created a refreshing blueprint for every leader who is striving to create a healthy and intentional learning organization. If you are a leader searching to create opportunities for deep connection and learning through PD, this book will take you on a transformative journey and push you to design PD that shifts thoughts, feelings, and behaviors of every human in your care. Elena and her team truly "pull the curtain back" on fostering environments for change—her work and her generosity are a true gift to leaders and PD practitioners."
—Shawna Wells, CEO of Wells Coaching and Consulting and B is for Black Brilliance

"In a time of professional alienation and teacher attrition, Elena Aguilar and Lori Cohen offer us a hopeful, liberating vision for professional learning. *The PD Book* sits at the intersection of theory and practice, modeling from start to finish the authors' assertion that 'storytelling is medicine.' The chapter on navigating power stands out as deeply relevant for the societal moment we find ourselves in. Leaders at all levels who are looking to transform compliance-based PD: get this book, highlight and dogear it, and in its pages, find a pathway to realizing the adult learning environment that you long for."
—Shane Safir, Author, Coach, Facilitator, Listening and Leading for Equity

The PD Book

The PD Book

7 Habits That Transform Professional Development

Elena Aguilar
Lori Cohen

JOSSEY-BASS™

A Wiley Brand

Published by John Wiley & Sons, Inc., Hoboken, New Jersey.
Published simultaneously in Canada.

For general information on our other products and services or for technical support, please contact our Customer Care Department within the United States at (800) 762-2974, outside the United States at (317) 572-3993 or fax (317) 572-4002.

Wiley also publishes its books in a variety of electronic formats. Some content that appears in print may not be available in electronic formats. For more information about Wiley products, visit our web site at www.wiley.com.

Library of Congress Cataloging-in-Publication Data:

Names: Aguilar, Elena, 1969- author. | Cohen, Lori,
  author.
Title: The PD book : 7 habits that transform professional development /
  Elena Aguilar, Lori Cohen.
Description: Hoboken, New Jersey : John Wiley & Sons, Inc., [2022] |
  Includes bibliographical references and index.
Identifiers: LCCN 2022008010 (print) | LCCN 2022008011 (ebook) | ISBN
  9781119843351 (paperback) | ISBN 9781119843375 (adobe pdf) | ISBN
  9781119843368 (epub)
Subjects: LCSH: Teaching—Vocational guidance. | Teaching—Practice.
Classification: LCC LB1775 .A395 2022 (print) | LCC LB1775 (ebook) | DDC
  371.102—dc23/eng/20220225
LC record available at https://lccn.loc.gov/2022008010
LC ebook record available at https://lccn.loc.gov/2022008011

Cover Art: © Shutterstock | Golden Wind
Cover design: Paul McCarthy

SKY10034430_051122

Tomorrow belongs to those of us who conceive of it as belonging to everyone;
who lend the best of ourselves to it, and with joy.
Audre Lorde

For every child, every day.
E.A.

To Amy and Buster: loves of my life.
To California Redwoods: my courage ancestors.
To my students: my reason for every word I wrote in this book.
L.C.

CONTENTS

ABOUT THE AUTHORS

Elena Aguilar is the author of *The Art of Coaching, The Art of Coaching Teams, Onward: Cultivating Emotional Resilience in Educators, The Onward Workbook, The Art of Coaching Workbook,* and *Coaching for Equity*. She was a longtime contributor to Edutopia and EdWeek and frequently publishes articles in Educational Leadership. Elena is the founder and president of Bright Morning Consulting, an educational consulting group that works to transform education. Bright Morning offers in-person and virtual workshops and online courses based on Elena's books. Elena is also a highly sought-after keynote speaker and hosts a podcast called the Bright Morning Podcast. You can learn more about Bright Morning at https://brightmorningteam.com.

Elena lives in Oakland, California, with her husband and son. She also writes fiction, essays, and memoirs. When she's not writing, coaching, or teaching, she enjoys being in nature, reading fiction, making art, and traveling abroad.

Lori Cohen is an educator, writer, artist, and coach. Lori has written articles and blogs for *English Journal*, EdWeek, the California Teacher Development Collaborative, and Bright Morning Consulting, and she was a contributing author of *The Art of Coaching Workbook* (2020). Through her coaching, consulting, and professional development design, Lori works to create the conditions for everyone to thrive. She currently works at Bright Morning Consulting as the Developer of People and Programs. She lives in Portland, Oregon, with her partner and her dog. When Lori isn't consulting, coaching, leading workshops, or writing, Lori is running through the gorgeous landscapes of the Pacific Northwest, drinking delicious coffee, or scoping out the latest restaurant.

ACKNOWLEDGMENTS

From Elena

So many people have launched me, keep me going, remind me of why I do what I do, and make what I do possible. What follows is a brief acknowledgment of some of those people.

My gratitude for Lori Cohen has grown exponentially since we first met. I would not have written this book without her—her contributions were vital, and this is a far stronger book on PD because of her coauthorship. But Lori is not only a gifted facilitator of learning, a masterful storyteller, and a brilliant thinker: Lori is also a generous friend who is very funny and very courageous. It was an honor to witness her growth and learning while writing this book.

I could not have written this book (or many of the previous ones) without Amy Fandrei and Caitlin Schwarzman. Amy is my editor at Jossey-Bass, and I cannot imagine a more responsive, encouraging editor. I'm also grateful for all the autonomy and creative freedom. Caitlin has provided meticulous feedback and editing on six of my books. Her work on this one was invaluable as she patiently supported me and Lori to meld our voices, stories, and styles, while also honoring our individuality.

I appreciate everyone who has attended a PD session with me and provided thoughtful feedback. I also thank those who have written reviews of my books or the podcast and who engage with me on social media. Those affirmations keep me going through long stretches of solitary writing.

I am endlessly grateful to my coaches. Liz Simons was my first coach role model, and I aspire to emulate her curiosity. Leslie Plettner set me on a most rewarding path. Eloiza Jorge coached me through the most challenging PD experience of my life. Elana Bell has ushered me into a new dimension of truth. Coaches need coaches, and I don't know where I'd be without the guidance of these women.

I am also grateful to the many people I've reached out to—for this book and previous ones—for an endorsement. Often under tight deadlines, these readers have provided meaningful reviews, and their encouragement means so much. I'm especially grateful to Zaretta Hammond, who has been a good friend and colleague for many years.

I work with an incredible group of people. I wouldn't be able to do a fraction of what I do as a writer, facilitator, podcaster, or leader without my Bright Morning team that currently includes LesLee Bickford, Lori Cohen, Rebecca Blackmer, Debbie Daly, Abby Butler, Jennifer Liu, Becky Barstein, Nick Cains, Maria Dyslin, Nita Creekmore, Jess Levasseur, and Jocelyn Fabello. These are wonderful, fun, kind, thoughtful human beings whose presence I truly enjoy.

My Kenyan dada, Carol Owala, is my co-dreamer, my favorite person to ask, "What if. . .?" and to imagine schools that serve every child, every day, in every corner of the world. As we take steps toward manifesting these dreams, I am endlessly excited by what we will create together.

Jeff, Larry and Louie, and Vyetty, Sharon, Barlin, and Dennis remind me of why I do what I do, which is not simply for the sake of justice and liberation, but for the potential of expansive love.

My aunt, Jeanne, and my father, Gilbert, have been cheering me on me since the day I was born. They are not educators, but they read everything I write, listen to my podcast, and do everything they can imagine to encourage me.

My son, Orion, has seen me through the publication of seven books. This translates into something like 7,000 bean and cheese tacos on the nights when I had no energy to cook. (Thank you, also, to the many people who delivered takeout when he couldn't eat another bean and cheese taco.) It's a cliché, but this isn't a book about motherhood, so I'll just say it: My son is my primary source of motivation and joy. Gratitude feels like only a hint of what I feel toward him.

My husband, Stacey Goodman, is my everything. He makes me possible. In the final week of preparing this manuscript, when I mentioned all that was on my plate, his response was, "Just let me know what I can do to help." His commitment to support me to be whomever I want and to do whatever I want has always been limitless.

Finally, I must acknowledge the nonhuman creatures who bring me tremendous joy every day. These include the hummingbirds who drink at the feeder outside of my office window, and my cats—Mango, Serena, and Clementine.

I am in awe of the love I receive from so many beings. To all of you: thank you.

From Lori

First and foremost, I'd like to acknowledge Elena Aguilar for bringing me on this life-changing journey. If someone told me several years ago that I would work with Elena Aguilar *and* eventually coauthor a book with her, I would have fallen out of my seat and told them to get out of town. A series of joyful "talk about our work" conversations soon morphed into a project and then into a book. Throughout the writing process, our collaboration nudged and nourished me. Elena's mentorship, guidance, partnership, and encouragement have transformed the way I coach, teach, write, and lead PD. I have grown exponentially and am fundamentally changed through working with Elena. My gratitude is as vast as the Pacific Ocean.

Caitlin Schwarzman, our editor, has been a gem and a necessity throughout the drafting stages. Her careful editing and reassurance allowed me to produce stronger and stronger work with each chapter draft. Caitlin's influence is on every page.

I am a firm believer that we never do anything alone, and this book was largely produced in community. I thank the lineage of mentors who created the conditions for me to lead adult learning: Jane Haladay, who inspired me to be a teacher; with wisdom, wit, and love, Jane taught me to be the best version of myself in classrooms—and in life. Kathy Dixon and Area 3 Writing Project Consultants at UC Davis taught me that "teachers teaching teachers" honors the dignity and expertise of adults; I cut my workshop teeth in those A3WP summer institutes. Janet McGarvey saw my leadership potential, sponsored me, and provided me a platform to lead workshops for California independent school educators. Lise Shelton fostered my ongoing growth and commitment to equity, designing optimal pathways that allowed me to coach and lead adults at our school.

There are not enough exclamation points to communicate my gratitude for my former and current Bright Morning teammates. My former teammates: Noelle Apostol Colin, Janet Baird, and Jessie Cordova buoyed me with intentionality, brilliance, and humor as I learned how to facilitate Bright Morning workshops. Helen Park Truong's reassuring words affirmed me; her incisive equity lens ensured everything I produced would best meet the needs of all workshop participants.

My current teammates: LesLee Bickford sparks my imagination and ignites my spirit; I credit her for green-lighting the approach to the *Artful Design and Facilitation* workshop, a series that inspired this book and brought me infinite joy. My teammate Rebecca "eagle eye" Blackmer is a careful reviewer, a heart-centered leader, a brilliant human, and a dear friend. I can't imagine this stage of my professional and personal journey without her. And my teammate Debbie Daly—the paragon of compassion—offers love and support that gives me solace.

I am grateful for the extended wolfpack who supported me throughout the drafting process—LesLee Bickford, Rebecca Blackmer, Elizabeth Denevi, Shoba Farrell, Juna Kim McDaid, Helen Park Truong, Lise Shelton, and Tamisha Williams—for having conversations that sparked my thinking, sharing provocative ideas and asking probing questions, reading chapter snippets and drafts, sending "car polos" and text threads and Bitmojis and notecards that said the exact right thing at the exact right moment, and being an inspiring crew of co-facilitators, co-conspirators, and co-creators of the world I want to inhabit.

I am also grateful for every co-facilitator, co-designer, and collaborative partner with whom I've worked. There are too many to name. I hope the pages in this book are reflective of what I learned with and from you.

Finally, I want to thank the loves of my life, Amy and Buster. Buster (whose age perplexes me) is my ride-or-die canine companion. Whether he's alive or not by the time this book is published, he's always going to be the adorable little creature who snores through all the PDs I lead. He teaches me acceptance and keeps me humble. Amy is my partner, my best friend, my favorite person, and my best cheerleader. She believes in a version of me that I strive to become daily. I cannot imagine writing this book without her support.

INTRODUCTION

On the final morning of a three-day retreat that Elena facilitated, she held time for questions. A participant raised her hand hesitantly. "It's okay if you don't want to answer this," she said. "Because maybe you can't reveal your secrets or maybe it's magic or something, but how did you know to put us with the others in our home groups? I love these people so much," she motioned to the three people at her table, "and I can't imagine a better grouping!"

Chatter filled the room as people said things like, "Me too! I love *my* group." Someone else said, "And I also love everyone else I've met in these days outside of my home group!" There was more chatter as participants concurred.

Elena smiled and observed the 60 educators who had convened for this residential professional development institute on emotional resilience in educators. They had traveled from across the United States to a retreat center in the mountains above Santa Cruz, California, for three nights and three-and-a-half days. A few participants came from the same organization, but most were strangers when they'd arrived. Knowing this, Elena had grouped them into "home groups" of four or five people.

On the first evening, after dinner, Elena asked them to spend two hours telling stories in home groups. They could sit around one of the outside fire pits or in the massive infinity hot tub that overlooked the redwoods, and they had a protocol to follow and storytelling prompts. That evening, Elena wandered around and observed these educators, who had met only six hours before, tell stories about heartbreak and life-changing decisions, about fears and hopes and dreams. She observed them listening to each other, affirming each other, and building community.

Throughout the retreat, home groups sat together for sessions, had delicious meals together and went on walks in the forest, and processed and practiced all the content. They also interacted with other participants in the retreat, but they spent a lot of time in their home groups.

The design of the retreat was complex, but the answer to the question "How did you know to put us together?" was simple.

"The truth is," Elena said, "your groupings were totally random. Sometimes I'm super intentional about creating groups—usually when I'm meeting with folks for multiple sessions, but in this case, I knew very little about you." Elena remembers feeling a little embarrassed revealing this—she had wanted to say, *oh, it was all so intentional! Every single thing!* But that wasn't the truth, and it wasn't what made the retreat so powerful.

We, the authors of this book, work for Bright Morning, an organization founded by Elena Aguilar, which brings transformative learning experiences to educators working to create equitable schools. In our workshops, we teach people the art of connecting to themselves, to each other, and to those in their communities. Sometimes the learners in our sessions are amazed by what we orchestrate and experience the facilitator as having access to magic. Obviously, we're not wizards, and because we aspire to teach others the strategies we use, we pull on the thick ropes of the stage curtains to reveal how we create powerful PD.

This entire book is an attempt to pull back the curtain all the way and share how we design and facilitate learning experiences. We want to tell you how to design and facilitate professional development that transforms how participants think, feel, and what they do—and sometimes feels magical.

We'll come back to Elena's workshop and hear how she pulled back the curtain for the benefit of the participants. But first, we want to usher you into this book by inviting you to recall a transformative learning experience that profoundly altered what you do, how you think, and how you feel. This could have been a cooking class, a communication seminar, a meditation course, a trip abroad, a lecture, or anything that felt like it opened up possibilities and potential.

Pause and remember that experience of transformative learning.

Visualize where you were and the people who were around you. Try to recall how you felt, maybe what you were thinking. Do you remember exploring new ideas and acquiring new skills? Can you recall the intellectual buzz of being challenged and stretched in a good way? Do you remember connecting meaningfully with someone else during the process? If you had a sense of your own growth at the time, did you feel satisfied or excited or hopeful? Think about how you've applied your learning and how doing so changed your life.

Now that you remember this experience, can you identify what made it so good? Perhaps you were pursuing interests and passions: Maybe you'd wanted to learn to play an instrument all your life and it felt good to finally begin learning. Maybe the experience provided you with skills you could use immediately. Or perhaps what made the experience so memorable were the other people—you made new friends or had profound conversations.

Sometimes powerful learning happens alone: Traveling abroad, reading books, and backpacking solo can be transformative. Often powerful learning happens with others, perhaps under the guidance of a mentor or teacher. In the positive learning experience that you just recalled, who was with you, and who guided you? How did other people contribute to your learning experience?

If you didn't recall a learning experience in which you had a teacher or guide, see if you can remember a time when someone facilitated a powerful learning experience for you. Reflect on these questions:

- How did your teacher make you feel?
- How did you know you could trust your teacher?
- What did they do to build community if you were in a group with others?

If you've had firsthand knowledge that transformative learning *is possible*, then recalling the physical, social, emotional, and intellectual memories of your own experiences can be a source of energy and insight. Those memories can guide you toward a holistic vision for adult learning.

While we hope that you've had an opportunity to experience masterful facilitation, if you haven't, we know that you can still become a transformative facilitator because we've guided thousands of educators toward that end. You'll need to draw on other kinds of positive learning moments—from when you were a kid to recent forays into developing a hobby or learning within your professional field. Your bank of memories might contain only fragments of transformative PD (perhaps you experienced a dynamic speaker or an engaging activity or a beautiful setting), but you can piece together the elements of transformative PD. And we're going to tell you so many stories in this book that you'll be able to round out your imagination with visions of what could be possible.

"I've learned that people will forget what you said, people will forget what you did, but people will never forget how you made them feel."

—Maya Angelou

A Couple Notes on Anonymity and Terminology

When we use the term *we*, we mean both Lori and Elena, unless we're explicitly referencing a larger group or we identify others we're including. When we tell stories and write about other people, we change their names and other markers that might reveal their identities. Also know that we use the traditional pronouns *he* and *she*, and in recognition of nonbinary gender identification, we also use *they*.

Pulling Back the Curtain

When Elena revealed the truth behind the random groupings at the workshop, some people looked disappointed. "However," she quickly added, "I think this is a question about how to get a bunch of strangers to connect quickly and deeply around what really matters." Heads started nodding. "You're asking about how I created *the conditions for learning*, the conditions in which each of you could show up fully. What created the conditions for learning that would have allowed you to develop a deep connection with anyone here—because it was about the conditions that I created for you as individuals and for all of you as a group." A lot of heads were nodding at this point.

"Yes! So how did you do that?" someone asked.

The participants in Elena's workshop fell silent. What they all wanted to know was how the magic happened. Elena hesitated. Rather than giving them the answers, she wanted participants to identify the critical moves. Doing so would help them become stronger facilitators. "Well," she said, smiling, "what did you observe me do to create the conditions for learning and deep connection?" Elena invited silent reflection and then provided time for participants to discuss their reflections with their home groups.

As Elena and participants pulled back the curtain together, the participants were able to identify many of the design and facilitation moves. They could see that what had happened wasn't magic. They could see how they could replicate what Elena had done back in their schools and organizations.

What they'd noticed, and what Elena expanded on, were the following design and facilitation moves:

- Elena made the *why* and the *what* for the institute explicit, over and over and over, in many places. Starting with the registration process, she went overboard in explaining the purpose for the learning experience and what would happen hour by hour. She emphasized the time for reflection and processing with others, and the immersive nature of the experience, and she provided a lengthy list of objectives and intended outcomes.
- Elena made expectations for the retreat very clear in the description, in emails and video messages from her that participants received before it started, and, finally, on the first day in person. For example, in the description of the institute, she wrote, "Participants must commit to being present during the entire institute: Your presence is expected from the first to the last minute. If you are not able to make the entire retreat, please do not register." She also stated (over and over) that cell phones could be used during breaks and before and after our sessions, but that otherwise they would need to be off and out of sight. She also explained that she was making this request for the sake of the community that would be built. These expectations helped to describe the *how* of the institute.
- Elena built buy-in to these outcomes and expectations on the first day. She engaged participants in activities around hopes and fears for the institute, community agreements, and how everyone could show up as their best selves. She guided folks toward making authentic connections to the objectives. She clarified that her role was to provide learning structures and facilitate processes, but that everyone shared collective responsibility for what happened.
- Elena paid attention to every little detail. She had thought through timing and learning sequence and snacks. She'd considered materials and music, the comfort of the seats, and the pros and cons of air conditioning versus open windows. She'd planned activities to meet the needs of introverts and extroverts and to play to different learning intelligences, and she'd planned how to best explain each activity and how to transition between them. And there was so much more. Her facilitator's agenda was 28 pages long—an indication of the level of detail in her preparation.
- Elena was flexible and responsive to requests. She made adjustments to the schedule based on feedback. When she observed that an activity needed more time, she had a set of criteria with which to make quick decisions.

- Elena gave participants many choice points. For example, she said, "During this 90-minute block, you can pick from four activities." After explaining the options, she gave participants a chance to make thoughtful decisions and communicated confidence in the choice they made.
- Elena modeled vulnerability, risk taking, and transparency. She shared her own emotions, including her enthusiasm for the community that she saw developing and the learning that was happening. She also modeled setting boundaries. For example, after one long afternoon, she said, "I'm feeling a little drained, which isn't a surprise given that I'm super introverted, so I'm going to take a walk alone and recharge. I'll see you all later!" This gave participants permission to take care of themselves, to share their emotions, and to take risks.

After Elena pulled back the curtain, participants recognized that they could have been in any configuration of a home group and they likely would have cultivated deep, authentic connections. The magic was not in the groupings, but in the design and facilitation of the learning experience and in the conditions that were created for the retreat.

Having peeked behind the curtain, participants also recognized that they could use the same tools and strategies that Elena had used to create transformative learning experiences for the folks they supported. Elena wanted them to be able to create for others what she'd given them—and in the feedback she's received in the years since this retreat happened, she knows that many of them have done so.

We can't wait to share our philosophy, habits, tips, and tricks for creating transformative professional development sessions like the one Elena facilitated. But we're going to take this step-by-step, and the next step is to ensure that we're aligned on some terminology, specifically on what we mean when we say *professional development*, a term that's used so broadly as to be almost meaningless. This book is called *The PD Book*, but what exactly is "professional development"?

Defining Professional Development

There have been far too many times when we have observed something that was called professional development, but we've thought, *this is not PD. There's no learning going on in this room. The facilitator just wants participants to nod and accept his opinions and do what he says.* When we have found ourselves in a faculty room or a conference hall watching educators grade papers in their laps during a professional development, we feel deflated. There's no learning going on in the room, and we can't blame the participants.

The term *professional development* (PD) can be used to mean a lot of different things from this kind of mindless training to sessions with the HR team about insurance options. Before you continue, take a moment to think about how you define *professional development*, how it's defined where you work, and, perhaps, what you wish PD meant.

The Definition

Let's start with naming the obvious elements of PD: It's a way that you continue developing your knowledge and abilities after you've met the baseline requirements for a position.

Many professions have expectations around ongoing development. You may need to renew a license or certificate in order to continue practicing in your field or you may need to develop additional skill sets to be promoted. In many organizations, there's also an assumption that the baseline may change: Although you're qualified when you're hired, you'll face new challenges and will need to continue developing skills. Whether you're in education or medicine or insurance law, we can count on the fact that changes in policy or demographics, advances in research and knowledge, or a shift in an organization's commitment will require continued learning. In schools, continued learning is required when a region experiences an influx of immigrants and teachers need to learn how to teach English learners, when new findings on the neuroscience of learning require that teachers acquire additional skills for teaching math, or when a school board adopts a resolution to create equitable schools.

We may also need to engage in professional development to refine a particular skill set. For example, the skills needed by positional leaders are extensive—whether they lead a school or a nonprofit. Even after leaders complete an administrative credential or get an MBA, they might need to further develop communication skills, emotional intelligence, or the ability to work across lines of difference. No one is ever done with their learning, and when learning happens in the context of a profession, it's called PD.

Refining the Definition

Can you recall a PD session you attended in which you felt, during the session or by the end of it, that you had changed? That you had new insights into yourself, your students, or your situation? That you had acquired new skills?

Can you recall another PD session that you attended where perhaps you felt ambivalent about in the moment but later the ideas from that session percolated into your mind? Maybe those ideas prompted you to try something different at work?

Elena recalls a slew of PD experiences as a teacher that resulted in her growth and development: a district-wide August training for 300 third-grade teachers on a new math curriculum during which she spent days exploring manipulatives and being a "student" as a master teacher demonstrated the lessons; a series of arts integration PD sessions in which Elena was given time to plan lessons and get feedback on how she had incorporated the arts; a two-year teacher inquiry project in which Elena did action research in her classroom. Each of these learning experiences changed, and improved, what Elena did as a teacher.

In contrast, Elena also remembers other so-called PD sessions that she was asked to attend, from which she walked away mumbling something like, "a total waste of time."

We've all attended meetings that were called PD in which the facilitator clicked through a massive slide deck, shared too much background, disconnected data, and a few dictionary definitions, and gave mandates. We may have taken in the information and complied with the mandates, but there was no learning going on inside of us. Perhaps it appeared that our behavior changed—we did what we were told. But we did so out of compliance and fear of repercussions, not because we'd learned and grown. Those meetings, therefore, were not professional development.

Let's stop using the term PD when what happens doesn't involve learning.

PD Structures

Identifying the structures in which PD happens helps us home in on an understanding of PD. In schools, PD typically happens in the twice-a-month all-staff PD meetings or on a Wednesday afternoon or during the two intensive days in August before school starts when the district convenes teachers for training on a new initiative. PD can also take other forms: When teachers who are part of a professional learning community (PLC) undertake an inquiry project together, that's PD. Instructional Rounds can also be PD. Individual and team coaching is PD. And PD can also take place via an online course, at a conference, or through a book study.

While any of these structures—and there are many more—can house PD, we don't know whether true PD is happening until we consider *development*. And here we get at the core of our definition of *PD*: The goal of PD is to change practice.

The Goal of PD

Professional development is defined by its impact. PD is successful if, after the learning experience, the learner can do something else, or do something different. PD isn't PD if the learner doesn't change, if the learner doesn't *learn*. Sometimes this learning is evident in the PD session itself, and sometimes the learning isn't evident until a later date, but it's the learning that defines PD.

Transformative impact is the result of a shift in behaviors and beliefs. Every action we take emerges from a belief. New behaviors—new changes in practice— come from new beliefs. New behaviors can generate new beliefs, and new beliefs can generate new behaviors. We'll explore this more in the next section.

Transformative Professional Development

This book's premise is that all PD can and must be transformative. To understand what transformative PD is, let's start with its opposite: transactional PD. PD that is transactional is characterized by the following:

- Learners are seen as passive subjects who need to be filled with knowledge that they are lacking.
- An expert on the stage transmits knowledge to learners.
- The emphasis of the learning is on acquiring new knowledge.
- The unspoken goal of the training is to ensure compliant behavior from the subjects.
- Rewards are often offered for acquiring knowledge and performing desired behavior; veiled threats may be suggested for not doing so.

If you've ever attended a sit-and-get training, you've experienced transactional PD. If you've felt like PD sessions were packed and you didn't have a moment to think and you were a little nervous about whether you were doing the right thing and whether the presenter would call you out and embarrass you, you may have been in a transactional PD session. If you've attended a PD session where you knew there were right and wrong answers, you were likely in a transactional PD session.

So, what makes PD transformative? To answer that, we need to begin with defining *transformation*. On an individual level, transformation occurs in the domains of "the Three Bs"—in a person's behaviors, beliefs, and ways of being (Aguilar, 2013). Transformation is not just about doing something different, but also about unpacking the mindsets connected to the actions.

Let's understand this by comparing two PD sessions on diverse representation in curriculum. In what we'll call Session A, teachers are presented with a slideshow and lecture explaining the research on "mirrors and windows" (Sims Bishop, 1990). (A mirror is a story that reflects your own culture and helps you build your identity; a window offers you a view into someone else's experience.) Subsequently, they are presented with a list of books that they must teach to diversify their curriculum.

In contrast, in what we'll call Session B on the same topic, teachers are guided through a reflection on their own identity experiences, they explore their beliefs about the need for students to read books that are mirrors and windows, and they have opportunities to discuss the emotions that arise when teaching books with characters whose identities they don't share. They might also review some of the research and listen to portions of books that could be adopted into the curriculum.

Which of these sessions could be transformative? In Session A, there's no learning going on. In Session B, there's the potential for learning.

Here's another example. At some point in their careers, many teachers attend PD on classroom management. When the PD consists of being told to do this and that, or *don't* do this or that, very little learning is happening. A transformative PD session on classroom management likely includes the following:

- An exploration of how to develop relationships with students and of the beliefs that teachers have about power, control, and respect
- Opportunities for teachers to practice using new strategies and to get feedback
- Time for teachers to recognize and acknowledge the stew of emotions that they experience in the profession
- A deconstruction of the beliefs the lie beneath traditional approaches to classroom management, and an opportunity to redefine *management*
- A chance for learners to make the connection between management strategies and their vision for themselves as teachers and people

Transformative PD—PD that changes behaviors, beliefs, and ways of being—is holistic and comprehensive. Too many PD providers focus exclusively on behavior change, and while ultimately facilitators of transformational PD aspire to see changes in practitioners' behaviors, we know that we must also address, explore, and change beliefs and ways of being. Behaviors will change permanently, and the outcome will be transformative only when we also reckon with our beliefs and ways of being.

In writing this book, we grappled with a choice: to label our approach to professional development *transformative professional development* or to write about *professional development* without the adjective *transformative*. Because we define PD as something that changes participants, we believe that the term PD should always refer to learning experiences that are transformative. And so, when we talk about PD, we mean *transformative* PD. That said, in this book, we'll often include the adjective *transformative* to remind you of our vision for PD.

In Table 0.1, you'll read a synopsis of our definition of professional development.

Table 0.1   What PD Is and Isn't

Professional development is. . .	Professional development isn't. . .
A transformative process in which learners are actively engaged and for which the aim is to explore and expand behaviors, beliefs, and ways of being; a learning process that results in a change of practice.	*A transactional process in which learners are passive subjects who are asked simply to change their behaviors.*
• A structure for learning. The purpose of PD is to help people change their practice through exploring their beliefs and ways of being. • Required for everyone because we all need to learn and grow. • A dynamic, holistic experience. Humans learn with and through our minds, hearts, and bodies. • A process to cultivate self-awareness and understanding, social awareness and understanding, community development, and individual and collective empowerment. • A vehicle for social transformation.	• A thinly veiled form of control. The goal of PD is not compliance. • An opportunity for massive amounts of information to be forced on someone. • A punishment for not performing well in a position. • An isolated experience, a one-time event. • A vehicle to maintain the status quo.

Creating the Conditions for Learning

When Elena pulled back the curtain for participants at the end of her three-day workshop, she revealed that much of the magic was in creating effective and inspiring "conditions for learning." In effect, this whole book is about creating the conditions for learning—for transformative learning. But what are "the conditions" in which learning happens?

Learning happens when:

- Learners understand the purpose for the learning they're involved in, and the purpose is clear, relevant, and meaningful. It's easy to see the benefits that will come from the learning.
- The social, emotional, cognitive, and physical needs of learners are met. This includes feeling that you can share your thoughts, that the teacher or facilitator has your best interests at heart, that you are being appropriately challenged, and that other learners will support and encourage you as you learn.
- The design for the learning experience is carefully, thoughtfully constructed and based on learner needs.
- Every last detail of the learning experience is anticipated and planned.
- Facilitators skillfully execute the learning plan and adapt, responding to learners when necessary.
- Facilitators are reflective, see themselves as learners, have a high degree of emotional intelligence and self-awareness, and can motivate people and inspire them to take risks and to stretch outside of their comfort zones.

These are the conditions for learning. We've taken these, and everything we know about designing and facilitating professional development, and categorized them into seven habits. To help you remember them, we've also come up with an acronym: PARTY. This stands for: Purpose, Audience, Routines, Technique, and You. We hope that Figure 0.1 will help you remember the core ideas and habits in this book.

The Seven Habits

Habits are behaviors that you enact so often that you internalize them and they become routine. For example, you probably brush your teeth every day without having to think about how to angle the toothbrush—you just do it. Once a behavior is a habit, it doesn't take as much cognitive, physical, or emotional energy as when you started.

Figure 0.1 How to Create Transformative PD: PARTY!

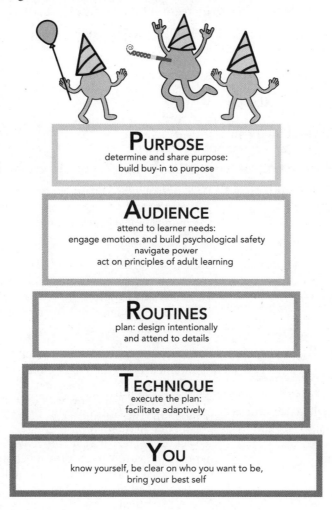

PURPOSE
determine and share purpose:
build buy-in to purpose

AUDIENCE
attend to learner needs:
engage emotions and build psychological safety
navigate power
act on principles of adult learning

ROUTINES
plan: design intentionally
and attend to details

TECHNIQUE
execute the plan:
facilitate adaptively

YOU
know yourself, be clear on who you want to be,
bring your best self

Many of the strategies we'll describe in this book might sound like they'd take a lot of time and energy—and they do at first. But if you practice them over and over, you'll eventually find yourself doing them with much less intentional labor than you needed at first. Once you reach a stage of mastery or what's also called *unconscious competence* (Broadwell, 1969), the habit will be ingrained—and possibly almost effortless.

But let's back up, because a habit emerges from a belief: You brush your teeth because you believe that dental hygiene is important and brushing will prolong the health of your teeth. Beneath every habit in this book are beliefs that uphold it. We will make those beliefs explicit to increase your investment in mastering the habits. Table 0.2 summarizes the habits and content of this book. You'll also see how the habit contributes to a condition for learning.

Table 0.2 The Seven Habits

Habit & Chapter	Condition for Learning	Description
Determine Purpose (1)	Purpose	Transformative PD emerges from purpose. We identify and create purpose, and then we communicate it to learners and build their buy-in.
Engage Emotions (2)	Audience	Human beings have emotions, and we engage our own emotions and those of others to create the conditions for learning. We respond to challenging emotions and create psychological safety for individuals and groups.
Navigate Power (3)	Audience	Power is always present, and when we're in hierarchical organizations, we must learn how to use it. We make choices about what kind of power we work from, how we use it, and how we respond to power struggles.
Anchor in Adult Learning Principles (4)		We act on the research about what adults need in order to learn. We can provide choice, honor agency, access prior learning, and make the learning relevant.
Design Intentionally (5)	Routines	We honor the backgrounds of participants, consider the *why* behind design, and are deliberate in determining outcomes, selecting activities, developing learning structures, and sequencing learning.
Attend to Details (6)		Attending to details makes learners feel welcome, affirmed, valued, and psychologically safe.
Facilitate Adaptively (7)	Technique	Developing self-awareness, emotional intelligence, cultural humility, and clear communication enables you to respond appropriately to whatever happens in a PD session.

You

You might notice that Purpose, Audience, Routines, and Technique each get their own chapter, but none of the habits explicitly addresses you, or the *Y* in the acronym PARTY. That's because who you are—your behaviors, beliefs, and ways of being—are addressed in every habit. Think of the *Y* as reminding us of you, of the importance of your presence and of what you bring to every aspect of transformative PD.

A Learning Organization: A Contextual Condition for PD

For PD to be transformative, it helps if an organization is committed to being a *learning organization*. In a learning organization, everyone is committed to their learning, everyone is expected to learn, and everyone learns. This value shows up in goals and priorities, in evaluations, and in the adult culture. Table 0.3 offers a description of a learning organization. As you read each indicator, note whether there's evidence in your organization of the indicator—maybe jot down "yes," "no," or "some" in the margin.

We include this here to acknowledge the organizational context in which you lead and facilitate PD. If you work in an organization that doesn't have any of these indicators of being a learning organization and you are committed to designing and delivering transformative PD, we want to acknowledge that it's going to be hard—not impossible, but hard. If this is the situation you're in, you'll need to address the larger organizational culture, while also implementing the strategies we're sharing with you.

Table 0.3 Indicators of a Learning Organization

Learning Environment	
Psychological safety	We can disagree with colleagues or supervisors, we can ask any kind of question, we can make mistakes, and we can express divergent opinions.
Appreciation of difference	Our discussions surface differences in ideas, and we have healthy disagreements about ideas.
Openness to new ideas	We are encouraged to take risks and try new things, and we do so.
Time for reflection	We take time to pause, thoughtfully reflect on our processes, and learn from our experiences.
Feedback	We get feedback on our work from multiple sources (including from colleagues and supervisors).
Purpose	We feel that our work matters to us personally and is connected to something bigger than us.

(Continued)

(Continued)

Learning Processes and Practices	
Orientation	Our learning is connected to and in support of the organization's core purpose.
Generation	We generate new learning together.
Interpretation	We make sense of our learning together.
Dissemination	We share what we learn with each other and outside of our group and organization.

Leadership	
Listening and questioning	Leaders prompt dialogue and debate.
Honoring process	Leaders ensure time for reflection, generation, interpretation, and dissemination.
Openness	Leaders are willing to entertain alternative points of view.
Modeling	Leaders make their learning visible and model the practices of a learner.

Source: Based on Garvin, Edmondson, and Gino (2008).

What If PD Could Be More Like a Party?

When you became a teacher, it's likely that you formed a vision for who you wanted to be based on two things: who you aspired to emulate, and who you didn't want to be like. This may have been a conscious process or an unconscious one. But often a vision is shaped by what we've experienced and by what we strive to replicate and what we want to reject.

When we began providing PD, we had thoughts like, *I want to welcome people into the room the way I once observed Mr. G,* and *I never want to talk down to teachers like Mrs. K did.* We identified behaviors and ways of being we wanted to replicate and ones we intended to reject.

We also thought about the overall feeling of PD. We'd been to many PD sessions that felt tedious and dreary; we wanted to create learning experiences that felt refreshing and gratifying. We wanted people to say, "That went by so fast!" And, "When is our next session?" We wanted to observe participants walking to their cars together afterward still talking about the content and laughing and exchanging contact information. We knew that if PD felt good, participants would be more likely to want to come, to show up eager to learn, and to take risks and ask questions, and ultimately, we knew that more learning would occur.

We're now going to present an extreme dichotomy: When characterizing the atmosphere of PD, on one end of the continuum, PD can feel like a punishment, like a prison. On the other end of the continuum, PD can feel like a festive gathering of friends. Most of us have probably attended a lot of PD that falls in the middle: It's fine, but immemorable. We wonder, *what if PD could feel more like a party?*

This question elevates one of our primary beliefs about what it takes to create transformative PD, which is that transformative PD occurs when the learning atmosphere feels very different than what we're typically accustomed to. When we suggest that PD could feel like a party, we're not actually imagining a large, loud, raucous gathering in which people have superficial conversations. We're referencing the aspects of a party that are universally appreciated: a sense of celebration, a clear and meaningful purpose for convening, the possibility of being with others whose company you appreciate, and perhaps also something that makes the gathering feel special—whether that is the food, the location, the decorations, or just the way you're made to feel like your presence is truly welcome.

Imagining PD as being like a party—or *more like* a party—has become a conceptual aspiration for us. Again, just to be clear: Neither of us would say we love parties; no one we know would describe us as "party people." But we love the possibility embedded in thinking about PD as being *like* a party. This metaphor evokes an energy that is a sharp contrast to what characterizes most learning spaces, and so it serves as a useful counterpoint to work toward.

If PD was more like a party, you'd see teachers sitting in small groups around a fire telling each other stories; you'd hear people expressing affection and appreciation for each other and wondering how they'd been matched up in the same group together. You'd also see people having hard conversations and challenging each other's thinking, and you might witness educators grappling with new ideas and skills. PD would still be purposeful and rigorous and structured. But the atmosphere would be lighter, more joyful, and characterized by meaningful connections between participants.

When we say, "What if PD could be like a party?" we're pointing toward the possibility of a gathering that feels very different from traditional PD, toward the social and emotional conditions needed for deep connection and learning. That said, we're also not opposed to the occasional costume, streamer, or rock-paper-scissors tournament. As we share the habits you can use to create transformative PD, we'll occasionally bring you back to this notion that PD could be something that feels fundamentally different from the typical PD experience, that perhaps PD could feel more like a party.

The Principles of Transformative PD

While we've got one big vision for transformative PD feeling more like a party, beneath the seven habits we outline in this book are a set of deeply held beliefs. We want to surface these, name them, and share them with you so that you know where we're coming from. As you read our principles, consider which ones resonate with you. The following are the Principles of Transformative PD:

- Humans are bursting with untapped resilience, strength, and abilities. We have an unfathomable capacity to change and transform, to grow and learn, to love and connect with others. Given the right conditions, we can unlock our potential.
- Teachers create the conditions in which transformative learning happens; we embrace this opportunity as our responsibility.
- Learning is a basic human need. Human beings want to develop and grow and fulfill our potential, and then we want to grow some more.
- Learning is a social process. Human beings are social creatures—we need each other to learn; we learn exponentially more when we're in healthy community than when we learn alone.
- Learning is the pathway to justice, healing, and liberation. For justice, healing and liberation to exist, there's a tremendous amount that needs to change. The only way for us to change is by learning. The only way for us to heal and repair our beautiful, broken world is by learning. If we can figure out how to learn and how to create spaces for others to learn, we can be free.
- Learning is transformative when the whole range of human emotions are experienced, including joy and love.

Who We Are and Who You Are

If we were physically in the same room, we'd engage you in activities to get to know each other. One of our favorites when we do workshops is to name a number of categories and ask folks to stand (if standing is accessible to them) if the category applies to them. For example, we'll say, "Stand if you come from a family of educators" or "stand if you love teaching middle schoolers" or "stand if you serve the community in which you were raised." This is a quick activity that gives folks a sense of who is in the room. Sometimes we insert a humorous category so that we can get people laughing and help them relax. We follow this activity by introducing ourselves as your facilitators. We'll do the same thing, now, in written form, of course.

Who We Are: The Authors

We are both life-long educators who share a deep commitment to *tikkun olam*, the Jewish concept of healing and transforming the world. We also both love words; we love reading and writing, drinking coffee, and eating cheese; and we're drawn to the redwoods and the Pacific Ocean. We can be shy and socially awkward but thrive in healthy communities, so we seek to create communities where each person is seen for who they truly are. We both still design and deliver PD almost every week.

Lori has worked in both public and independent schools since 1999, as a teacher, instructional coach, administrator, and facilitator. Early on in her career, Lori realized she had two great loves in education: teaching young people and teaching adults. She has had the good fortune to do both, bringing an infusion of humor and heart to every learning experience. Throughout Lori's leadership journey, equity has been a central lens through which she creates the conditions for transformational learning. Lori identifies as a Jewish, queer, white, cisgender, English-speaking woman. She was a first-generation college student who put herself through school; this experience informs Lori's big questions about equity and access, power, and privilege.

Elena became a teacher in 1994 and spent 19 years working in the Oakland, California, public schools, where she was a teacher, instructional coach, leadership coach, and administrator. Following the publication of her first book, *The Art of Coaching* (2013), Elena founded Bright Morning Consulting and began delivering professional development sessions across the United States and abroad. Her trainings are based on her model of Transformational Coaching and on her books on team development (*The Art of Coaching Teams*, 2016), resilience (*Onward*, 2018), and educational equity (*Coaching for Equity*, 2020). Elena is also the host of the Bright Morning Podcast where she models coaching conversations. Elena identifies as Latina and Jewish, as a cisgender, heterosexual woman, as a Spanish-bilingual immigrant, and with the lower socioeconomic status of her childhood. In addition, she is a mother. These identity experiences profoundly affect how she thinks about education, learning spaces, and community.

Lori joined the Bright Morning team in 2019 and contributed to *The Art of Coaching Workbook* (Aguilar, 2020). Writing this book together has been a tremendous learning experience. We're amazed by how we've grown individually, by the way our partnership has deepened, and by what two heads (and hearts) can create.

Who You Are: The Readers

We are assuming you are tasked with designing and delivering professional development in the education world. Although we're writing to you as "PD providers," we know readers of this book serve many different roles. Some of you might be instructional coaches responsible for delivering PD at your sites or across your district. Others might be site administrators, perhaps principals who (on top of everything else) lead PD. Perhaps some of you are external consultants who partner with schools and organizations and who have curriculum you've created that you want to share with others. We're guessing that many of you might be teacher leaders—perhaps a department chair or an Instructional Leadership Team member who has volunteered or been asked to provide PD. We hope that there are folks reading this book who are in roles with titles such as Director of Professional Development or Chief Academic Officer. Whatever role you serve in, we hope you'll learn strategies to create true cultures of learning.

Our assumption is that your roles and responsibilities beyond designing and delivering PD shape your work as a PD provider. As we describe the habits in this book, we'll explore the nuances of holding these different roles and the impact of positional authority on how you deliver PD. We also want to be mindful of how much time you have and how stretched you likely are. We recognize your commitment to delivering transformative PD, and we are aware of your capacity limits. Therefore, we'll often be direct and instructive about what matters most.

What Is in This Book?

If you were going to attend a PD session with us, we'd let you know before you showed up what to expect. We'd tell you what will happen and why, we'd tell you how the learning will happen, and we'd give you tips on how to get the most out of the learning experience. We might also assign pre-work so that you'd be primed for the learning. We hope you'll experience this book as a learning experience, so we want you to know what's in it—what you can anticipate, suggestions for how to read and use it, and what makes this book different from other books on PD.

Before you continue reading, we encourage you to pause for a moment and see if you can identify a few challenges you deal with when designing and delivering PD. Perhaps you don't know how to get everyone to participate. Or you design PD sessions but always run out of time. Or you often have grumbly participants who mutter, "Why do we have to do this?" Or folks engage in PD sessions, but

> **Tips and Tricks:**
>
> At the outset of a learning experience, ask learners to preview the agenda and identify what they're looking forward to. This allows them to find the portions that might be most relevant to them and therefore to cultivate positive anticipation. In addition, invite learners to share what they're looking forward to with each other. Often, these brief exchanges reveal that participants are looking forward to very different aspects of the agenda, which can help people buy into activities that they might not have been excited about.

when you visit their classrooms, they aren't incorporating any of what you taught them. What's hard for you about doing PD?

As you read the following pages, we encourage you to star or highlight the things you're excited to learn—to cultivate your own positive anticipation.

Seven Chapters, Seven Habits, and More

We hope you're getting excited about what's in this book. In each chapter, we'll dig into one of the habits and provide you explicit instruction on how to practice it. We'll also unpack the beliefs that underlie the habit, and we'll help you see how the larger context you're in might impact how you practice the habits.

In the process of exploring the seven habits, we include stories from our own work, both our successes and our challenges. We've both been designing and delivering PD for many years, and we share our journey with you so that you can see that we, too, have struggled and that we've changed. We hope you'll see yourself in our stories—in our struggles and our growth—and that you'll feel validated and be inspired to continue refining your facilitation skills.

Some features to anticipate:

- "Tips and Tricks" ideas that you can do immediately that can have outsized impact. You'll find these in boxes in each chapter.
- Mid-chapter opportunities called "Pause and Process" when the content is dense and we know you'll benefit from a midpoint reflection.
- End-of-chapter "Pause and Process" prompts to help you reflect on the whole chapter.
- A short list of key points to remember also at the end of the chapter.

How to Get the Most from This Book

The seven habits in this book build on each other, so we recommend that you read the chapters sequentially. You'll find that some chapters are heavier on theory and how to apply that theory. While we are committed to telling you *how* to do transformative PD, we also want you to know something about *why* what we're suggesting works—and so we'll dip quickly into adult learning theory, the neuroscience of learning, and research on emotional intelligence. We hope you'll note the balance between how we guide you through technical and adaptive habits.

Prior to March 2020, we hadn't done much virtual PD—all of the PD that we did at Bright Morning was in-person. As a result of the pandemic, we had to design and deliver virtual PD. We learned how to transfer our skills, acquire new ones, and create powerful learning experiences for hundreds of people at the same time on Zoom. We have come to appreciate the potential and opportunities in virtual PD and are excited to share our learnings with you. We hope that even if you don't do virtual PD, you'll find some ideas in these sections that you'll be able to apply.

What makes this book different from many others about PD is our commitment to equity. We are committed to dismantling systems of oppression and the way that they manifest in our culture, organizations, mindsets, and learning spaces. If you've read Elena's other books, you know that whether she's talking about team development, emotional resilience, or instructional coaching, she addresses race, class, and gender. You'll find the same attention to equity in this book: We'll expose how the ideology of white supremacy shows up in a PD session; we'll explore how values around efficiency push us to take on too much and undermine deep learning; and we'll consider the role of dominant culture in allocating authority. We'll show you how you can make decisions when you design and deliver PD that create equitable spaces. If learning about equity is new to you, we're excited to guide you through this first foray. We encourage you to stay open to the emotions that arise in you and to the content.

Finally, we hope you'll have an opportunity to read and discuss this book with others because we know that processing with others helps us learn. Check out the Bright Morning Book Clubs (https://brightmorningteam.com) if you're looking for guidance and other educators with whom to discuss this book.

We wrote this book to shift the PD paradigm. We aspire to guide you to see that your purpose as a PD provider is not simply to "deliver PD," but to create a community in which people can learn with and from each other. Are you ready for the nitty-gritty details, the explicit instruction, and the theory that upholds this model of transformative professional development? We're ready to pull back the curtain all the way and share everything we know and do with you so that you can join us at this PD party.

Before You Go

Pause and Process:
- How has your definition of *professional development* changed or expanded based on what you've read so far?
- Which Principles of Transformative PD (p. 18) resonate for you?
- Write or talk with a few colleagues about their positive learning experiences. What made those experiences good? What do they say makes for a transformative PD session?
- Return to your own transformative learning experience that you recalled at the beginning of the chapter. How has your understanding of that experience expanded or deepened based on what you've read in this chapter?
- In what ways do you imagine PD could be like a wonderful dinner party?

Remember:
- Transformative professional development is a process in which learners are actively engaged. The aim is to explore and expand behaviors, beliefs, and ways of being.
- Transformative PD changes practice.
- PD can change the world.
- PD can feel energizing, joyful, connecting, and even celebratory.

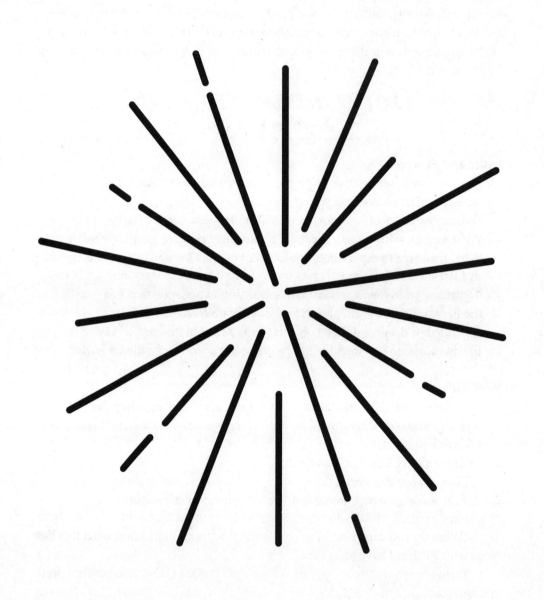

CHAPTER 1

Determine Purpose

At Curtis High School, Lori was about to lead her first workshop on Socratic Seminars, a student-centered approach to discussion. She was a newer teacher at the site, and this was her first time presenting to all the staff.

Before the session began, the school's principal, Dr. Deal, addressed staff in the dimly lit school library. "I know I normally lead professional development," she said, "but Lori Cohen is going to lead our session today. She came to my office last week after the College Success Conference and was *very* enthusiastic about this new method called Socratic Seminars. So I decided to let her share her learning with you." Before Dr. Deal could introduce Lori, a longtime math teacher, Dan, raised his hand.

"Isn't Lori an English teacher? What's the purpose of learning about this?"

"Yes, she teaches English, but she thinks Socratic Seminars might help any teacher. You can figure out how to adapt it." Dan looked at his math colleagues, one of whom shrugged. Marcus, the PE teacher, smirked and called across the library to Dan. "What do you care, Dan? You're retiring this year. I don't know what this has to do with PE, but I have to be here."

Trying to ignore the comments, Lori placed bowls of chocolate-covered pretzels and stacks of learning packets on each table. Dr. Deal continued, "Let's just see how this goes."

"At least we get snacks," Dan said. Laughter flickered across the room.

Undeterred, Lori flipped on the overhead projector, smiled, and shared an inspirational quote from one of her students who had recently participated in a Socratic Seminar. She didn't make explicit connections to other disciplines, but she talked about Socratic Seminars as a form of discussion that could be adapted to suit teachers' needs. Dr. Deal sat in the back of the library, filling out a grant application. She left halfway through the session, her walkie-talkie blaring a garbled message as she rushed out.

As Lori asked for volunteers for a mock demonstration, Dan raised his hand again. "Yeah, um, Lori, you seem really nice, and it's clear you put time into this presentation. I'm still hoping you can explain how this is relevant for over half the teachers in this room. It's midterms, and I have a lot of grading to do before the reporting period ends." Some teachers nodded their heads. Lori was silent, not sure how to respond.

Eileen, a respected history teacher and Lori's former mentor, interrupted. "Dan, I hear you. Those of us who have been here a long time have sat through a lot of PD that's had nothing to do with us. That's not Lori's fault." Dan nodded, but he was also thinking, *this too shall pass.*

Six volunteers (Eileen and Marcus included) participated in a brief Socratic Seminar. Dan ignored the demonstration and graded the stack of math quizzes he'd brought with him. Dr. Deal stepped back into the room with five minutes left in the session.

In the final minute, Dr. Deal thanked Lori for sharing her learning, and half the room clapped. Some teachers grabbed a final handful of pretzels and left their packets on the tables. A few told Lori, "Good job." Dan approached Dr. Deal on his way out of the room. "Lori did a nice job, but that PD served no purpose for me."

Dismantling PD Apathy

Recall a PD session you recently attended and reflect on the following questions:

- What was the session's purpose?
- How did the agenda and activities meet the PD's purpose?
- How did the facilitator make the learning matter for participants?
- What was the impact of the PD in relation to the purpose?

Getting Clear on Purpose

When the purpose of PD is clear, participants are more willing and eager to engage in learning and transformation becomes possible. When the purpose is not clear, participants become cynical and "this too shall pass" becomes the mantra. PD becomes a thing to endure, not something that helps people develop skills and knowledge.

In this book we ask, what if PD could be more like a party? What if PD could be a gathering for learning and growth? PD needs to be the primary vehicle through which adults acquire the tools, skills, strategies, and knowledge to ensure every child gets what they need every day to thrive. But if PD is thought of as an endurance test, it won't fulfill that potential. Our thoughts become our reality: To create a new mental model about PD, we must start by getting clear on purpose. Purpose is a key component of making more intentional systemic change, and it's the first step in transforming your PD.

This chapter offers a process for determining purpose. You'll begin by getting clear about the purpose of your PD and how that purpose might serve you beyond a single PD session. You will then explore how to use that purpose to develop outcomes and possible activities for your PD. You will learn how to make the learning matter by communicating purpose before, during, and after your PD. And you will receive guidance on how to assess the impact of your PD using multiple measures.

Throughout this chapter we're going to revisit the opening story, beginning with the moment when Lori walks into Dr. Deal's office, enthusiastic about leading PD on Socratic Seminars. We're going to imagine this story takes an alternate path, one where Dr. Deal says, "Lori, I love your enthusiasm. I think this is a great idea. But before we move forward and you present to staff, let's identify the *why* for this session. Let's make sure this PD can change teachers' practices and have an empowering impact on students." As we follow Lori and Dr. Deal's process, we'll see what might be possible for them—and you—when purpose drives PD.

Purpose: The Foundation for Transformational Learning

To get clear on purpose, we first ask w*hy*—not just once, but throughout the planning process. When the purpose is clear, everything flows from there—the planning process is more meaningful, and the time spent in the PD matters to participants more. When participants are clear on the purpose, they are more willing to learn and transfer that learning to their contexts.

Five Whys to Purpose

One structure that supports this clarity is an exercise called the Five Whys to Purpose, adapted from National School Reform Faculty. The Five Whys to Purpose helps you consider what's at the core of your PD. In systems thinking, this process is called *root-cause analysis*. This kind of analysis helps leaders and teams consider the root causes of systemic issues so they can respond strategically. The Five Whys to Purpose exercise guides you to articulate why your PD really matters. Here's how the exercise works:

1. Think of an upcoming PD session you're leading. Identify what you think the purpose for this session is and why this needs to be the purpose. Write down an initial purpose statement. Then answer the question "why?" underneath your purpose statement.
2. Complete this process four more times. Just let the ideas come without forcing your response. Doing this five times allows you to dig below the surface to uncover additional, and potentially deeper, purposes.
3. After the fifth *why*, review your responses and write your final purpose statement. You might find that your original purpose has changed and something more pressing has emerged. Or you might find that your *why* connects to something larger. A PD on Socratic Seminars, for example, may turn out to be less about a discussion protocol and more about student empowerment.

When participants in Bright Morning's *Artful Design and Facilitation* completed this exercise and shared their final purpose statements, many communicated amazement at where this exercise took them. One participant, Rosario, wanted to lead a PD on equity-focused conversations. Her initial purpose was "to provide tools for teachers to talk about sensitive topics." As she completed the exercise, she uncovered that the purpose was less about the tools themselves (though the tools are important) and more about "ensuring that our students feel seen and cared for so they can be affirmed at school." By the end of the quick exercise, most participants had jotted down purposes that spoke to larger systemic issues at their sites. Identifying these deeper purposes opened up more possibilities—and even imperatives—for educators to address in their PD.

The Five Whys in Practice

In the hypothetical scenario in which Lori and Dr. Deal work together to prepare for a PD around Socratic Seminars, Dr. Deal hands Lori a copy of the Five Whys exercise. After about 10 minutes, Lori produces the responses in Table 1.1.

Table 1.1   Sample Five Whys to Purpose—Socratic Seminars

What's the purpose of PD in Socratic Seminars?
To provide participants with a strong tool for student-centered discussions.

Why?
Because a lot of class discussions tend to be teacher-directed. Students come to rely on a teacher's wisdom rather than their own or their peers'. Also, Socratic Seminars invite dialogue over debate; in a Socratic Seminar students can consider their ideas and find their voices. They build courage to speak, they listen to one another carefully, and they select evidence that best supports their assertions as they build shared meaning.

Why?
Because right now in our classrooms, only some students' voices are privileged—those who talk the most, who are the quickest verbal processors, and often, who are male, white, and English-speaking. Not everyone's voices are heard.

Why?
Because our learning structures in school have been set up to support a narrow subset of students to succeed: Those students usually already have privilege or have assimilated into more privileged structures. This is inequitable at its core.

Why?
Because we haven't considered a different way of engaging our students in classrooms—particularly when power and privilege are the undercurrent of all we do.

Why?
Because we don't want to raise another generation of students who perpetuate an already inequitable status quo.

The purpose of your PD:
To reimagine classroom discussion as an opportunity for shared meaning-making and student empowerment. Class discussion can become a place in which dialogue is welcomed over debate and in which everyone can share their ideas.

Let's pause and consider Lori's final purpose statement for the Socratic Seminar PD:

To reimagine classroom discussion as an opportunity for shared meaning-making and student empowerment. Class discussion can become a place in which dialogue is welcomed over debate and in which everyone can share their ideas.

As you read this purpose statement, what do you imagine could happen in the PD session? What might be some ways to address this purpose?

This purpose statement opens possibilities for where this PD could go, beyond a presentation on Socratic Seminars. With this purpose in mind, Lori and Dr. Deal generate a list of approaches:

- Designing this PD so that all teachers can talk about student-centered discussion (with Socratic Seminars as a case study for one kind of model)
- Focusing on discussion-based classes first (history/social science, English) and perhaps split up the staff into subject-area groups
- Inviting additional teachers to lead PD on discourse structures that empower students and provide more options for teachers across content areas
- Talking about inequities in our classrooms, assessing what's currently happening and considering what we can do to reimagine what's possible

Lori and Dr. Deal choose the first bulleted idea on this list—how to make this PD a place where all teachers can talk about student-centered discussion—and decide to design PD based on that topic.

The Five Whys exercise isn't something you'll share with participants. It's something you (and your collaborative partners) do to create your own clarity. Doing an activity like the Five Whys can also catalyze conversation about systems-level change and the pathways to get there—and perhaps inspire possibilities that had not yet been considered.

In our hypothetical scenario, the Five Whys exercise allows Lori and Dr. Deal to get clarity on what the Socratic Seminar PD is ultimately about: shared meaning-making and empowering students. If "real life" Dr. Deal used this exercise at Curtis High School as a starting point for all PD, she and her leadership team might have gotten greater clarity about the purpose of PD; she might have collaborated with PD leaders like Lori and talked about how PD could lead to larger changes at their school site. Teachers might have experienced PD differently—not as a series of disconnected sessions or as a "this too shall pass" endurance test, but as an opportunity to transform teaching and learning to best meet the needs of their students.

While it's crucial to clarify the purpose of your PD session, the purpose is even more powerful when it aligns with your site or organization's mission and overarching PD goals. This kind of alignment allows the PD to feel less like an add-on and more integrated into the fabric of your site's approaches to PD. As you think about the purpose of your PD, align that purpose to your site/organization's mission and connect your purpose to your larger PD goals as well. Together, this alignment provides you with a clear guide for decision-making, clarifying, and sequencing your learning in ways that can best meet the needs of all those involved—most importantly, your students.

Purpose, Power, and Educational Equity

Determining purpose is a crucial first step in creating transformational PD. It is also important to consider the role of power as it relates to purpose. Who decides the purpose of PD? Who has a say in how purpose is decided? If purpose is decided by one sole PD provider, consider additional ways to get input from stakeholders or invite collaboration in the planning process.

When Lori became her school's Dean of Faculty, she went from being a classroom teacher and coach who collaborated with colleagues on all decision-making to the sole person overseeing all PD. She was excited for this role, but she didn't feel right about doing this work in isolation. As a teacher and coach, Lori knew collaboration and shared expertise yielded stronger outcomes for students, so she decided to bring a collaborative practice into her leadership. Each August, Lori met with senior staff and department leaders to identify the site's needs and the PD arc for the year ahead. They reviewed student experience surveys, student outcome data, and teacher performance data to identify areas to address in PD; they surveyed staff about topics they most wanted to learn about. Together, Lori and school leaders collectively determined the purpose of the year's PD. They created a calendar with topics for each month and shared this calendar with all staff. In collaboration, Lori was sharing her power *with* school stakeholders rather than power *over* (a concept we'll describe in greater detail in Chapter 3).

When Elena was a middle school humanities teacher and was preparing to teach a unit on slavery in the United States, she invited the parents and caretakers of her African American students to a planning meeting. She wanted their input into how this history would be taught to their children. As she developed unit plans, she shared those with this group of caregivers and asked for their feedback.

If you're a site leader, how might you design and lead PD with input from school stakeholders? If you are a sole provider, how might you connect with members of your professional community in this process? A single individual might be able to lead transformational learning; but systems transformation requires more of us to work in community to make changes that best support our students. We don't have to do this work alone.

Create Purposeful Plans

Purpose needs to be infused in everything you do. Once you've identified your purpose, then you're ready (and possibly eager) to map a plan of action: identifying your ideals, assessing your gaps, analyzing data, and understanding learning needs. This plan will allow you to generate meaningful outcomes and learning structures that align purpose with action.

Four Steps for Purposeful Planning: Outcomes, Gaps, Possibilities, Priorities

In our Bright Morning workshops, *The Art of Coaching Teams* and *Artful Design and Facilitation*, participants take their work on purpose and put it into action using the four steps outlined next. By the end of this process, they see how a strong purpose can guide their plans and how this practice offers a meaningful structure for designing and implementing professional development.

Step 1: Generate Ideal Outcomes. Once you identify the core purpose of your PD, it's time to generate some ideal outcomes: what you hope to achieve with your PD. Eventually, you may put these outcomes on your agenda, but at this stage, these outcomes are aspirations—all the things you hope to be true as a result of your PD. The following questions can help you envision your ideals.

As a result of this PD. . .

- What do you want PD recipients to know and do?
- What do you want PD recipients to say and feel?
- What outcomes do you hope to see for students?

Let's consider an example. Leanne, an assistant elementary school principal, designed a workshop for department leaders to give meaningful feedback to their colleagues. Her site had a culture of niceness, where department leaders often shied away from giving critical feedback to teachers to support their growth. After doing classroom observations alongside department chairs, Leanne noticed that department leaders would share critical feedback with her, but not with teachers directly. Leanne wondered if department leaders felt equipped with the tools to offer feedback. When generating ideal outcomes for her workshop, Leanne wanted to department leaders to understand some structures for giving feedback and to know the neuroscience behind feedback. She imagined staff would say things like, "I now have a couple good tools to help me process feedback," "my beliefs about feedback have changed," and "feedback is a gift that supports teacher growth and student learning." She wanted participants to feel prepared for their next feedback conversations. When she imagined these outcomes, she got excited about what was possible.

Step 2: Identify Gaps. After generating ideal outcomes, the next step is to identify gaps between where participants are and where they need to be for students. When we say gaps, we are referring to areas for learning and growth, not deficits. To identify gaps, it's helpful to consider what the data tells you. If you are an internal PD provider at your site, data sources may be more readily available to you. If you're an external provider, you may have to consider what data you need to collect. In this step, the following data sources and questions can support you:

- *Student performance data and experience surveys*: What do these data sources tell you about student outcomes?
- *Performance evaluations*: What do performance evaluations indicate in terms of what people need to know and what skills they need to develop?
- *Focus groups, conversations, and informal check-ins*: What have you learned from conversations (formal and informal) that indicates adult and student learning needs?
- *Surveys*: How will you gauge the knowledge or skill PD participants have in relation to this topic? If you're surveying adults, questions like these can be helpful to ask:
  - What do you already know or do in relation to this topic?
  - What do you hope to learn in relation to this topic?
  - What questions do you have about this topic?
  - What should the PD leaders/committee consider when designing learning around this topic?

After assessing learning needs, you can review outcomes and determine the following areas for growth:

- Participants' knowledge and skill gaps
- What people are currently saying and feeling about this topic
- What student data tells you

Sometimes the data will reveal that participants have several areas for learning and growth, and you may need to adjust your outcomes to meet the needs of participants. Or you might find you need to develop a sequence of PD sessions to address participants' gaps.

When Leanne gathered data for her feedback workshop, she reviewed three data sources to identify gaps: performance evaluation data, department leaders' classroom observation notes, and an anonymous survey she sent to department leaders. Performance evaluation data revealed that teaching practices had not changed much after department leaders' observations. Classroom observation notes indicated areas for teacher growth, but Leanne wasn't sure if or how these growth areas were communicated with teachers directly. When Leanne reviewed the anonymous survey results to gauge department leaders' feelings about feedback, she noted how folks' comments ranged from "I don't know how to give feedback well" to "I'm afraid I won't be liked if I'm honest with teachers about their practice. My department might think I'm being mean." Leanne matched these data sources to her ideal outcomes and recognized that she would need to address department leaders' fears and shift their beliefs about giving feedback.

Step 3: Brainstorm Possible Activities. Once you are clear on participants' gaps, brainstorm a list of ideas for how to close the gaps. When brainstorming activities, consider ways to build participants' knowledge and skills and think about the kinds of activities that will allow participants to be empowered in their learning and implementation.

Planning for her feedback workshop, Leanne brainstormed the following possible activities to address participants' gaps:

- Hopes and fears reflection related to giving feedback
- Role-play a feedback conversation with low-stakes scenarios
- Create a feedback action plan
- Group-guided process to shift beliefs about giving feedback

Step 4: Prioritize Topics—considering the **why** *of each topic.* When reviewing the list of possible activities, notice what feels most important, relevant, or purposeful for participants. You might then underline or put a star next to the activities that you suspect will have the greatest impact. In this phase of the process, it's also helpful to articulate the purpose of each activity you select, as identifying the *why* will help when you communicate your plan.

For her workshop, Leanne prioritized addressing participants' hopes and fears around feedback; she wanted to normalize the emotions people were experiencing. She also prioritized an exercise to shift beliefs about feedback, because she imagined department leaders were operating with mental models that were getting in the way of giving critical feedback. Mental models are our beliefs, assumptions, and ideas about how things work. In this example, department leaders were operating with the mental model, or belief, that giving critical feedback meant they were mean or that they might not be liked. But the culture of niceness wasn't serving students, and Leanne hoped that if department leaders could examine their underlying fears and beliefs about giving feedback, they could eventually shift those beliefs and form new ones that supported student learning. Leanne also prioritized practice with low-stakes feedback scenarios so department leaders could see what a shift in beliefs looked like—and ultimately, how feedback could be a tool for growth.

The Four Steps in Practice

Now let's look at how Lori and Dr. Deal might have put these four steps together to create plans for Lori's Socratic Seminar PD. Let's also imagine they had a conversation about data sources, and then they sent a staff survey asking about what discussion methods teachers use in their content areas, how discussions contribute to student learning, how often discussions happen, and what people already know about Socratic Seminars. Table 1.2 illustrates what Lori and Dr. Deal create from this process.

Table 1.2   Socratic Seminar Outcomes, Gaps, Possibilities, Priorities

Current Conditions and Gaps	Possible Activities (*priorities*)	Ideal Outcomes
Gaps • Skills: Giving students tools to facilitate their own discussions • How to gradually release students into their own student-led discussions • Cultural competency: Potential cultural competency gaps based on what some teachers say about what students know (deficit thinking)	• *Do a fishbowl of a Socratic Seminar • How to choose high engagement texts • *Determine what discussion looks and sounds like in your subject area • Create a gradual release plan in pairs/ teams to determine how to make classroom discussions more student-centered • *Create an action plan of one student-centered discussion method a week; check with an accountability buddy before the next PD session	Know and do • Teachers are able to create structures and conditions for students to lead their own discussions. • Teachers create psychological safety in classrooms that support student empowerment.

(Continued)

Table 1.2 (Continued)

Current Conditions and Gaps	Possible Activities (*priorities*)	Ideal Outcomes
<u>What people are saying/feeling about this topic</u> • "I see its importance, and I want to learn ways to make discussions better for all my students." • "My students can't do this. They need the language and the tools to do this well." • "Right now, all the students who participate are more extroverted. How do I do this in a way that allows my quieter students to engage?" • "I have a lot of curriculum to get through. I don't want this to slow me down."		<u>Say and feel</u> • "It's amazing how student-centered discussion methods allow students to find their voices." • "When I get out of the way, students have so much more to contribute." • "I feel proud of my students for what they are able to contribute."
<u>What student data tells us</u> • Extroverts participate in discussions more than introverts. • Students who participate more in discussions are getting more attention from their teachers.		<u>Outcomes for students</u> • Students can grapple with learning independently rather than relying on the teacher all the time. • Students feel proud of their contributions in class. • Students feel psychologically safe so they are readier to take risks.

After Lori and Dr. Deal fill out this document and go through these steps, they have a conversation about what they notice so they can make decisions about which topics and activities Lori might lead in her upcoming PD. Lori notices some deficit thinking ("these students can't") in the Current Conditions and Gaps column, but she also sees alignment between what teachers say about extroverts and what the student data reveals: that introverts participate less and that those who do participate in discussion get more attention from their teachers.

Looking at Table 1.2 allows Lori and Dr. Deal to consider a lot of possibilities to make this workshop purposeful: how to address the knowledge, skill, will, capacity, emotional intelligence, and cultural competency teachers have in relation to this topic, how to make the learning matter to participants, and how to create greater engagement. Based on their assessment of data compared to their desired outcomes, Dr. Deal and Lori talk about the specific, high-leverage activities that would best work to address teachers' gaps. Based on their assessment, Dr. Deal and Lori land on the activities listed next. They generate a brief purpose phrase about each activity to support their decisions:

- *To activate prior knowledge and honor teacher expertise*: Determine what discussion looks and sounds like in your subject area.
- *To model a student-centered discussion strategy*: Do a fishbowl of a Socratic Seminar.
- *To build accountability*: Create an action plan of one student-centered discussion method you might try; check with an accountability buddy before the next PD session (perhaps do some peer observation to gather more data).

When selecting activities, it's helpful to talk about the purpose of each activity or write mini purpose statements next to each one. It may seem like overdoing it, but returning to the *why* helps all of us—newer and more experienced PD providers—hold ourselves accountable for creating the conditions for transformational change.

Communicate: Make the Learning Matter

Communication is key at all stages of planning and facilitating PD, and we'll come back to this topic throughout this book. In terms of communicating purpose, it's beneficial to consider what communication will look and sound like before, during, and after your PD. The following tips can support you in making the learning matter, and they are broken down into three categories: before the PD, during the PD, and after the PD.

Before the PD

Communicate the purpose in advance. Instead of just sharing the next PD topic with participants, consider writing an enticing blurb that articulates the *why*. You might explain what problem you will be solving with this PD. If this PD is a one-off event or if you have a professional learning day, you might consider writing an email that frames this topic for your participants (Chapter 6 offers a sample of what this communication might look like). Generating anticipation in advance may create greater engagement on the part of your participants.

Audre, a middle school principal, was introducing a peer coaching program to empower teachers to support one another. Prior to the first training, Audre made a short video explaining the purpose of peer coaching and the goals of the first PD session; she talked about the impact of coaching on her growth and how coaching offers a set of tools anyone can use regardless of role. This framing language allowed participants to come to the PD with greater curiosity and openness about what lay ahead.

Assess your audience and leverage relationships. It's critical to assess levels of trust in your organization, the role of power, and whose voices and values are centered. If you've been at your site for a while, consider leveraging relationships. Identify a couple of key colleagues, ones who may have influence in the community and share your excitement about the upcoming PD. Perhaps even involve these colleagues in the workshop. If you don't know people well yet (or you're an external provider), identify someone you can ask about the context (the culture and levels of trust), so you know what to expect during the PD.

When Lori led monthly PD seminars at her site, she leveraged her relationships with the instructional coach and with department leaders. She asked them to be partners in generating excitement for upcoming sessions; in their team meetings, department leaders announced upcoming PD sessions shared how the upcoming session connected to departmental goals. As external providers, Bright Morning consultants ask clients about what matters most to participants—what topics, stories, or experiences are most important—so they can connect the purpose of the workshop to what participants value.

Activate your audience's intrinsic motivation. As you design your session, consider the principles of adult learning (Chapter 4) as you activate to your audience's motivations. Are there portions of your PD that might invite participant input or expertise? Consider the problem your PD will solve and how participants might contribute to that solution. Both before and during your PD, consider how to tap into adult strengths, prior knowledge, and their desire to learn as you frame your PD's purpose.

During the PD

Frame the PD at the beginning. Consider sharing the intended outcomes for your PD and why this PD matters, particularly in relation to student outcomes. Even a couple of sentences of framing can be a powerful anchor for your audience. In Bright Morning's *Onward* Book Club, a PD series that meets monthly, presenters begin each session with the intended outcomes and identify how those outcomes support the PD's overarching purpose: to cultivate emotional resilience so educators can thrive. When educators are thriving, they can create conditions for children to learn and thrive.

Communicate purpose through your agenda. The agenda itself can include the purpose in clear, succinct language. You might write it at the top of the agenda or put purpose statements next to each activity. In our Bright Morning workshops, facilitators share a "What-Why-How" agenda, a three-column agenda that articulates topics and activities (What), the purpose of each activity (Why), and how participants will learn (How). (We'll explore this in depth in Chapter 5.) Facilitators also explain why they're using certain learning structures, for example, when they balance some quieter reflection with group discussion to meet the needs of both introverts and extroverts.

Anticipate questions or concerns. Anticipate that someone might ask, "Why are we doing this?" Script possible answers to likely questions in advance so you can be responsive to your audience and be ready for what comes. Participants in Bright Morning's equity workshops sometimes wonder why race-based affinity groups are offered for small-group discussion. Elena and Lori anticipate this question and are prepared to answer with their reasoning: "Participants who identify as Black, Indigenous, People of Color (BIPOC) can decide whether they want to be in a BIPOC breakout group for the session. Racial affinity discussion groups allow for participants to reaffirm and explore aspects of their own identities without the emotional labor that can come as a result of cross-racial discussion groups. Our hope is that all our discussion groups are places to support healing and growth, and in turn, be a catalyst for individual and collective transformation."

After the PD

Solicit feedback and follow-up. At the end of your PD session, build time in your agenda for feedback. Remind participants of the purpose of your PD on an end-of-session survey. Ask your audience to rate on a scale of 1–5 how well you met that purpose. Or ask participants to articulate the purpose in their own words—you hope that what you receive aligns with your intentions. The following month, send a quick survey or do some informal polling about what people are still thinking about related to your PD, or what they have transferred or tried; this information will help you consider additional steps, such as how to sequence future PD related to this topic, or what additional data might be needed to assess the impact of your PD.

How Lori and Dr. Deal Make the Learning Matter

In our hypothetical scenario, Dr. Deal and Lori consider their context: teachers who may be holding negative views and a "this too shall pass" mental model about PD. Lori and Dr. Deal consider how to communicate purpose to colleagues like Dan, Marcus, and Eileen (among many others). They think about how to tap into their colleagues' strengths and leverage good relationships. Lori and Dr. Deal craft a plan to communicate purposefully and make the learning matter to everyone, from start to finish.

Dr. Deal encourages Lori to reach out to Eileen and ask her to help set the tone for the session. She knows if Eileen participates early on, others might as well. Lori then asks Eileen's advice about who would be good models for the role-play. Eileen tells her that Dan and Marcus are extroverts and love to volunteer when they know what's coming; she also shares the name of some additional teachers who could have a strong influence on the group. With Eileen and Dr. Deal's support, Lori reaches out to these teachers, shares the purpose and topic of the workshop, and asks if they would like to help by volunteering for the model discussion.

Dr. Deal writes a brief blurb in her staff digest about the upcoming Wednesday PD. She also poses a question for teachers to think about in advance: *What student-centered discussion methods have been most empowering for your students?*

Lori spends a couple hours refining her agenda and creating a document that articulates the purpose, outcomes, and activities of the session. Dr. Deal and Lori review the agenda to ensure the purpose is clearly stated at the top of the document and next to each activity. Finally, Lori creates a feedback form and makes sure there is time at the end of the session to fill it out. She includes a question that asks teachers to articulate the purpose of the session in their own words. The time Lori and Dr. Deal have invested in determining purpose has given them greater clarity on why this PD matters.

Putting It All Together

Let's revisit the dim school library where Lori will deliver her PD—this time having engaged with Dr. Deal in planning around purpose. As you read, identify how purpose shapes the direction of this session, from how it is communicated to how it shifts how participants engage in the learning.

Socratic Seminar PD Revisited

Dr. Deal addresses the staff: "I know I normally lead professional development, but as you know from last week's staff digest, Lori Cohen is going to lead our session today. She recently came to my office, *very* enthusiastic about a student-centered discussion method called Socratic Seminars. This topic fits beautifully with our school's mission: to empower students to become courageous leaders of the future.

"The purpose of this session is to help us reimagine classroom discussions as a place for all students to have access—where everyone can share their voices, where dialogue is welcomed over debate, where shared meaning-making can happen (even with competing viewpoints), and where the teacher creates conditions for student empowerment. You'll see it written at the top of Lori's agenda, too. We also know you have lots of your own ideas and strategies to help us reimagine class discussions. Your input was invaluable in helping shape today's plans so we can best center the needs of all our students. Thank you. I'll now pass it along to Lori."

Lori steps to the front of the room, flips on the overhead projector, and posts the following question for teachers to discuss: *What student-centered discussion methods have been most empowering for your students?* She says, "Take the next five minutes at your tables, and generate a list of methods."

Teachers gather at their tables and brainstorm discussion methods. They write their lists on flip charts and post them in the front of the room. Lori facilitates a discussion on themes people see across all the lists. She then asks, "What do you notice about these themes?"

Eileen raises her hand. "Some are related to our subject areas, but a lot of these are good techniques for any of our classes." Lori thanks Eileen for sharing. A couple more people share.

"The purpose of starting with this activity is twofold," Lori says. "First, I know, even after a short time at this school, that the wisdom and the expertise are in the room; I've learned so much from people here. Second, I invite you to consider today's topic on Socratic Seminars as a case study for one kind of discussion method. I'd like you to consider what you might use from this session, what you might adapt. Ultimately, I hope you can walk away with at least one strategy that will be empowering for student-centered discussion." A few heads nodded. "And if not, you have the feedback form at the end to share your input." Dan laughed. Lori smiled.

When Lori asks for volunteers from different subject areas to engage in a mock demonstration, Dan raises his hand to participate. Marcus does, too. They both are extroverts and have prominent voices in the community. Dan makes a joke about math teachers and discussions, which brings some levity to the demonstration. Eileen volunteers, too. So does Dr. Deal.

At the end of the session, Dr. Deal asks teachers to write down one action item, something they'll try in their own classrooms. "I'll be asking you to let us know how it went in next month's PD session," she says.

Lori saves five minutes at the end for teachers to fill out the feedback form. As Dan walks out of the library, he approaches Dr. Deal. "That was fun," he says. "Not all these techniques might apply in math, but the brainstorm at the beginning of the PD got me thinking about something I could try."

Assessing Impact

Lori once worked with a colleague who was always energized at the end of the workshops they co-led: "That went really well!" he usually said.

Not trying to burst his bubble, Lori would follow up with, "How do you know? What changed for people?"

"I can just sense it," he would say.

As much as we might be able to sense whether a workshop went well (perhaps participants are smiling on their way out of the session, or they are talking about what a great workshop it was), we don't really know whether the PD fulfilled its purpose until we assess the impact, until we measure the changes in practice. The more measures we use, the better.

Five Measures of Impact

How do you measure the impact of your PD sessions? How do you know whether you met your purpose and whether participants learned? As you look at the questions listed next, consider which ones you might use to assess the impact of your PD. What other topics and questions would you include in this list?

- *Participants' responses to the workshop*: How did they feel about the experience?
- *Participants' learning*: What did participants learn, and what can they do as a result of this PD?
- *Organizational change*: How does participant learning support site and systems-level change?
- *Participants' application of new knowledge or skills*: How are teachers applying this learning in classrooms?
- *Student learning outcomes*: How are students benefiting from this PD and getting what they need to thrive?

These topics and questions, influenced by Thomas R. Guskey's work on evaluating professional development (2002), allow PD leaders to determine the impact of PD from the participant experience to how the PD creates change for students. Each of these measures—from the most immediate to the long-term, and from what we can most influence to what we have the least control over—allow PD leaders insight into what's working, what isn't, and what's leading to transformational outcomes for adults, and ultimately, for students.

Participants' Reactions

"If you get the inside right, the outside will fall into place."

—Eckhart Tolle

The most immediate feedback PD leaders will receive is participants' reactions—the responses participants have as a workshop ends. This is an area you have the most influence over. You might do a visualization before your PD and imagine what people will do, say, and feel as a result; perhaps imagine your workshop as a party with honored guests, and as they leave you identify some things they might say to one another on the way out of the room, such as "That was so purposeful" or "I wish PD was always like this." Thoughts are powerful, and they can shape the reality we create.

Through feedback forms and formal/informal conversations, a PD leader can learn almost immediately how people felt about the experience. As Dan leaves the library in our hypothetical scenario, he says to Dr. Deal, "That was fun." In the chat at the end of Bright Morning virtual workshops, participants often share enthusiasm for the experience, making comments like, "Best PD I ever experienced" or "This was transformative. So many tools I can try immediately."

Like Lori's former colleague, sometimes you can actually just sense how a PD went. Facilitators with a high level of self-awareness or a strong intuition can sometimes feel when a PD is successful; the mood in the room feels good, there's lively chatter after a session, or people leave energized. These may not be formal pieces of data, but they are important indicators of a PD's success, at least in the immediate moment.

Unfortunately, when participants have an unpleasant experience in a PD, they rarely share their feedback directly with the facilitator. Sometimes people silently walk out of a room saying nothing to the facilitator (ouch), or participants fill out an anonymous survey with scathing feedback or low ratings. These types of responses can sting. In moments like these, it can feel personal. In Chapter 2, we offer tools for how to engage the emotions—pleasant and unpleasant—you or participants might be having in PD. Chapter 7 also provides a process to facilitate adaptively when your PD goes off course.

Tips and Tricks:

Buddhist practitioner Ruth King (2018) offers a mantra we use when our PD doesn't go as we intended: "It's not permanent, personal, or perfect." This mantra allows us to loosen our grip on self-criticism and the unpleasant feelings that can come when a workshop or session doesn't go well.

Participants' Learning

The second measure of impact is identifying what participants learned or are taking away from the experience. This measure gets at the practical ideas and big takeaways of the PD—ultimately, what participants now know or can do as a result of what they learned. This assessment happens during a PD session as facilitators check for understanding or circulate the room as participants engage in activities. This assessment also happens at the end of a workshop as participants identify key learnings and which activities were most useful.

At the end of Bright Morning workshops and on our final feedback form, we ask participants to identify specific takeaways from the experience; sometimes we also ask participants to create an action step or two based on these takeaways. This data helps us understand which activities and resources had the greatest impact. Some PD leaders might ask participants to fill out an "exit ticket" that describes their experience. One of Lori's favorite exit tickets is a process called "Triangle, Circle, Square," which asks the following:

- *Triangle*: What are three big points you're taking from this PD?
- *Circle*: What is a question or topic that is still circling in your mind?
- *Square*: What is something that is "squaring" (resonating) with you from this session?

Flipping through the index cards with participants' responses, Lori can assess how the feedback successfully fulfills the PD's purpose. She can also use the "circle" portion of feedback to inform future PD sessions she leads.

Organizational Change

The third measure of impact asks how learning is supported beyond the workshop and how changes are implemented over time. This is a measure you have less control over, especially if you are outside an organization. This is a measure that may not be immediately visible either.

Perhaps participants were transformed in the workshop itself, but more work may need to be done to make change at the organizational level. Perhaps staff are working on conversation practices to build a healthy school culture, but shifts in culture take time. If the PD is a one-off experience, it might not lead to the kind of organizational change a site is seeking (which is also why we advocate for PD that is ongoing).

PD providers measure this by looking for evidence of cultural shifts or policy changes that occur as a result of the PD. Participants in Bright Morning's *Art of Coaching Teams* workshop often cite how the tools from the book and the workshop change the culture of how their teams work together. One statewide organization attended a series of Bright Morning *Coaching for Equity* workshops, and in a six-month follow up, leaders in the organization shared the equity conversation protocols staff use and how these workshops "have changed the kinds of conversations we're having." It's helpful to follow up a month, six months, or even a year after a PD to determine its impact.

Participants' Use of New Knowledge or Skill

The fourth measure assesses how participants are using their new knowledge or skills, which also is implemented over time. If you are an internal PD provider, you have better access to whether participants are using what they learned. If you're an external provider, you may be able to follow up with participants, though sometimes you may need to trust the process; ideally, if participants were transformed by the PD, then they will apply what they learned.

Site leaders and coaches might use formal and informal modes of data gathering to assess how teachers are applying what they learned. Professional learning communities (PLCs) might share strategies they are trying along with student work samples. Classroom walk-throughs, peer observations, coach observations, and student performance data are all ways to learn about how learning is transferred from PD into classrooms and schools.

In our hypothetical scenario, Dr. Deal shares how she wants teachers to bring an "artifact of practice" to the next PD session. In real life, when Lori first learned about Socratic Seminars at the College Success Conference, she tried them in her class the following week; the implementation of this discussion method took a few rounds before it became routine. From that point forward, though, Socratic Seminars became one of Lori's go-to routines, and students often asked for Socratic Seminars whenever they were about to have a class discussion.

Student Learning Outcomes

Finally, the fifth—and most important—measure of impact is how PD creates meaningful outcomes for students. After all, that's why we're all in this field. We hope that participants will leave PD with the knowledge, skills, and habits to create equitable learning conditions for students. We hope that as educators walk through classrooms or review student work samples or build relationships with young people, they see clear evidence of student engagement, learning, and growth.

To measure impact on student learning, it's helpful to gather a range of data beyond quantitative measures, data that also measures how students feel and what skills they can demonstrate—what they can apply and create that's not necessarily reflected on a mandated exam. As you think of the PD you're leading, what student data would best reveal the impact? How might you look for evidence of change for students?

More than two decades have passed since Lori led that first workshop on Socratic Seminars. Among the many lessons Lori has learned about PD since then, the most fundamental one has been this: When purpose is clear, everything else falls into place. With a clear purpose, the outcomes are stronger. The activities are more relevant, and participant engagement is greater. The learning is more meaningful, oftentimes more joyful. The facilitation is easier. Lori also learned that the process for determining purpose doesn't have to be done in isolation. It takes all of us to contribute to systems change that can best support our students. What might be possible if your PD is guided by purpose?

Before You Go

Pause and Process:

- What is the role of purpose in your PD?
- Among the ways to determine purpose outlined in this chapter, which ones might you try?
- How will you communicate the purpose of your PD?
- What measures might you use to assess the impact of your PD?

Remember:

- Purpose is foundational for transformational professional development.
- For everything you do in relation to your PD, ask *why*.
- Communicate purpose before, during, and after your PD.
- Use multiple measures to assess the impact of your PD in the short and long term.

CHAPTER 2

Engage Emotions

Elena suspected that the 26 teachers would arrive feeling anxious and distracted. They'd had very little notice about the PD session and were being pulled out of their classes for three days. They were struggling first-year teachers, most of whom had not entered the profession through a traditional route—they themselves would have admitted that they had no idea what they were doing. Elena understood: This PD was an intervention. It needed to get all the teachers anchored in their purpose, back on their toes, and equipped with a small set of immediately implementable, high-leverage teaching skills.

When the teachers arrived in the school's library, Elena could see the exhaustion and apprehension in their expressions. Several walked in and didn't make eye contact with her, looking at the floor and shuffling into a seat. Sighing, one teacher said, "So this is where all the bad teachers are sent, huh?"

Elena greeted each teacher, handed them a name tag, and directed them to the bagels and coffee. The day's agenda was projected on the wall, written in blue ink on a transparency. A "Do Now" below the agenda asked teachers to identify three words that they hoped students would use to describe their teacher at the end of the year and to write those words below their name. One teacher wrote "Alive, intact, employable" below her name.

Elena wasn't surprised, but she recognized she'd need to reach a little deeper into her bag of tricks to effectively facilitate the session she'd planned. She started the session by naming the emotions she observed and sensed in the room: "I see the fatigue on your faces. I hear it in your voices. I recognize it, and I know it. I've been there. I hear your fear and self-doubt, I hear the sarcasm that you're protecting yourselves with. I know that, too. And I also hear the hope below that turmoil. I know you wouldn't be here if you didn't have hope. I'm really glad you're here."

By the end of these sentences, just two minutes into the session, there'd been a change in energy. Many of the teachers sat up a little bit straighter and looked up from their half-eaten bagels. Elena continued: "I know this might be hard, but I want you to imagine we're wrapping up our three days together and you're leaving this room. How do you want to feel then?" Elena waited for a moment. "Would anyone like to share?"

A teacher named Ali raised his hand. "I'll be honest. I want to feel like I can go back to school and not feel like a complete failure all day, and like there's a tiny chance I could make it through this year." Elena thanked Ali for his honesty. Several other teachers shared, echoing Ali's sentiments.

"Turn to your partners now and add anything else that might be a hope for these days," Elena said. Within seconds, every teacher was either talking animatedly or listening to their partner. Elena felt energized by the buzz in the room.

"We're going to spend the first part of today re-anchoring in desires, commitments, and passion. What brought you into education? Why do you want to teach?" Elena asked teachers to write for seven minutes without stopping and then, in groups of four, to tell each other their stories. When this activity ended, an hour later, one teacher said, "I didn't think this was what we'd be doing today, but I already feel so much better."

Elena nodded. "Storytelling is medicine," she said. She continued: "I've got a lot planned for us for these days, and my intention is to leave you feeling a whole lot more confident and capable." Elena paused and then said, "I'm also afraid—I don't want to let you down. But I've been where you are, and I have a lot of ideas for how to help you get where you want to go. I'll be soliciting your input and feedback along the way so I can make adjustments to our agenda, so I hope you'll be honest." Although some teachers had entered feeling apprehensive or resentful or annoyed, Elena could see that they were now willing participants: Their body language had shifted. When they spoke, Elena could hear the openness in their voices.

Three days later, 100 percent of the teachers reported that their hopes for the PD had been met. "I really didn't believe you could help me feel happier," Soraya said. "And I didn't believe you could help me plan the rest of this unit. But you did." On his feedback form, Ali wrote, "I appreciated the opportunity to share my feelings. As a man, and a Middle Eastern man, I usually feel like I can't be vulnerable or talk about my fear. It's just not acceptable. But I'm leaving here feeling lighter and freer and more hopeful—and I think this is because I got to talk about my feelings."

Every teacher had stayed for the entire training and had been more engaged than Elena had imagined was possible. The feedback indicated that the participants had been changed—they were leaving feeling ready to tackle what lay ahead. Reflecting on the feedback, Elena acknowledged that the way she'd responded to the teachers' emotions had been the key. She had recognized their distressed emotional states at the door and had responded to that reality. That attention and action cleared the way for the teachers to dive deep into the community building and the content.

Pause and Process

Before we share our beliefs about emotions, take a moment to identify and name your own beliefs.

1. Complete this statement a few times: *Emotions are. . .*
2. Read the following statements and consider your level of agreement with them on a scale of 1–10.
   - Emotions are annoying.
   - Emotions are things we just have to deal with.
   - Emotions are a source of power.
   - Emotions are irrelevant in a work environment.
   - Emotions are a waste of time.
   - Emotions are energizing.
   - Emotions get in the way of doing important work.
   - Emotions are scary.
   - Emotions are my friends.
3. Where do you suspect your attitudes about emotions come from? What has influenced them?
4. How do you think your gender and race/ethnicity affect how you think and feel about emotions?

What You Need to Know about Emotions to Deliver Transformative PD

Human beings have emotions. All the time. For so many people emotions are an untapped source of power, and when we learn how to work well with emotions, we can do incredible things. Coming to understand this deeply can be difficult because all of us so often experience emotions as draining, as burdens, or as aspects of our being that need to be managed. In this chapter, we hope to help you shift your relationship with emotions (both your own and those of others) and help you see the potential in them.

We also want to be clear: It's imperative that if you aspire to deliver transformative PD, you must learn how to understand, expect, and embrace emotions; and then you've got to learn how to decolonize emotions. Here's why:

- It's likely that at some point you have, or will, experience what you might feel is resistance. Resistance is all about emotions, and understanding emotions can help you prevent resistance as well as develop a range of strategies to respond to it.
- Emotions are a potential source of energy that can carry us through the challenging moments of teaching and learning.
- Our experience of emotions is culturally constructed and sometimes distorted by the dominant culture. To be free, we need to unearth our underlying beliefs about emotions and release those that don't serve us.

Figure 2.1 summarizes what's in this next, meaty section. We hope it'll serve as an anchor and reminder of these essential foundational concepts. Finally, as we explore these ideas and strategies around engaging with emotions, you might also find that they are relevant to your lives outside of being a PD provider.

Understand Emotions

How did you learn about emotions? Social-emotional learning is still rare in formal schooling. Although some of us learn about emotions in therapy or from books, many of us know little about them. Knowledge is empowering, so here's a quick primer on emotions.

An emotion is a cycle of mind-body experiences. Emotions occur in our bodies and often have a mental or psychological component. First, there's an event—something happens and our bodies respond—and then our minds create meaning. A colleague smiles at you and says, "Good morning," and your body produces dopamine (a feel-good hormone) and you think: *I'm glad to see her* and you feel happy. Or a seventh-grade student rolls her eyes at you, your body produces stress hormones, your heart beats a little faster, your breath gets shallow, and you think: *She's so disrespectful. I'm sick of teaching ungrateful kids,* and you feel annoyed and hurt.

Figure 2.1 What you Need to Understand about Emotions

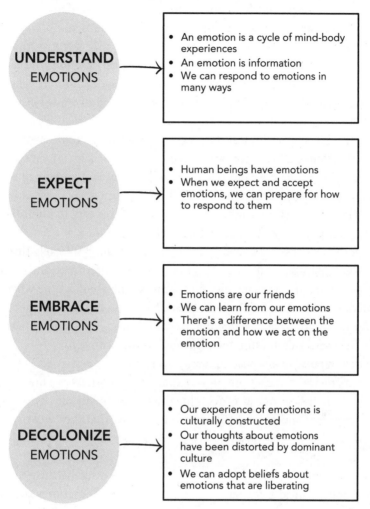

UNDERSTAND
EMOTIONS

- An emotion is a cycle of mind-body experiences
- An emotion is information
- We can respond to emotions in many ways

EXPECT
EMOTIONS

- Human beings have emotions
- When we expect and accept emotions, we can prepare for how to respond to them

EMBRACE
EMOTIONS

- Emotions are our friends
- We can learn from our emotions
- There's a difference between the emotion and how we act on the emotion

DECOLONIZE
EMOTIONS

- Our experience of emotions is culturally constructed
- Our thoughts about emotions have been distorted by dominant culture
- We can adopt beliefs about emotions that are liberating

Learning to listen to our bodies, and understand what they tell us, is critical. Our bodies communicate a lot of emotions: When we don't feel well physically, it can be a sign that we're not paying attention to uncomfortable emotions.

In the cycle of mind-body experiences, what matters most is the conclusion we draw when something happens. Our conclusion often dictates our emotional responses. And how we respond can take two directions: the path of freedom or the path of suffering. If we think, *That student is so disrespectful*, we travel down the path of suffering. If we think, *I wonder what she's experiencing? I wonder which of my needs aren't being met in this moment*, we travel the path of liberation, recognizing that emotions are messengers and we can learn from them.

An emotion is information. An emotion is the primary way that our body sends us signals about what we need. When our needs are met, we feel pleasant emotions. When our needs are unmet, we feel unpleasant emotions. The process of moving from thought to emotion is not quite this black and white because all emotions exist along a continuum. We experience some emotions as especially pleasant or unpleasant, but many will feel only slightly pleasant or unpleasant—in fact, we may even experience these emotions as neutral.

Sometimes when an emotion shows up, you may not recognize what it is or what it's trying to tell you. Appendix A: "The Core Emotions" (also downloadable from https://brightmorningteam.com/), is an invaluable tool to identify emotions. Think of a recent time when you felt upset and then look at this tool and see if you can spot the words that convey what you were feeling. It's likely that by simply naming those feelings you feel a little bit better. The Core Emotions is also helpful as a tool to understand other people's emotions. Think about a time when you were with someone who was upset. Look at the document and see if you get any insight into what they might have been feeling. Naming emotions is a precursor to understanding them and ascertaining the information they convey.

We can respond to emotions in many ways. When emotions show up, we can respond in many ways. Sometimes, if we experience emotions as a flood that sweeps us away, we might lash out at others, hurting people with our words. Or sometimes we suppress, ignore, or avoid emotions, fearing that they will overwhelm us or could damage our relationships. We pretend they're not happening and try to work around them.

Emotions will always search for a way to be expressed because they're trying to communicate critical information about our needs. Sometimes they come out unproductively in our words or in our silence. This can be harmful—to ourselves and sometimes to others.

For emotions to be helpful, we must welcome them, identify them, learn from them, and express them without blame or judgment. When we are open to emotions, we'll not only be more equipped to respond to uncomfortable or unpleasant feelings, but we'll be more accepting and responsive to pleasant ones. In shutting ourselves off from emotions, we deny ourselves a whole lot of joy.

Let's be really clear: There is nothing wrong with experiencing an emotion. We all experience anger, rage, disgust, shame, sadness, and so on. And there's a difference between *experiencing* and *expressing* an emotion. You can feel angry and say mean things or smash a wall—and this expression would be harmful. Or you can feel angry and identify your unmet needs and ask for what you want—and this expression could help you process the emotions, release them, and get your needs met. We can experience our emotions, understand them, and express them in ways that build community and connection.

Expect Emotions

Again: Human beings have emotions. When we deny emotions or downplay them, when we tell someone, "It's okay, you'll feel better tomorrow" or "It's not a big deal, it's not a reason to be angry," we communicate a lack of acceptance of emotions. A healthier relationship with emotions begins with normalizing emotions.

One reason why emotions can feel tricky or challenging is because we don't expect them. Folks who work in schools are likely to experience a broader range of emotions more often. Being around young people and their fluctuating emotions provokes a lot of emotions on our part. This may be obvious, but it's surprising how often educators receive the message that they need to just suck it up and deal with whatever happens, or leave their emotions at the door.

Furthermore, when adults engage in professional development, we should expect strong emotions: For true learning to occur, we have to take risks, which will feel a little uncomfortable. When emotions show up, either our own or other people's, we can feel disoriented and nervous. Learning to expect and accept emotions allows you to prepare for how to respond.

Embrace Emotions

A monumental shift we could make in how we relate to emotions would be to recognize them as messengers. Imagine what it would be like if, when an emotion arose in us, we greeted it warmly, invited it in for tea, sat down with it, and said: "Hi! I'm listening. What do you want to tell me?" To do that, we'd need to first recognize when we're experiencing an emotion, and then we'd need to hold a value that emotions are worthy of our time and attention.

It's important to remember, again, that emotions are not the same thing as the *expression* of our emotions. Having emotions is normal and necessary; however, we can act out our emotions in ways that are harmful and unnecessary. There's nothing wrong, for example, with anger—it can teach us a lot about boundaries and grief; there is something wrong with screaming at people and breaking things. Often we think we're afraid of strong emotions, but what we're really afraid of is how people act on those strong emotions.

We can increase our willingness to listen to our emotions by recognizing that emotions aren't obstacles to learning—they are a resource. Learning is risky, and in most classrooms and PD sessions, you're likely to hear and see and sense fear. This can look and sound like participants doing any of the following:

- Not asking questions or sharing an opinion
- Asking questions, but not asking what they really want to know—it can feel like you need to read between the lines
- Not participating in activities, or participating only to the extent that they really have to
- Multitasking or disengaging
- Pushing back on a facilitator's request for engagement

There's nothing wrong with fear being present. It's there to inform participants about what they need in order to get the most out of that learning space. As a facilitator, it's your job to welcome fear, listen to it, learn from it, and use what you learn. Emotions are messengers.

When you are facilitating PD, embracing emotions looks and sounds like the following:

- *Normalizing feelings*: "It's likely that the data I'm going to share will elicit some strong feelings. That's normal."
- *Asking about feelings*: "I'm sensing some discomfort in the room right now. Would anyone like to share your feelings?"
- *Validating feelings*: "I can see why that interaction felt so painful to you. I appreciate your honesty."
- *Inviting curiosity about feelings*: "Take a moment to acknowledge the emotions that might be arising as you look at this data. What's coming up for you?"
- *Appreciating feelings*: "Ali, thank you for being vulnerable and sharing your fear."
- *Not trying to quickly deal with an uncomfortable emotion so that you can get back to the agenda*: "It's seems like this activity brought up some sadness for some of you. I want to hold some space for that before we move on. If you'd like to talk to a partner, go ahead. If you want to take a few minutes to journal or just stand up and get some air, go ahead."
- *Communicating your feelings to participants*: "Today I'm worried about my daughter. She's been having a hard time in school."

- *Being vulnerable*: "I'm going to ask you to do an activity that I've never led with a group. I believe it'll be a powerful learning experience, and I'm nervous so I want to ask for your grace as we try it out. I definitely want all your feedback."
- *Holding time to process your own feelings when needed*: "Can you give me a moment before I answer that question? I'm noticing a lot of feelings coming up for me and I want to get clear before I respond."

Depending on your background, feelings about emotions, as well as on your identity markers, you may feel like it would be uncomfortable to say many of these statements. It might be at first. And then it will get easier.

Shifting our feelings about feelings would make a tremendous difference in how we experience learning spaces. If we saw emotions as messengers, then when a student rolls her eyes, we might wonder about what's going on for the child. If we saw emotions as messengers, then when we're delivering PD and someone walks in late and we feel intense irritation, we might become curious about what's being triggered in us. Emotions are messengers; they appear so that we can learn from them.

Decolonize Emotions

We see and interpret emotions—our own and those of others—through a socio-political lens. This is because the meaning we make of emotions is culturally constructed. All humans experience the same basic emotions—sadness, anger, joy, fear, pride, and so on. But we ascribe different meanings to those emotions depending on the emotional person's race or ethnicity, gender, age, and class. We also have different rules about the acceptable expression of emotions given someone's identity markers. This means that how you respond to people's emotions depends on your identity—your race or ethnicity, class, and gender, and theirs. Furthermore, other people will express their emotions to you differently, based on their identity markers and experiences and on how they perceive your identity.

What exactly does this mean? Take crying: Women are perceived to be more emotional, and therefore, women's tears (and particularly white women's tears) are more accepted. Men are raised to be stoic and unemotional, and their tears are acceptable only if they're intoxicated, at a funeral, or at their daughter's wedding. Or consider niceness: What we perceive sometimes as niceness—especially in women—can be a mask of avoidance, fear, or disagreement. That's why sometimes niceness feels inauthentic and suspicious. In most of the world, women are expected to be peacemakers and nurturers who deny their own needs in deference to the needs of others. Because of that, women can act "nice," but that action doesn't come from kindness. Think about attitudes toward anger: White men's anger is often perceived as justified. However, a Black man's anger marks him as dangerous. Finally, think about assertiveness: A white woman who is assertive is congratulated for "leaning in." A Black woman who is assertive is often seen as being pushy, loud, or angry.

Dominant culture is racist and misogynistic, and dominant culture has distorted how we make sense of emotions. Racism and misogyny have profoundly shaped our beliefs about who should express which emotions; this is what it means to say emotions have been colonized. But at their core, racism and patriarchy are *ideas*—toxic ideas that have manifested in toxic systems, institutions, and structures. Because these are ideas, we can deconstruct them and, ultimately, abandon them if we want. If we learn how to identify these poisonous ideas and systems, if we extricate them from our minds and systems, and if we heal from the harm that they've done, we can decolonize emotions. Then we can develop a healthy relationship with what is a normal, natural part of being a human being.

If you are committed to facilitating transformative PD, you need to understand what it means that emotions have been colonized, and you need to know how to take action to rectify that history. Otherwise, you are perpetuating the inherently inequitable status quo, and your PD will not be transformative.

You can start by understanding that emotions are culturally constructed; that the way you express your emotions (including when you're facilitating PD) is culturally constructed; that the way you respond to other people's emotions (including when you're facilitating PD) is culturally constructed. This means you may feel more irritation when one person asks you a question than when someone else with different identity markers asks the same question. This means you might respond to a woman's doubt or nervousness differently than you'd respond to a man's. Depending on your identity markers, and your awareness of the cultural construction of emotions, you might feel one way if a Black woman challenges something you say as a PD facilitator and another way if a young white woman challenges you.

Awareness is a critical start, and it's not enough. You must take action when you see how inequitable our organizations are, how your own emotions have been colonized, and how you may have inadvertently contributed to the oppression of others—especially if you are in a leadership position. If you don't take action, you send a message to others that you condone the inequities.

You can learn the skills to interrupt inequitable dynamics—although of course this will take time and practice. You will experience many emotions along the way. You deserve time to do this learning and to explore and process the feelings. In the meantime, if you are facilitating PD, you need to take action. Here are a couple of concrete ways to address inequities and the colonization of emotions in a PD session:

- When you invite whole-group discussions, pay attention to patterns of participation: Who speaks first? Notice if there are patterns of women refraining from speaking or going last. Women's body language may seem deferential or apprehensive, which can reflect feelings inferiority and fear. To interrupt this dynamic, when you invite discussion or questions in a group setting, say something like, "I'd like to invite those who haven't spoken yet today or who often hold off until last to get us started," or you can say, "I've noticed a pattern that women seem hesitant to speak up. I'd like to invite you to be bold and do so."
- Challenge assumptions that are made about authority.
- Communicate value in different kinds of knowledge and authority: When people speak up in a whole group or small groups or pairs, who speaks with authority, and what is that authority based on? Do you see patterns based on race, gender, age, or class background?

> For more on the connection between identity and emotions, read Elena's book *Coaching for Equity*.

Grumpiness, Pet Peeves, and Triggers

Before considering how to respond to other people's emotional expressions, you need to reflect on your own emotions and how you respond to them. Recognizing and engaging with your grumpiness will make you a better facilitator.

Grumpiness is normal. It happens to all of us. But what can you do when you're in a bad mood and you need to deliver a PD session, and you know that your mood will set the tone for the session? Or what about when you're facilitating PD and you're in a good mood, and then you get triggered and annoyed? What can you do then?

The good news is that there's a lot you can do to shift your mood. You can learn to understand and engage with your own emotions in a way that will feel empowering.

Identify Your Pet Peeves and Triggers

Let's start by normalizing the emotional terrain of a PD facilitator. We know that you care a great deal about what you're doing, and you want to be successful. We also know that many leaders rarely feel that they get the kind of appreciation that they deserve. Leaders work and work, deal with all kinds of things, and step up and take risks, and often they get heaps of criticism and little recognition.

We also know that many of us (human beings) have loads of fears and insecurities. We want to be liked. We bring all of our past experiences, unique psychologies, personalities, and preferences to our work, and these contribute to the weather of our emotional terrain. As described earlier in this chapter, we can learn to understand, expect, and embrace our emotional terrain.

Here's a way to do this. List your pet peeves: When you are presenting, what kind of participant behavior gets on your nerves? Maybe people arriving late or being on their cell phones or having side conversations? Next, investigate the meaning you make of their behavior. When people are engaged in side conversations, how do you interpret that behavior? What's the meaning you make of someone scrolling through social media on their phone while you're demonstrating an instructional strategy? You could interpret that behavior as disrespect, or perhaps as a response to an activity that doesn't feel relevant to the person. How we respond to other people's behaviors has a great deal to do with the meaning we make of their behavior.

While pet peeves are annoyances, triggers activate stronger emotions. Recall a moment at work when you were triggered. Who said or did what? Which feelings came up for you? Often when we're triggered, we experience a mix of anger, sadness, and fear, and sometimes these feel especially intense because we aren't expecting them. Emotions that are evoked by triggers feel sudden and can knock us off our game.

There are two helpful ways to understand triggers. First, they often indicate that a boundary has been crossed. The boundary might be a value or belief you hold deeply. For example, many educators believe that every child can learn and, therefore, are triggered when other educators disparagingly use the phrase "these kids," as in, "Well, *these kids* can't do that." When a boundary is crossed, we can feel angry and defensive.

Take a moment to think of something that triggers you. Can you see the connection between the triggering comment or action and one of your values or deeply held beliefs?

Triggers can also reveal an unhealed wound from previous harm. For example, Elena is triggered when she observes a teacher using a red pen to correct spelling. She experiences a surge of irrational anger. She jumps to the conclusion that the teacher doesn't believe that the students deserve to express themselves. Elena is triggered because she remembers her own stories covered in red ink by teachers who told her she couldn't write. Because she didn't spell well when she was a child, she was placed in remedial English classes and given clear messages that she was inferior to other children. For Elena, this is a sore spot that hasn't healed. With this awareness, however, Elena is triggered less often. When she sees red marks all over student work, she says to herself, *ouch—that spot still hurts in me*, and then she can pivot and coach the teacher without bringing her history to the conversation.

Take another moment to think of something that triggers you. Can you make the connection to any experiences in your life when you might have been harmed by someone's actions or words and from which you haven't fully healed?

When you see your triggers as an invitation for inquiry, you can relate to them differently. You can say to yourself, *Oh! I'm triggered by that comment—I wonder what that's about? I wonder what I can learn about myself by exploring the roots of that trigger?* You might even get excited by being triggered because you recognize that it indicates an opportunity for deeper self-understanding. But yes, sometimes triggers are tricky with when you're facilitating an activity on a Wednesday afternoon with 50 tired teachers and you're behind in the agenda and the video you'd embedded in your slide deck isn't playing and you're also a little hungry. And then someone says something that triggers you, and it feels absurd to try to get curious about yourself in that moment. When that happens (it will), acknowledge that you're triggered, and make a promise to yourself that you'll come back to that incident and unpack it so that you can understand what your strong emotions are trying to tell you. Sometimes just making that pledge to yourself will decrease the intensity of the emotion in the moment.

If you want to learn how to navigate your emotions and moods, it helps to know what sets them off. This takes the surprise out of the situation, and you can be prepared to respond. Create a list of your pet peeves and triggers. Keep it somewhere that's visible to you so that you can add to it; or remember to explore your triggers, or just know that they exist.

So what can you do when you're emotionally activated (which is what happens when you're triggered) or when you're just in a bad mood, and you need to present a training or lead a meeting or show up in a way that creates the conditions in which others can learn? Before we share our suggestions, take a moment to identify the strategies you already use—we're sure you've got some!

Ten Strategies to Shift a Mood

What's described in Table 2.1 can be useful before or during a PD session when you find that you're in a mood and you want to shift it. Each strategy in the table is reflected in a self-talk phrase to make it memorable.

As you read these, recall a time when you wish you could have shifted your mood, and imagine whether the strategy could have helped. Not all of these will help everyone. Not all of these help in every situation. Your task is to identify a couple that resonate and might be useful.

Table 2.1 Ten Strategies to Shift a Mood

Self-Talk Phrase	Explanation and Purpose
What's most important right now?	Anchor in your core values and sense of purpose. Sometimes we're irritated by little things that don't matter. Stepping back from the situation and anchoring in what's most important in that moment might help you to let go of those little things.
What's within my influence or control?	It's easy to get annoyed by things that are outside of our control. When we recognize that, we can focus on what we can influence or control which is empowering, and ultimately, the only thing we can really control is our response to a situation.
Is there any other way I can interpret what's going on?	Often our interpretation of someone's behavior or something that happens contributes to our suffering. Considering other ways to see the situation can expand our perspective and help us not take something personally. Remember, the behavior you see in someone else is the tip of an iceberg. You can't see their histories, lives outside of that moment, and much more.
Everyone is doing the best they can, including me.	Activating your empathy and compassion, for yourself and others, can create softness in a difficult moment. Sometimes someone's best isn't enough, and you have a choice about who you spend time around, but recognizing that people are doing their best can be a relief, as it can allow you to accept the current reality.

(Continued)

Table 2.1 (Continued)

Self-Talk Phrase	Explanation and Purpose
What do I need right now?	Acknowledging your needs and identifying them can feel like an act of kindness toward yourself, even if you can't meet those needs in that moment. You might recognize that you need respect at work, or rest, or that you need to talk to a friend. Often a bad mood is a sign that we need to take care of some part of ourselves. Acknowledgment is a start.
Nothing is perfect, personal, or permanent.	Sometimes when we're grumpy or emotionally activated, those moods feel permanent. Remind yourself that everything changes. It can be hard to accept that nothing is personal, but nothing is personal. And nothing, and no one (yourself included) is perfect. This injunction can generate some kindness toward yourself and others.
Have I ever acted this way?	When you're triggered by someone else's behaviors, sometimes humility helps. Recall your own learning journey and development as a human. Can you see yourself in the other person? Allow this reminder to soften you.
What's unhealed in me?	Triggers can indicate an experience in which you were hurt or harmed and from which you haven't healed. Make a pledge to yourself to investigate those sore spots. You deserve healing.
What do I wish I could say right now?	There's a difference between what you wish you could say and what you can say when you're triggered or in a bad mood. Identifying what you wish you could say can be powerful because it allows you to hear a part of yourself that needs expression. If possible, write it down. Do this before or during a PD session to release steam.
Get in the bubble.	Imagine a translucent bubble of safety. When you are inside of it, nothing gets under your skin. No one's words can hurt you. When you're in a situation that feels especially difficult or toxic and you're triggered or in a mood, visualize stepping into the bubble and staying in there until you are safe. Later you've got to figure out how to get out of the toxic situation, but in the moment, you can draw a boundary. Yes, moods are contagious, but you can also step into a bubble, and do a lot to prevent catching the toxic mood.

Grumpiness, triggers, and pet peeves are invitations to learn more about yourself. Remember: Emotions are messengers. They are trying to give you information. If moods stick around for a while, if you find that you're sad, annoyed, or anxious a lot and without relief, we encourage you to learn more about depression and anxiety and to seek out professional support.

We hope that this section has inspired you to continue learning about emotions. Your emotions matter and how you relate to them might just be the key to living your values, fulfilling your sense of purpose, and helping to create a more just and liberated world.

Creating Psychological Safety

When Elena was a new coach, she struggled to build trust with teachers. She perceived many of them as being resistant, and she was frustrated a great deal of the time. Fortunately, Elena had a skillful, brave coach named Leslie Plettner who changed Elena's life when she said, "No one can learn from you if you think that they suck."

Take in those words: *No one can learn from you if you think that they suck.* Think about your own experience: Can you imagine being an open and receptive learner in front of a teacher who dismisses your abilities, your thoughts, your feelings, and perhaps even your humanity? Now, think about your experience as a facilitator of learning. Be honest with yourself. Have you ever dismissed the abilities, thoughts, and feelings of the people you taught?

When Elena heard those words from Leslie, she realized that she had, indeed, thought that many of the teachers she worked with were incompetent. She sensed what it must have been like to be in their shoes in a PD session she led, and she understood why they hadn't been open to her leadership. Elena became an effective coach and facilitator of PD when she shifted into believing that every adult wants to learn. As her mindset changed, her behaviors also changed: She responded to what she perceived as resistance with curiosity, she created more opportunities for teachers to share their expertise, and she invited feedback more often and heeded that feedback. Finally, Elena prioritized creating psychological safety. This last item, psychological safety, is one we talk about when designing classrooms for children, but we rarely focus on what it means for staff at a school.

Many habits in this book contribute to psychological safety in a PD setting. When you share the "why" behind an agenda item, build community among learners, attend to details, and use power with (as opposed to over)—you build psychological safety. We'll spend time learning about each of these habits in later chapters. We'll begin the learning in this chapter with a summary of the science on psychological safety and a deep dive into the emotions of psychological safety. You'll learn how to contribute to psychological safety by cultivating your own emotional intelligence, cultivating a group's emotional intelligence, teaching communication skills, using norms and community agreements, and addressing conflict and breaches in psychological safety.

But first, a caveat: You can do a great deal to create psychological safety—far more than you've probably ever imagined—but you can't *guarantee* psychological safety. Aim to create "safe-ish" spaces, or "safe enough" spaces. We'll unpack precisely what this means later in this chapter.

A Very Short Summary of the Research

Psychological safety is a prerequisite for transformative learning to occur because, as Leslie Plettner said, no one can learn from you if you think that they suck. Here's why: Our brains shut down when we're afraid—this is true for children and adults. If we feel like someone poses a threat to our physical or psychological well-being, our body lurches into protection mode, preparing for battle, diverting blood to our large muscles, and generating hormones and neurochemicals to help us survive. Our attention narrows and focuses on the little cues that indicate when to fight, flee, freeze, or appease. Yes, even if we're in a PD session in the library.

When our bodies respond this way, we might notice that we're not really following the PD anymore, or that we're losing interest, and later we may not remember much of the presentation. This is because our prefrontal cortex (the part of the brain where complex thinking happens) has slowed down. This is what can happen when our psychological safety feels threatened, what happens when we sense that the presenter thinks we suck. Clearly, understanding the research on psychological safety is a prerequisite to creating learning spaces for others. Why battle how the brain works?

The research of psychological safety in group settings is especially compelling. Google sponsored a well-known study on highly productive teams. The results found that emotional intelligence and psychological safety was "far and away the most important dynamic that set successful teams apart" (*New York Times*). This finding can be applied wherever people gather to do something together, including to learn together in a PD session, meet in professional learning community, or collaborate in an instructional leadership team.

Professor and author Amy Edmondson, an internationally recognized expert in psychological safety, writes:

> ". . .psychological safety makes it possible to give tough feedback and have difficult conversations without the need to tiptoe around the truth. In psychologically safe environments, people believe that if they make a mistake, others will not penalize or think less of them for it. They also believe that others will not resent or humiliate them when they ask for help or information." (2012)

Can you imagine what our PD sessions could be like if we felt like we could make mistakes around each other and not feel anxious about what our colleagues would think?

The ability to ask for help also contributes to creating psychological safety. Edmondson explains:

> "This belief [that others will not resent or humiliate them when they ask for help or information] comes about when people both trust and respect each other, and it produces a sense of confidence that the group won't embarrass, reject, or punish someone for speaking up." (2012)

Imagine a PD session on developing relationships with parents and caregivers that was characterized by psychological safety. You might see teachers role-playing a conversation they want to have with caregivers; you'd see them stumbling over their words, receiving feedback from colleagues, throwing up their hands in frustration, trying again and again, throwing up their hands in celebration, laughing, receiving more feedback and trying again, talking about their own identity markers and those of their students and their students' parents, and asking each other challenging questions like, "What is the belief you're holding about his mom when you say she doesn't care about her kids' education?" Or saying something like, "It's racist to insinuate that her father probably snuck across the border." The room would be buzzing with conversation, and then perhaps quiet with reflection, and you might see tears and you'd hear people say, "I don't know!" and you'd hear others say, "Try this. . ." You might sense moments of discomfort, but the room would be buzzing with energy and learning—and you'd be witnessing transformative PD.

Okay, let's get into *how* to create psychologically safe PD sessions.

Cultivate Your Emotional Intelligence

When you facilitate PD, everything starts and ends with you, including the degree of psychological safety that's possible. In part, this has to do with the fact that emotions are contagious. Our brains contain *mirror neurons*, and we literally catch what others are feeling. When you facilitate PD, you hold power, so learners look to you for cues about how you feel—and they mirror your emotions. If judgment oozes from your pores, the folks you are trying to teach will shut down. If instead you communicate openness and acceptance—if you feel that learners are likely skilled, capable, smart, caring people—it is much more likely that your participants will be open and receptive. What you think and feel is everything.

Emotional intelligence is the ability to do two important things well. First, emotionally intelligent people recognize their own emotions and relate to them in a healthy way. Sometimes this healthy relating to emotions is called *regulating* or *managing* emotions, but we prefer phrases like "gaining insight" and "generating resilience." The second thing emotionally intelligent people do is recognize other people's emotions and relate to others' emotions in ways that also generate resilience in those folks.

Imagine what happens when an emotionally intelligent leader facilitates a PD session and a teacher shows up grumbling and grouchy. As the teacher pushes her chair around noisily, complaining about the furniture, the leader pauses to recognize her own emotions—maybe she notices a flicker of annoyance. Then that annoyance passes as she activates her curiosity, wonders what's going on for the teacher, and feels empathetic. The leader does not take the teacher's behavior personally. This distance allows the leader to approach the teacher. "Hey, I'm glad you're here," she might say, and maybe she asks a question or two. "How was your day?" she might ask, or maybe she thinks better of it and, remembering that a mood can shift, decides to let the teacher be.

Contrast that scenario with this one: A grumpy teacher shows up at PD. She's grumpy because she didn't have lunch, because she had to meet with a parent, because the lesson she'd spent hours planning didn't go well, and because she's had meetings after school every day all week. When she walks into the library, the instructional coach tells her that she needs to sit with her grade-level team and tells her to get started on the Do Now. The teacher gives the coach a dirty look, and the coach gives the teacher a dirty look, and a low-intensity conflict has ignited.

You can continue learning about emotional intelligence in Elena's books *The Art of Coaching Teams* and *Onward*.

Cultivate a Group's Emotional Intelligence

Creating an emotionally safe learning environment takes a leader with emotional intelligence, but an emotionally intelligent leader is not enough. You might be skilled at using empathy to connect with a grumpy teacher, but when that teacher sits down with her colleagues, they might be triggered by her mood, and a new ripple of tension starts.

If you're a PD provider, you'll be a whole lot more effective if, regardless of what you're providing PD on, you incorporate opportunities to teach people about navigating their own emotions and the emotions of others. This can be simpler than it sounds. Here's an activity that takes five to seven minutes to do at the start of a PD session:

1. Ask people to identify three words that describe how they're feeling. This allows people to bring awareness to their emotions, something we often feel like we don't have time for or simply don't do.
2. Give folks a resource like Appendix A to find words that most accurately reflect their emotions in that moment. This tool (which provides hundreds of terms for emotions) helps put language to our feelings, expand our vocabulary for emotions, and gain insight into the nuance of emotions.
3. Invite folks to share the words they came up with that describe their emotions or to talk about why they're feeling the way they are.

This activity creates self-awareness and is an opportunity for people to cultivate understanding and empathy for each other. When a grumpy teacher shares that she feels "frustrated, disappointed, and despairing" and explains that the lesson she'd worked so hard on didn't go well and she's doubting herself, her colleagues will soften. They might relate and be less inclined to take her behavior personally. As the teacher explains her feelings, there's a chance that the intensity of her emotion will shift, especially if she receives empathy from her colleagues. Whenever you can cultivate empathy, do so. Judgment seriously undermines psychological safety, and by cultivating empathy, there's less space for judgment.

It should be acknowledged that temporal grumpiness is different from chronic grumpiness. In the last scenario, team members are likely to soften on hearing the teacher's reflections—unless the teacher is in a bad mood at every single meeting. If that's the case, further intervention is needed, and we'll address strategies for intervention in the upcoming section on conflict. For further learning on how to cultivate emotional intelligence in a group, see *The Art of Coaching Teams* and *Onward*.

Teach Communication Skills

Most of us have spent far more time learning advanced mathematics than we've spent explicitly learning how to skillfully communicate with each other. Imagine how different our personal and professional lives would be if we had advanced listening and speaking skills. Because so few people learn communication skills formally at any point in our schooling or career development, this is something else that PD providers should incorporate into PD.

Psychological safety and effective communication go hand in hand. Can you recall a meeting or PD session when you checked out because you felt like you weren't being heard by colleagues? Or because someone interrupted you and talked over you? Or because you felt like others judged your ideas?

Two specific actions that seriously undermine psychological safety are interruptions and unsolicited advice (Edmondson, 2012). When people interrupt us or give us unsolicited advice, they aren't listening; they are angling to insert their own arguments, experiences, and beliefs. The result can be that we feel like we don't matter or that we aren't truly seen or heard. Being interrupted and getting unsolicited advice can also make us aware that someone is trying to assert their power over us. As a result, many of us shift into a defensive mode in which we're less able to learn.

In Bright Morning workshops, we often explore communication skills. We teach people to cultivate awareness of what happens in their mind when they are listening: Are they getting distracted and spacing out? Are they looking for points they can argue with? Are they listening for ways to fix the situation? We also teach people ways of listening that are conducive to psychological safety and connection, such as listening for possibility and listening with compassion and curiosity. But just learning about something isn't enough to change a behavior, so we structure opportunities to practice listening—and that's when the learning happens.

In our workshops, we also teach the skill of asking nonjudgmental questions. This, too, is something that requires practice. Asking nonjudgmental questions is not just a technical skill—it's not just about formulating the right words—it's about what's going on inside of you. A nonjudgmental question comes from a nonjudgmental person. In exploring communication, we explore deeply held thoughts and feelings.

Poor communication is often at the root of many problematic adult cultures in schools. When people bemoan that they just "don't feel understood" or "don't feel heard," they aren't primed for learning. Fortunately, PD providers can do something about this. Maybe you're reading this, and you provide PD on how to integrate technology into curriculum or a reading program, and you're thinking, *and now I* also *have to teach people to listen and rid themselves of judgment?!*

Well, yes. Possibly. If you aspire to create the optimal conditions in which adults can learn and if you aspire to contribute to psychological safety, you might need to incorporate mini-lessons (and mini-practice sessions) on listening and speaking. These can be topics for mini-lessons in any PD session, regardless of the focus or topic:

- How to actively listen
- How to probe for deeper understanding
- How to disagree
- How to support someone and help them feel more empowered
- How to challenge ideas
- How to understand nonverbal communication

Start by inviting individuals to reflect on their communication skills and to identify which skills they'd like to work on together. Once we normalize the fact that all of us could benefit from refining our communication, that none of us was really taught skillful communication, this can feel a lot easier. For further learning about listening and asking questions, see *The Art of Coaching, The Art of Coaching Teams*, and *The Art of Coaching Workbook*.

Use Norms and Community Agreements

Community agreements (or norms) are a way for people to align on how they will treat each other and understand, or buy into, a set of expectations for group behavior. If a group doesn't have community agreements, psychological safety will be tenuous.

Ideally, community agreements are co-constructed by all members of a staff or a team. But they don't have to be. If you are a PD provider and you are working with a group for only a day or a few sessions, it can be appropriate for you offer a set of norms. In Bright Morning workshops, we usually offer the following community agreements:

- Take care of yourself.
- Be fully present.
- Take risks.
- Be mindful of other learners.

We emphasize that these contribute to the well-being of the whole group, we provide brief definitions of what we mean by each norm, and we explain how adhering to the norm will help everyone learn. For example, we say, "When we talk about being mindful of other learners, we're asking that we keep some awareness of things like being back on time from breaks, not having side conversations, and using technology in a way that doesn't distract others." We invite learners to "try these on" and "see what happens." But we also say, "We're asking you to hold these."

Having norms is the first step. The second step is to ensure that they mean something, that they are upheld. Doing this is complicated, and we encourage you to read the chapter in *The Art of Coaching Teams* on community agreements. Here, we offer you a quick story about what Elena did when she was delivering a two-day workshop and she observed the community agreements being ignored.

During the afternoon of the first day, Elena began noticing that some of the 150 learners were engaging in conversations during silent activities, and others were responding to emails during small-group activities. Elena's first thought was, *Well, if they aren't finding this useful or relevant, that's their choice to check out and do what they need to do.* But she was also concerned about the deterioration of the learning environment, and furthermore, she observed that engaged learners were noticing that she was observing the breakdowns. Their eyes went from the person on their cell phone (who was clearly on a popular shoe shopping site) to Elena, who was looking at that person on their cell phone. Elena could almost hear the thoughts of the folks who observed this: *Elena sees that this person is not engaging in the group activity. Is she going to do anything or will she ignore this?*

In that moment, Elena knew that she risked losing the trust of the engaged learners and risked a deterioration of the psychological safety that had been developing through the morning. As she recognized her responsibility to say something, Elena noticed her anxiety surge. She embraced her fear, saying to herself, *It's okay to be afraid. You want to take a stand for something that matters, and your fear is telling you that this is important. It's worth it, and you'll be okay.*

This is what she said to the group, right before a scheduled afternoon break:

"I'm feeling uncomfortable right now, but I have to name something I'm observing. Over the last couple of hours, during several independent activities, pair shares, and small-group activities, I've noticed that some folks have disengaged from this learning. My concern is about the impact that's having on others in your groups. And some of you have noticed that I've noticed this happening—you're watching me watch what's going on. I realize that I risk losing your trust that I can hold a safe, focused learning space unless I name that I'm seeing the breakdown of the norms that I invited everyone to hold. This feels awkward to say, but it's my responsibility to ensure that this a learning space. If you're unable to participate in these activities for whatever reason, I invite you to step out and return when you are. If you're in this room, I ask you to recommit to these community agreements and keep this space focused on learning."

As Elena spoke these words, her heart raced, and her palms got sweaty. She worried that participants would feel that she was attempting to control them. She was surprised when she said, "Okay, let's take a break," and half of the people in the room started clapping. Several participants approached her and said they appreciated her comments and the modeling of an important leadership move. When she reflected on this incident later, she recognized that her fear had transformed into courage and that she'd felt aligned to her values and sense of responsibility to the group, and that had felt good.

As the facilitator, you are the primary person responsible for cultivating psychological safety. When you see breakdowns in community agreements, you've got to do something. You can start by simply saying, "I'm seeing a breakdown in how we're holding our community agreements." You can follow that by asking if anyone else sees that and if anyone else is concerned and wants to address what's going on. Another option is to make a request, which can sound like, "I'm hearing a lot of side conversations and seeing a breakdown in our agreement to be mindful of other learners. I'd like to ask that we recommit to this for the sake of everyone's learning." Although we know this might feel uncomfortable, it's your responsibility. If you're nervous about speaking up, first identify the emotions that are arising in you (probably fear), and then take a deep breath, consider the consequences of not saying anything, and try it. See what happens. Speaking up is rarely as bad as you think it will be.

If you work with a group on an ongoing basis, you might notice trends in how psychological safety breaks down—for example, you might see that people interrupt each other a lot. You can name what you observe and engage participants in identifying what can be done. But the key here is always that there are norms or community agreements in the first place—without them it's much harder to attend to breakdowns.

Address Conflict and Breaches of Psychological Safety

The final strategy to create psychological safety is to address conflict when it arises. Unfortunately, most of us have been in teams or PD sessions where we can sense or even hear outright conflict between people; sometimes such conflict grows week after week. Unattended conflict, even between just two people, will negatively affect the whole group. There's a range of conflict that can occur in a group—from situational and infrequent conflict to chronic, toxic conflict. In a highly functional organization, conflict is addressed quickly by the leader or a member of the group. Here are some key ways to address conflict:

- Identify the signs of conflict, and note when they happen.
- Name when you perceive tension and say something like, "I'm noticing that there's disagreement about how to use this engagement strategy. I'm going to create time at our next meeting for us to hear different perspectives and work this out." Or you might also decide to address the tension within that meeting. You might ask for consensus to do this, or you might say something like, "This issue has been coming up repeatedly, and the tension is getting in the way of us learning from each other. I'm going to hit pause on our meeting so that we can address this issue."
- Offer sentence stems for how to engage in productive conflict. (You can find suggestions in *The Art of Coaching Teams*.)
- Institute the use of "process observers." Process observers help a group recognize when they are no longer upholding their community agreements and help figure out how to get back on course. (See *The Art of Coaching Teams*.)
- Name breaches of psychological safety. For example, "Alex, I've noticed a couple times that you've interrupted Tracey when she was sharing her ideas."
- When community agreements continuously break down, suggest a reset. "I've noticed it's really hard for us to hold these. We need to pause in our learning scope and sequence and get to the heart of this because otherwise we're not going to get the most from this learning experience."

To effectively address conflict, a facilitator must have keen emotional intelligence. You can't get freaked out by other people's strong emotions. Many people avoid conflict or have fear of it, but conflict can provide opportunities to build trust in each other and in our leaders. It can teach us about ourselves and others.

We'll continue to explore how to address conflict in Chapter 7, but for now, let's commit to the idea that in order to create and hold psychologically safe learning spaces we need to be willing and able to address conflict when it inevitably arises.

Recognizing Your Sphere of Influence

There are factors that can make it hard, or even impossible, for a facilitator to create psychological safety. Recognizing these factors allows you to be clear on your sphere of influence and determine next steps. Pervasive organizational toxicity and complex individual psychologies are the two factors most likely to limit your influence as a facilitator.

Pervasive organizational toxicity usually results from many years of poorly managed change, rampant instability, transactional leadership, high staff turnover, and a dehumanizing adult culture that hasn't been interrupted. In organizations character-ized by this kind of dysfunction, people talk about each other behind their backs, spread false information, openly attack each other, and disengage from learning opportunities. There's rarely accountability for holding to behavioral (or sometimes even professional) standards, and there's a general atmosphere of fear and mistrust.

Lori and Elena have attempted to provide PD in toxic organizations. We've attempted to create psychological safety and named the conflicts we'd observed with participants and leaders, but we hit brick walls. Sometimes you need to know when to go. We've said something like, "The PD you want us to provide isn't a match for what people here need. Our time and energy, and theirs, will be wasted. If you want to discuss getting to the root cause of this toxicity, we can support you, but this PD isn't going to result in people learning."

Perhaps you aren't an external PD provider who can walk away from a toxic organization. Perhaps you are the Director of Curriculum and Instruction and you recognize that your district is toxic. If you choose to stay in your district, commit to addressing the problem. Start by considering your own role in creating or per-petuating the dysfunction. Own your part—at least to yourself. Then find allies with whom you can address the dysfunction and take action. If you can't find any allies, maybe it's time to leave. At the very least, recognize the limits to your sphere of influence in creating psychological safety and therefore the limits in your ability to design and deliver transformative PD.

Complex individual psychologies are another obstacle to creating psychological safety. People are complex, and the hard truth is that you can't create psychological safety for every single person. Elena once coached a principal who complained end-lessly about her superintendent. When the superintendent led PD, Elena observed the principal disengage. "I just don't trust him," the principal explained to Elena. "I never feel safe around him." Several conversations later, the principal broke down in tears and explained that her superintendent triggered her unhealed childhood trauma. "There's probably nothing he could ever say or do that would make me feel safe with him," the principal said. "It's unfair, and it's not him, but this is the case."

Many people have unhealed trauma. A facilitator can do a lot to create a psy-chologically safe learning space, but there are limits. Sometimes you might have an insight into what someone is dealing with, but often you won't. Recognizing the limits of your responsibility can help you not take things personally. When you hit brick walls, whether with individuals or organizations, see what is possible if you listen from a place of compassion and curiosity. But also remember that you have permission to draw boundaries and a responsibility to hold a safe-ish learning space for a group of people.

It can be hard to figure out where to draw the line between "it's worth trying more" and "I've tried enough." This is why you need colleagues, your own coach, or a supervisor you trust. Additional perspectives can help you see your specific situation more clearly. If you don't have those support systems, your next step should be to find your own professional community.

Mitigating Dominant Culture: Creating Safe-ish Spaces

When we consider how to create conditions in which people can learn, we must acknowledge the role of power dynamics, dominant culture, and systemic oppression. This consideration has implications for how we create "safe" learning spaces, whose psychological safety we center, and how we use norms and agreements.

Identifying Dominant Culture

Dominant culture manifests in everything: in the way we greet each other, in how we communicate welcoming and belonging, in what we value and prioritize, in what we praise and appreciate, in how we ask questions and listen, in what kind of knowledge is most valued, and in what we think we should spend time doing. In the United States and many settler societies, the dominant culture is a culture of white supremacy: European (and white) values and practices are considered the norm and the standard. For example, Christmas is paid time off. If you practice another religion that has a different important holy day, you need to take personal time off if you don't want to work on that day. Another example is what is considered professional clothes: Elena's first principal wore a tailored skirt and jacket, nylons, and high heels every day. If she had worn a sari, she would not have been considered to be wearing professional attire.

Dominant culture plays a role in determining psychological safety. In the United States, those who appear to be white and male, and those who are English speaking, enjoy the greatest physical, social, and psychological safety. This is true whether folks are bird watching, driving, jogging, shopping, wine tasting, or barbecuing. Those who appear to be white, male English speakers are afforded a level of safety by their skin tone, gender, and linguistic privilege. Walking into a PD session, they bring that sense of safety with them. In contrast, many people of color, women, and folks for whom English isn't their first language can experience a sense of inferiority or not-belonging in institutional spaces, including in PD sessions. When we create psychological safety, we need to be aware that people have different levels of need for psychological safety—the playing field isn't the same for everyone when they enter learning spaces.

Consider Catalina, a teacher who immigrated to the United States from the Dominican Republic when she was a teenager. Catalina lives in a small city in Oregon. She speaks English fluently, although she has an accent. When she's in a PD session, sometimes she hesitates to ask a question because she's shy about her accent. Sometimes she is reluctant to share her opinions because she feels like everyone else, having been raised in this country, knows more about the education system than she does. She has internalized beliefs that her knowledge and experiences are less valuable and reliable than those of her American-born, white counterparts. Sometimes when she's shared her beliefs, her colleagues have dismissed her views and inserted their own. In a PD session, Catalina's needs for psychological safety are greater than for many of her colleagues because of the context that she is in. If Catalina was teaching in a school in Brooklyn, alongside other teachers who are immigrants or the descendants of immigrants, perhaps where there is more understanding and acceptance of her identity markers, Catalina's needs for psychological safety might not be as great.

Here's another example. Michael is a Black man who teaches at a private school in a suburban West Coast school. Although his school promotes progressive values, there have been countless times when he's enthusiastically expressed an opinion or shared an idea and his white colleagues said things like, "Your tone of voice is making it hard for me to hear you because it's so aggressive" or "You always sound angry" or "That's a good idea, but that's not how we do things here." What he experienced was bias (conscious or unconscious—it had the same effect on him), and it didn't take too long before Michael began to silence himself.

Our organizations, schools, and districts typically reflect the dominant culture in which they are situated. It is absurd to consider that folks who have marginalized identities, who are not considered by some to be as knowledgeable or valuable or fully human as others, can make a distinction between how safe they feel in the rest of the world and in a PD session. It takes great awareness and diligence to create a truly "safe learning space" when the culture in which we are embedded is harmful to so many people.

Furthermore, in much of the world, dominant culture has been profoundly shaped by capitalism. In a capitalist system, outcome, product, and efficiency are elevated above all else—including above relationships and emotions. These values affect how we think about PD: When facilitators focus on "getting through the agenda" and when they minimize or eliminate practice and processing time, their actions reflect the internalization of this ideology. In a capitalist system, emotions are disregarded and considered an obstacle to the important goals; after all, it's inefficient to the accumulation of wealth to have workers bemoaning their exploitation. Inadvertently, sometimes education leaders and facilitators adopt a mindset that conversations and feelings are a waste of time. When PD is thought of as an opportunity to deposit information into the minds of teachers, that's a reflection of a capitalist mindset; the result is not transformative learning.

If we want to transform our schools into places that embrace the full humanity of young people and adults, we'll need to slow down. This will be counter cultural, and we'll need to learn how to navigate the urgency of what needs to get done for children with the reality of the pace at which adults learn and change—but we'll need to divest from the capitalist mindset. This mindset places product above human beings; it says that it's a waste of time to talk about feelings; it purports that we don't need relationships in order to learn together. This mindset contributes to astronomically high burnout rates and disengagement; it's hurting everyone.

On White Fragility and Discomfort

White fragility is a term coined by author and teacher Robin DiAngelo in her 2019 book by the same title. It refers to what happens when white people center their own emotional needs (often their fear or hurt) at the expense of those of people of color or as a way to avoid talking about race.

Here's an example of how white fragility can show up in PD: Some years ago, Elena observed a principal she coached facilitate a session on implicit bias. The principal had edited together a video of classroom observations and asked teachers to track data points, including how often teachers called on Black or Latinx students, as opposed to white students. The data was upsetting. It was clear not only that teachers called on white students far more often, but they were also far kinder and more patient with them, asked them higher-order thinking questions, and praised them far more. A white teacher started sobbing. "I just feel like you're trying to humiliate us," she said to the principal. "I love my students, and I feel like you're saying I'm a terrible teacher." Another teacher said, "I don't think this activity is helpful. We don't feel supported by administration. This feels like an attack."

In this situation, the teachers used the expression of their emotions to attempt to hijack the session. The principal had anticipated this response. She skillfully allowed teachers to name the underlying feelings and acknowledge their fear, and then she guided them through the rest of the session. The problem wasn't the *emotions* the teachers were experiencing; it was that they were attempting to manipulate the situation by using their emotions. We can learn both to interrupt dominant culture and also to accept and embrace emotions.

How to Interrupt and Disrupt Dominant Culture in Learning Spaces

If you are committed to creating the conditions for learning so that *everyone* can learn, then you must consider how dominant culture (and all of its problematic, dehumanizing values) manifest in every space in which we convene. Yes, this might feel massive and overwhelming, but addressing the unhealthy impact of dominant culture is something you have to do if you aspire to create transformative PD. Here are some things you can do:

- Continue learning. As a facilitator, you bring your unconscious and conscious biases to every learning space. Cultivate your cultural competence. Learn how to understand, work with, and support folks who don't share your identity markers. Learn about your own identity markers, how they intersect, and the privileges conferred on those identities. Learn about dominant culture and white supremacy culture and how those show up in our organizations and schools. Hone your ability to identify indicators of white supremacy culture and your skill at interrupting those behaviors and beliefs. Learn about Tema Okun's research (see Appendix F: "Resources for Further Learning"). Keep learning. We've been indoctrinated with racist ideology for more than 500 years; it's going to take some time for us to extricate it from our minds and organizations. Learning is the antidote.
- Center the psychological safety of folks who have marginalized identities. Pay close attention to how they engage and communicate. Observe how others communicate with them. Just like you would in the classroom, pay attention to patterns of participation. If you ask a question to a group of 50 people and 5 people raise their hand to answer and one of those is a teacher who has a marginalized identity like Catalina (or Michael), invite their response first. This messages that you value what they have to say. Depending on how you identify, or depending on whether you have more dominant identities, you may need to hone your skills to notice whom you call on. Invite a trusted partner or colleague to observe you facilitate. Ask yourself this question, *Whose needs am I centering?*
- Aim to create "safe-ish" spaces. Remember: For the majority of people of color, as well as folks from other marginalized identities, we live in such a profoundly unsafe world that it sounds disingenuous to suggest that a PD session could be a "safe space." People don't drop their biases and bigotry at the door. Acknowledge that safety is relative and that you are committed to seeing how power, privilege, and dominant culture manifest in a PD space that you facilitate; be

clear that you are committed to doing all you can to create an equitable, safe-ish space for learning.

- Create optional affinity group learning spaces. Whether during one PD session or throughout the school year, give people of color the option to meet with other people of color (and/or to meet in identity group-alike configurations). These will likely be *safer* spaces and more conducive to learning for those participants.
- Develop norms, and processes to uphold norms, that are inclusive. If you are working with a group more than once, be sure to involve members of this group in developing the norms and be sure that a diversity of perspectives is shared. Scrutinize norms for ways in which they might inadvertently uphold dominant culture.
- Develop accountability structures, such as the process check, for meetings. Also do inclusion checks and ask, "Whose voices are not here as we do this learning? What are the implications?"
- Gather feedback (see Chapter 5) and pay close attention to feedback from people of color. Ask questions that explore a sense of psychological safety ("Do you feel listened to? Do you feel like your ideas are taken seriously? Do you feel safe to take risks in our learning spaces?"). Believe what people of color say (especially if you aren't a person of color). If they say, "I don't feel safe here," don't argue or ask them to defend themselves. Don't ask them to solve the problem (the racism they experience), but invite their ideas and suggestions, and commit to taking steps toward creating safe-ish spaces.

For People of Color Who Facilitate Learning, from Elena

As a person of color working in organizations that most likely reflect dominant culture, you've got extra work to do—and this is not fair. Here are a few suggestions for how to interrupt and disrupt dominant culture in learning spaces. First: Keep learning. We've internalized a lot of white supremacist ideology, as well as ideology that marginalizes other folks. This manure is toxic. The first step to getting rid of it is to be able to spot it and understand it.

Second: Keep healing. You deserve healing from the violence of white supremacy. Find ways to heal your mind, heart, body, and spirit.

Finally: Build community. Especially if you're in a place where there aren't too many other people of color around you, you're the only person of color on staff, or you present PD to majority white groups, build your support system. Find friends, colleagues, a coach, and a supervisor who are people of color with whom you can process. You probably don't need me to tell you that you need support; find it. You'll struggle to create safe-ish learning spaces for others if you don't feel safe-ish. You can feel safer if you have support.

Psychological safety, or safe-ish spaces, should not be our ultimate aspiration. "Safe" feels like the minimum required condition. So what kind of emotional tenor would you want to experience in a learning space? Perhaps absorbed, calm, centered, connected, curious, energized, engaged, enthusiastic, exhilarated, fulfilled, intrigued, joyful, and satisfied. Perhaps you'd like to experience a state of flow. Safety is a prerequisite to accessing these feelings and experiences—but aim for the feelings beyond safety.

When Elena delivers PD, she likes to think of herself as a manipulator of neurochemicals, or as a conductor of emotions, which sounds less nefarious. A great deal of what happens on our emotional landscape is influenced by what happens in our brain and body. When you intend to deliver transformative PD, you need to decrease the production of cortisol (the stress hormone) in learners and increase dopamine, oxytocin, and endorphins (which make us feel good and connected to each other). The purpose of activating pleasant emotions is not simply so that participants leave the PD and say, "That was great! It was so much fun!" Feeling good and having fun is important, but it's not enough. It's also important that the learners like you—even love you! But it's also not enough. You create spaces that are psychologically safe, and full of joy, so that people are primed for learning.

"No laughter, no learning."

—Jane Vella

How to Orchestrate Pleasant Emotions

There are both proactive and reactive moves you can make to guide people toward pleasant emotions. Many of these can be planned; others need to be called up when the need arises. Here are some ways to activate pleasant emotions in a PD session:

- When participants are arriving and settling in, play upbeat music—just don't play it too loud.
- At the start of the session, play a short video that is heartwarming or humorous and that connects learners to the content for the session.
- Place fresh mint plants on tables. The smell of mint is energizing, and we can use our senses to activate emotions.

- Include images in your slides that evoke connection, love, and joy. We're big fans of using natural imagery and animals, especially baby animals.
- Use color in slides and materials. Color lifts our mood.
- Include storytelling at the start of sessions. Research finds that just a few minutes of storytelling between people generates oxytocin, the "bonding" hormone (Zak, 2014).
- Get people out of their seats at least once an hour. Moving our bodies generates endorphins. Of course, be mindful of mobility issues. Make sure that out-of-seat activities are easy and accessible (i.e., stroll around the room and find a new partner to talk to; take a 10-minute walk and talk), but also invite people to "dance like a toddler" or throw tennis balls to each other.
- In tense moments, invite people to stop and take slow, deep breaths. Five deep breaths resets the nervous system.
- Read the room: Pay close attention to nonverbal communication. Sense the energy. If you see that people are starting to look tired, even if a break isn't scheduled, call a short break. Invite people to stand and stretch, get a snack, or get some fresh air.
- Use humor. Plan your jokes or bust them out spontaneously, but lighten things up. Most of us take ourselves too seriously.
- Give folks an opportunity to be playful with each other. Rock-paper-scissors tournaments are great fun. There's loud chanting (which means deep breathing, which is good for our mind and body) and laughter and clapping.

Perhaps as you read an item on this list you thought, *I hate it when facilitators do that.* That's okay. Some people won't like every single thing you do. Some people will hate it when you ask them to get up and dance (and those people will rush off to the restrooms), but others will like it. Your job isn't to please everyone, all the time.

Tips and Tricks:

Keep silly activities short, and make sure they have relevance to the content of the PD (and name those connections!). After asking participants to engage in silliness, invite participants to debrief. Allow them to identify the emotions that came up for them and also to make connections between the activity and the PD session. Finally, guide people to identify how fun activities help them feel more open to learning.

Purpose Is Primary

Let's get back to the reasons for doing what we do: the *why* that drives all our decisions in creating transformative PD. The purpose of cultivating positive emotions and helping folks to process uncomfortable emotions is to prime people for taking risks, building connection with each other, and learning. As you plan for PD, consider how to cultivate pleasant emotions and keep the big picture in mind (what are the session's goals or outcomes?) and then think about the conditions in which learning happens. You need to create those conditions, and at the top of the list of conditions is how we feel.

A commitment to purpose emboldens Elena (who is rather shy) to lead a goofy mood booster called, "Let's All. . .!" The facilitator begins by calling out, "Let's all. . ." and then naming a behavior like *howl like coyotes!* Or *Dance like sixth graders at their first dance!* Or *Sing if you're happy and you know it!* The group echoes back, "Yes! Let's!" And then everyone does it, and it's silly. After a minute or so, when someone else is inspired, they call out an action: "Let's all pat our heads and rub our bellies." And the group echoes back, "Yes! Let's!" And so on for around five minutes.

When Elena leads this she usually feel awkward and self-conscious—after all, she has to enthusiastically howl like a coyote, dance like a sixth grader, and do whatever anyone else throws out there—and often she's on a stage. Yet these feelings quickly dissipate as people engage. Afterward, when the group debriefs, many participants admit their discomfort but say things like, "It really wasn't that bad, and actually it was kind of fun." Many of us are attached to our professional, adult selves; it can be good to take a break from those selves once in a while. Being silly and feeling joy can prime us for deeper learning—and Lori and Elena are willing to do whatever it takes for PD to be meaningful.

If PD is going to feel like a party, facilitators have to know how to engage emotions. But that need not feel like a draining task. What we seem to have forgotten is that emotions give us access to connection and energy and celebration. What if, for both facilitators and participants, PD sessions could feel exhilarating? Joyful? What if creating such sessions could be easier than we think?

Before You Go

Pause and Process:

- What emotions did you experience as you read this chapter? Why do you think you experienced them?
- Which emotions do you long to experience when you present?
- Of the ten things to do when you get emotionally activated, which two might be most helpful? How can you remember them?

Remember:

- Human beings have emotions.
- Emotions are friends that want to give us information.
- A transformational facilitator needs to understand, expect, and embrace emotions.
- Dominant culture profoundly influences how we understand our own emotions, how we express them, and how we interpret other people's emotions.

CHAPTER 3

Navigate Power

As soon as Terry walked into the library, Elena could tell that the PD session would be a battle. Terry was 15 minutes late, she was noisily crunching on tortilla chips, and when she registered that the meeting had already started, she loudly whispered insincere apologies and said, "I'll go to timeout! So sorry, so sorry." She proceeded to sit in a chair on the other side of the room and pulled out a red pen and a stack of papers to grade.

"It's okay, Terry," Elena said, "we're just getting started. You can sit with your grade-level team."

"That would be disruptive," Terry said. "And anyway, I've done this activity before. You're probably the third person from the central office who has tried to get us to do this." Terry's phone buzzed, and she looked at the screen and laughed. She looked up at Elena. "It's okay, you go on back to them. I'm sure they need you. I'll be fine here."

Terry was a department chair who held a lot of social capital in the school. She was liked and respected, and many teachers took their cues from her. Elena was a new instructional coach. She didn't know what to do in response to Terry's behavior, and she could see that other teachers were observing their interaction. The objective for this PD session was for teachers to identify ways to better understand students. Elena had opened it with "I am from" poems written by the school's eighth graders, poems in which students had shared heartbreaking anecdotes.

"Terry," Elena said, trying to stay calm, "your grade level needs your participation. What will they think if they see you opting out?" Terry's phone buzzed again, and she picked it up.

"Oh, sorry," Terry said, "I need to step out." She stood and walked through the room, loudly saying, "Sorry, everyone, sorry! I'll be back, don't worry! Keep on!"

Elena turned back to the group of teachers. She was irritated that Mr. H, the school's principal, hadn't shown up; usually the teachers were better behaved when he was there. She began explaining the next activity when the algebra teacher raised his hand. "It's great that you're trying so hard," he said, his tone patronizing, "but we could really use this time to grade papers. Now that admin is asking for progress updates so often, we don't have enough time to grade. Couldn't we do this during the summer?" Affirmations echoed throughout the room.

"Or maybe this can be optional," said the music teacher. "If you want to do this PD with Elena, you stay. I don't have papers to grade, but I could use the time for something better."

Terry returned, taking in the uprising. "The thing is, Elena, what we really need to talk about is our discipline policy. These kids need us to hold high expectations for their behavior, they need clear consequences, and they need us to enforce those." Terry scoffed as she noticed the poems on the tables. "We don't need to read their poetry."

"Fine," Elena said. "It's your choice if you want to leave. I'll let Mr. H know who makes this choice. Your checks will be docked as this is contracted time."

Terry sat down in the chair in front of Elena. "Let's go, then! Let's learn about our students!" Her tone was falsely enthusiastic. The algebra teacher leaned back and crossed his arms over his chest. The music teacher opened his computer. Another teacher rose from her seat, complaining of a stomachache and said she'd stop by the office and fill out a sick-leave form. Terry walked in and out all afternoon taking calls. Elena knew that the teachers who stayed did not meet the objective; she doubted that any empathy was built for students. She suspected that the primary outcome of the PD was strengthening staff resistance, and by the end of the afternoon, as Elena left school with a major headache, all she could think about was how she needed to find another job.

What Elena didn't understand as she loaded her bags into her car was that she was dealing with power: The teachers felt disempowered and were trying to find a way to have input into PD; the principal had abdicated power and, as a result, created an unstable situation; and Elena was trying to figure out what her power was and how she could leverage it. The "problem" in this moment was not Terry or the teachers or Elena—it was that no one was skillfully navigating power.

The most common question we get about coaching and delivering PD is about resistance. "How do you deal with resistance?" someone will inevitably ask in every workshop, and the room will fall silent. The philosopher Michel Foucault wrote, "Where there is power, there is resistance" (1978: 95–96). The inverse is also true, so it makes sense that questions about resistance are really questions about power: how you understand power, how you use your own power, and how you respond to other people's engagement with power.

In the opening anecdote, Elena felt like she was experiencing resistance (which she took personally), but she was unknowingly in the epicenter of a larger power struggle. Frustrated and feeling they had no say (power) in determining the focus of PD, the teachers reached for what's called *coercive power*, and their behaviors showed up as resistance. Elena also reached for coercive power by making threats. In the end, none of these attempts at grabbing power really worked. Everyone felt drained and defeated; the experience and outcomes for children did not improve.

Where there is power, there are emotions, often uncomfortable emotions—and especially fear. A chicken-and-egg situation can emerge in situations in which unhealthy power dynamics exist: Power generates emotions, and emotions generate power. And so, to respond to resistance, you must know how to recognize and navigate power—your own and other people's, and you must understand how to respond to emotions—your own and other people's. This chapter will help you understand the many layers of complexity in a situation like Elena's, and it will help you identify possibilities for action.

This chapter also has applicability beyond your work as a PD facilitator. It'll help you think about how you move through hierarchical systems and relate to power in social contexts outside of work. First, we'll explore the sources of power, how people acquire power, and how power can be used. Then we'll offer ways to navigate power in a PD context. The questions in Table 3.1 will guide us as we explore the sources of

Table 3.1 How to Navigate Power

Source	Which sources of power am I drawing from? Who grants me authority and credibility? What role does dominant culture play in how I source power?
Leverage	How am I leveraging power? Why am I using it that way?
Impact	What impact am I having? Do I truly want to have this impact? Does this impact align with my intentions, my core values, the values of my organization? Who do I want to be?
Possibilities	What possibilities exist for how I source and leverage my power?

our power, how we leverage it, and the impact it has on others—and new possibilities for how we wield power and respond to its presence. By the end of this chapter, we know you'll feel empowered to deal with power!

Sources of Power

Social psychologists identify six sources of social power: position, coercion, rewards, expertise, relationships, and information (French and Raven, 1959). None of these sources is inherently good or bad, although coercive power can definitely undermine the health and well-being of many. In systems of

> Which sources of power am I drawing from? Who grants me authority and credibility? What role does dominant culture play in how I source power?

oppression, coercive power is relied on by those at the top of the hierarchy more than any other source. For example, in the majority of schools, children's behavior is controlled through threats of expulsion, suspension, or exclusion. However, coercive power can be used as a tool for making change; for example, when people strike, they use coercive power, withholding their labor to generate fear in their employers.

The problem with coercive power is that it often results only in compliance; that is, it is more transactional than transformational. Laborers might win a strike, and the bosses might comply with their demands, but the bosses' fundamental attitude toward the workers doesn't shift—the demands were met out of fear, not basic respect for the dignity and well-being of other human beings. Children might comply with school rules because they fear the consequences, but they don't gain an internal locus of control. Coercive power won't help us guide adults and children to become fully realized or connected to individual and collective purpose; coercive power alone won't help us create kind, equitable, just, and liberated school communities.

Like coercive power, reward power can be limited because it relies on external motivation and doesn't fuel long-term change efforts. That said, reward power can be used as an important, temporary scaffold. For example, if a parent draws from reward power by offering a privilege for desired behavior, and if that allows the child to be successful, the child might develop confidence and skills to enact the behavior. The reward is a scaffold allowing the child to tap into intrinsic motivation to enact a concrete behavior like getting up on time. For reward power to work, the rewarded person has to have the skills and knowledge to enact the desired behavior—or has to be able to develop these skills fairly quickly.

Table 3.2 describes the origins of the sourcing and provides examples. As you read these descriptions, see if you can come up with other examples of people who draw power from each source.

Table 3.2 Sources of Social Power[1]

Source of Power	Description
Position *(Positional power* or *legitimate power)*	• Comes from a formal right to issue directives or make key decisions because of position in an organization. • Granted by a title, role, and/or status. • Examples: a superintendent determines a district's annual goals, a principal spearheads an equity initiative, a teacher decides on grading policies. The Director of Curriculum and Instruction introduces the year's PD focus at the first all-teacher PD session. She says, "The data from last year's benchmark assessments indicate that there's a breakdown in how you assess students' progress toward mastery. So this year, everyone will be expected use daily formative assessment methods to track progress and adjust course when needed."
Coercion *(Coercive power)*	• Comes from the ability to punish someone for noncompliance. Consequences can be losing a job, public shaming, being kicked out of class, or being socially ostracized. • Often relies on punishments that are vague and obtuse. • Relies on fear to induce compliance. • Can be explained as "the ends justify the means." • Examples: dictators, bullies, and the teacher who at the start of a PD session says to the facilitator, "Why are *you* presenting this session? You don't know our students." The district adopts a scripted literacy program and hires curriculum coaches who are charged with ensuring fidelity to the program. They do unannounced classroom visits to make sure that teachers are on the designated page for that day. The names of teachers who are not delivering the assigned lessons are reported to the principal.

(Continued)

Table 3.2 (Continued)

Source of Power	Description
Rewards *(Reward-based power)*	• Comes from the ability to issue rewards such as a promotion, high grade, public compliment, or group approval. • Can be coercive if rewards are used to achieve compliance. • Reward-based and coercive power are typically tied to positional power, but not always. • Examples: a district gives bonuses to teachers whose students score high on standardized tests, a promise of Friday afternoon free time if everyone turns in the week's homework. During an activity, the PD facilitator says, "While you all practice, I'm going to circulate and listen in. I'm hoping to hear a few great examples of how to use this strategy so that after the practice time, I can ask those folks to share with the whole group."
Expertise *(Expertise-based power)*	• Comes from someone's experience or knowledge, and/or from reputation or qualifications. • Expertise doesn't have to actually exist, but the perception of expertise must exist. • Examples: a leader with a Ph.D., a teacher who won a "teacher of the year" award. A fifth-grade teacher is invited to present a PD session on how to develop classroom community because he's been at the school longer than almost anyone else and everyone says he's a "great teacher."
Relationships *(Relational or referent power)*	• Comes from being trusted or respected. • Based on personality and interpersonal skills. • Isn't contingent on positional power. • Examples: the beloved school custodian who treats everyone kindly and who has been at the school for decades; a student's parent who is a community organizer; the staff member who leads a rebellion against a leader's equity initiative. The newly hired principal leads an all-staff PD session and begins by saying, "My vision for this time is that you'll teach me. I will facilitate the structures in which we'll learn together and make sure this time is useful to all, but all of you are the experts on our students. I am eager to learn from you."

(Continued)

(Continued)

Source of Power	Description
Information *(Informational power)*	• Comes from access to facts and knowledge that others find useful or valuable. • Can result from and indicate relationships with power holders. • Builds credibility. • Examples: the department head who attends meetings at the central office and is informed about upcoming changes, the student's parent who knows all the kids in the neighborhood. The grade-level team lead informs teachers that they need to revise the scope and sequence of their units. He says, "In the Leadership Team meeting, our principal explained changes to funding sources, and while it's too complicated to explain, we need to do this."

[1] French and Raven were the first to write about power in these ways, and they used *legitimate power* for what is now commonly referred to as *positional power* and *referent power*, which is commonly known as *relational power*.

The first step in navigating power is getting really clear on where you are drawing power from. Often, we draw from multiple types of power simultaneously, although it's also common to have a tendency to habitually draw from one or another source. Once we consider the ways to use power and the impact we have, we'll be able to evaluate our decisions. But the place from which we draw power is complicated by where we are, whom we are leading, and how we respond to dominant culture. That's what we'll explore next.

Pause and Process:

• When have you worked from coercive power?
• From which sources of power does your supervisor operate most often?
• From which sources of power do you most often operate in your role?
• From which sources of power would you like to draw on in your role?

Where Does Credibility and Authority Come From?

Imagine you're in a dark auditorium waiting for the new superintendent to come on stage. You know little about him, except that he's a man. The room is abuzz with curiosity. Your district has been in transition for some years, and folks are eager for a leader who will create stability. Now imagine a tall, slender white man wearing a tailored suit walks out. He seems to be in his 40s, has short graying hair and a broad smile, and greets everyone warmly. How would you feel?

How would you feel if the new superintendent rolled out in a wheelchair, appearing to be in his 60s and speaking with an accent? He, too, smiles and greets everyone warmly. Which of these two superintendents do you think you'd immediately grant more power to? Whom do you think you'd instinctively trust?

Extensive research on biases has found that the majority of people immediately grant more power to the tall, slender white man in his 40s. Now, you may not be among these, and you might welcome the perspectives of an older man in a wheelchair. But dominant culture has conditioned us to value youth, physical abilities, height, thinness, and wealth; we have been conditioned to think that people who are older, who aren't conventionally attractive, who are in a wheelchair, who don't appear to be of European descent or who are dark skinned, who don't wear "nice" clothes or have gleaming straight white teeth, and who speak with an accent are inferior. We grant status—almost instantly—to the superintendent in a suit; we withdraw status from the superintendent with an accent.

The majority of the people who hold political and economic power—the leaders of our institutions—are white and male, are cisgender and heterosexual, identify as Christian, speak English, have access to wealth, and are physically able. This is true when we look at who is on TV, who is in the superintendent's office, and who occupies corporate corner offices and the Senate chamber. We have been socialized to think this is just the way things are—and worse—that there's something innately better about those people who make it into positions of power.

This mindset, when unexamined, will affect how you lead PD. It can affect how you think about your sources of power and your credibility and authority. This mindset can generate the feelings associated with imposter syndrome.

If you aspire to create transformative schools, it's imperative to apply a sociopolitical lens. This means that you analyze relationships, mindsets, decisions, systems, and just about everything through an understanding of dominant power. Because how we feel about our own power, and who we grant power to, has a great deal to do with how power manifests in larger systems and in our culture as a whole—and right now, in the United States and the Western world, that dominant power is patriarchal, capitalist, and white supremacist.

It can be hard to tease apart our individual thoughts from the norms of the dominant culture, which is the culture produced by our country's dominant social, economic, and political systems. We are born into dominant culture, indoctrinated or conditioned into it, and unless we learn to recognize it, we may not be conscious of the way it affects us. And that can have a deleterious effect on us and the people we support. If you don't activate a sociopolitical lens to question power, you may, for example, not trust the superintendent who roles out in a wheelchair and has an accent—even though he may be the brilliant, phenomenal leader you've been hoping for. If you act unconsciously, drawing power from the same places that you see other leaders around you draw from, you may end up sourcing from coercive power more than any other kind—because so many leaders in our world do so— and you may not achieve your ultimate goals and act on your truest intentions.

When you critically analyze how power manifests in our larger systems, you won't feel like you constantly have to struggle to get credibility and authority. Using a sociopolitical lens is part of what helps us recognize our internalization of dominant culture and shift away from inequitable and unjust allocations of power and privilege. Ultimately, using a sociopolitical lens to deconstruct power allows us to see more pathways from which to source power. To transform our schools, organizations, and society, we'll need to see every possibility available to us. Honing your ability to identify where dominant culture is warping your mindset is liberating.

"The most common way people give up their power is by thinking they don't have any."

—Alice Walker

Imposter Syndrome

When Elena began delivering PD sessions, she often felt like she didn't have the authority or credibility to do so. She thought she hadn't been teaching long enough, she didn't have an advanced degree in education, and she had never been Teacher of the Year or received any formal acknowledgment of her expertise. Elena also questioned whether her colleagues would see her as credible: She hadn't attended a prestigious university (unlike some of her peers), she didn't feel articulate as a speaker, and she didn't look like the PD providers who came to her district. When Elena stood in front of other teachers, she did not project confidence or authority; her colleagues perceived this and unconsciously their trust in her ability to facilitate PD decreased. Elena suffered from imposter syndrome, and she didn't become a powerful presenter until she exorcised that mindset.

Imposter syndrome is the feeling that you don't have the skills or expertise to be in the position you're in, even if you have been or can be effective in the role. At its core, imposter syndrome is a stew of emotions that results in a sense of inadequacy. Often this includes anxiety about how different you are from people who have traditionally been in your role or who are in a comparable role. You think: *Someone else should be here, not me!*

Let's unpack that "someone else." Do you share that other person's social identity markers? Their gender, race, ethnicity, class background, physical appearance, and so on? When Elena began delivering PD, she had never seen a Latina in a leadership role in education (not as a superintendent, principal, or assistant principal) and had never attended PD facilitated by a Latina. Most of the PD providers she'd observed wore clothes and spoke in a way that seemed to indicate an upper middle class background; most were male; many cited their Ivy League alma maters. Because she didn't see herself in the people who were doing what she aspired to do (facilitate PD), and when she didn't engage her sociopolitical consciousness, Elena felt like she was unfit to deliver PD.

When you experience imposter syndrome, you feel like there's something wrong with you. But the problem is in the systems and dominant culture that's blocked you (and people who share your identity markers) from stepping into the role you're in—or that you want to be in. When you can see that the problem lies in systems and culture, you can more easily shift your mindset.

The antidote to imposter syndrome is to redefine your authority and credibility on terms that resonate for you, and for the folks you're leading, and continue to uproot unconscious beliefs that there's something inherently inferior about you. This is way easier said than done. Here are a few strategies that can help you eradicate a sense of imposter syndrome:

- Surface, name, and explore the emotions that come up when you feel a sense of inadequacy.
- Identify the link between your thoughts and emotions. For example, you may think that you're not equipped to be a guest lecturer in a teacher training program at a university because you don't have a PhD, and that thought makes you feel insecure and afraid. Or you may feel like you can't run for president because there's never been a person in that office who looks like you or shares your cultural background.
- Find evidence to counter your thoughts. For example, recall that some university lecturers don't have a doctorate; their legitimacy comes from their experiences in the field. Or identify all the people who were the first to do something that no one like them had ever done before.
- Decide whether you want to believe your thoughts. Do you want to believe that someone else could do whatever you're doing better? Or do you want to believe that you can do a fine job? Do you want to believe that only people who attended Ivy League colleges are competent leaders? Or that other criteria define quality leadership?

- Create new thoughts and beliefs, and recite those affirmations to yourself over and over. For example: *I know a heck of a lot about teaching, and I have a ton to offer people who are learning to become teachers.* Or *Maybe there is someone else who could do this better, but I'm here now, and I'll do a great job in this role.* Or *Just because no one who looks like me has ever been the president doesn't mean I can't run for president.* Elena's preferred affirmation is: *Fuck imposter syndrome; I don't have time for that.* Lori's preferred affirmation is: *I am meant to be here (and I am a badass).*

A point of clarification: We've found that those who share many traits with dominant culture (such as young, white men) can feel *insecure* in a new role—and this insecurity merits exploration. But in our research, this is distinct from what many people of color and folks who have marginalized identities describe when they talk about imposter syndrome—a deep sense of inferiority and not belonging, a deep fear of not being accepted or considered to be credible.

Before you continue reading, take a few moments to think about these questions. This reflection will help you process all the ideas we've shared so far, and make connections to your own experience as a facilitator.

- What gives you the authority to do what you're doing? The degrees you've completed, the institutions that granted those degrees, your life experiences or age?
- Think of someone you admire. What is that admiration based on? Is it something they've accomplished? Or how they treat you or others? Why do you grant them credibility?
- Do you have beliefs that limit your sense of what you are capable of? What are those? What do you get from believing them? What could you get from releasing them?

When Positional Power Is Murky

Many educators are in roles of quasipositional power. If you are a coach or division head, for example, you may have some authority to make some decisions, but you also might feel like you don't really have positional power. You might feel caught between what you're told to do by the principal or central office and what teachers want. You might be seen as having power, even if you feel like your position doesn't come with meaningful authority.

Let's consider an example. A principal asks a coach to facilitate PD on analyzing data. The previous year's test scores are out, the area superintendent has expressed concern about the school's data, and the principal believes that the next step is for all teachers to look at the data. The coach, feeling compelled to defer to the principal's authority and positional power, agrees. The coach may feel like this is the right direction for PD to go in, or not. Regardless, the coach feels like they have no choice—the principal is their boss. But when the coach stands before the 50 faculty members and begins the PD session, they sense pushback. The teachers feel that the testing data isn't useful; they feel that students scored poorly because of challenges outside the teachers' control. Finally, one teacher says it directly, "Looking at this data is a waste of time."

The coach squirms at the front of the room. Now that the teachers have pointed out the ways the data is compromised, the coach isn't so sure this PD makes sense. Perhaps the principal stands and makes a case for looking at the data, and the teachers comply—because the principal is their boss as well—and the coach proceeds with the plan, now feeling uncomfortable and torn.

Have you been in a situation like this or witnessed one? The power dynamics can be challenging to navigate, but there is a path forward: direct communication. When you feel squished among the hierarchies of an organization and you're presented with conflicting demands and desires, you need to *coach* or *manage up*. This term references the ways you shift to engage your supervisor in a conversation to align on actions. You'll need to skillfully share your perspective, the data that you see, and your suggestions for action; you'll need to listen closely to your supervisor and understand their perspective; you'll need to offer solutions, compromises, and partnership. That's what it means to coach or manage up. This can sound like:

- I understand that you've made the decision to create several combination classes for next year, and I have some concerns. Before it's finalized, could we consider the potential unintended consequences for teachers and students?
- I'd really like to hear more about your vision for our team, and I'd love to share mine as well.
- I know we're getting pushback from some parents on our ethnic studies program. I am here to support you in responding to that pushback, and I have some ideas to propose.

When you are in a role in which your positional power is murky, it's also critical that you provide and get clarity wherever and whenever you can. There's often confusion about a coach's role and responsibility: Does a coach report everything they observe in a classroom to administrators? Does a coach play any role in evaluation? Does a coach share their opinions on whether a teacher should be retained or not? If you're in a role that's murky, get really clear on what is within your power in terms of decisions and input. For example, a coach might manage up and say to their supervisor, "For me to lead this PD, I need some clarity on my role and your expectations." When you stand before others, be as clear as possible. This can sound like saying, "The decision for this PD session was made by consensus in the Leadership Team," or "The district has requested that we focus on this topic for PD this month, and I see value in it," or "Because I play a role in evaluations, during the practice time, I'll be sitting on the side so you don't feel like I'm hovering around and listening. I want you to feel completely comfortable with practicing and making mistakes, so I'll be out of the way just in case my proximity creates self-consciousness." Sometimes you'll be able to clear the murky waters, and sometimes you won't. In those instances, understand that you'll need to focus on building relationships and trust.

Establishing Credibility and Authority

How you establish credibility and authority will involve reflection on who you lead, where you lead, and how you respond to dominant culture. For example, if you are a department chair, leading a team of teachers in a school you've taught in for a decade, you'll likely lean on your experience and the relationships you've built to establish authority. If you are a new Diversity, Equity, and Inclusion Director, you're aware that this is a new role and that you are one of the only people of color in the district, and you're facilitating PD for the district's administrators, you may need to lean on your expertise and positional power. Pathways to credibility will vary. If you aspire to design and deliver transformative PD, here are some suggestions to establish credibility:

- *Script an introduction that conveys both confidence and humility.* Write out what you'll say when you begin a PD initiative, share it with colleagues, get feedback, and practice saying it. This can sound like, "I'm so excited to work with all of you on how we can better meet the needs of our English Learners. As the child of immigrants, I saw firsthand how challenging it was for my parents to learn English. I've been working in schools around language learning for 15 years, and I have a master's degree in language acquisition—and I have so much more to learn. Recently I've been researching language acquisition in children who have high literacy skills in their heritage language, and I'm finding this fascinating. I know that in your school you have a large population of Syrian refugees, and so I'm eager to hear your observations."
- *Show up as a learner.* This can sound like, "Although I've taught English for 25 years, in the last two years I've been learning about how to authentically diversify my curriculum."

- *Share your learning journey.* This can sound like, "I appreciated the feedback from our last session, which helped me see how I can diversify the assignments I give as well as the books I assign," or "When I first started coaching, I really struggled to hold off on giving advice. I still struggle with that, but I've found other coaching strategies that work better."
- *Be honest about what you know.* Don't be embarrassed to say you don't know something. This can sound like, "I appreciate that question, and I'm not familiar with the research you're citing. I will definitely take a look at it and get back to you next time." Or, "I've primarily worked in suburban schools, and while there are some similarities, there are a lot of differences with your rural district. I'm eager to learn from you and hear your perspectives."
- *Emphasize your commonalities and connections.* We rarely respect people just because they got this or that award or because their students scored high on an exam—in fact, boasts can lead us to withdraw credibility. Activate your empathy, find points of connections, and share those when you do. This can sound like, "Although I've never been a site administrator like all of you, I've lead many teams through hard moments of change. I know what it's like to have tremendous responsibility, to feel alone in a leadership role, and to be responsible to many stakeholders."

As you navigate the complexities of leadership and facilitation, ask yourself frequently what kind of leader you want to be. To be a transformational leader, you'll need to source primarily from relational power. Avoid coercive and reward sources of power—remember that those might result in compliant behavior, but they won't change beliefs or ways of being. Using coercive and reward power isn't transformative and ultimately might just serve to replicate the hierarchical status quo.

By taking into account how authority and credibility are granted, and by understanding the role of dominant culture, you can be more intentional about how you source power. This will help you also understand how, when, and by whom power is given to you.

We've taken a long look at where power comes from. Before we explore what you can do with power, review the sections you've read and consider doing one of the following:

- Draw a couple of sketches to represent the key ideas.
- Talk to a friend or colleague about your big takeaways or ah-has.
- Write in response to the reflection questions in the section on imposter syndrome.
- Take a walk and get some fresh air.

Leveraging Power

You can do a lot of things with fire: cook dinner, warm your toes, roast marshmallows, or burn down a house. Power is like fire. You've got a lot of options for what you do with it.

> How am I leveraging power? Why am I using it that way?

Before we explore what you can do with power, let's consider how you register the presence of power. Recall the last professional meeting or PD session that you attended in person. Do you remember what you thought as you entered the room? Perhaps you knew you could sit anywhere you wanted, and you found a seat in the back. Or perhaps you saw a colleague you avoid at one table and made a beeline for the other side of the room. It's also likely that you registered the presence of the facilitator. Perhaps you took in the expression on their face, what they were doing, and how they related to each person arriving. Part of what you were doing as you took in all this information was registering the presence of power.

Whenever we physically walk into a space, we unconsciously (or sometimes consciously) scan for power—we look to see who has power and how they are wielding it. If the facilitator stands at the door warmly greeting people, they are sourcing from relational power. If you are encouraged to sit anywhere you want, power is shared with you. If the facilitator is rushing around and doesn't make eye contact or welcome anyone, you might feel a little apprehension or some mistrust as you consider how this person with positional power might act. If you don't see the leader of the gathering, you might feel anxious, wondering where they are, what they're doing, and when they'll show up—their absence unsettles you because it means you lack the clues you're looking for about power. Part of our unconscious work when we scan a space for power is assessing it for risks and dangers—and figuring out, usually unconsciously, how to keep ourselves safe. Power can be scary, and we elevate self-preservation above almost everything else.

The job of a facilitator is to create the conditions in which learning happens. To do this, you need to pay attention to energy—both cognitive and emotional energy—and direct it toward learning. When your learners are spending energy trying to figure out how to stay safe, they have less energy for learning. By cuing learners from the moment they enter a PD session that they are safe, you reserve their energy for what's most important: learning.

When we think about power in hierarchical settings—which most schools are—what we probably notice most often is the way people leverage or use power, especially when it feels controlling or manipulative or when it is challenged and a power struggle erupts. As facilitators, we might notice power most glaringly when it shows up as resistance. Once power manifests as resistance, it can be challenging to address. But as we learn how to source from and use power intentionally, we can avoid a whole lot of resistance.

Sociologists explain that regardless of where we source power from, we can use it in different ways which they talk about as using power-over, power-with, and power-to. These are described in Table 3.3. As you read them, see if you can recall times when you used power in each of these ways—perhaps as a teacher, as a leader, or in interpersonal relationships.

Table 3.3 Ways to Use Power

Way to Use Power	Definition and Examples
Power-over	Power-over relies on concealed or overt force, coercion, or threats. An individual or group typically makes decisions for others, and compliance results from fear of consequences. Power-over rests on the beliefs that power is finite and must be protected and that one individual or group is superior to another. Those who source from coercive power often use power-over. Those who use power-over are often enabled by well-established systems and institutions and/or have high levels of social capital. This kind of power is often met with resistance. Looks/sounds like: • "I know we're over time, but we've got to get through this agenda today. If you stay on task, we should finish soon." • "We'll start at 2:00 on the dot. There'll be a sign-in sheet at the door. Please make sure to note the time when you arrive." • "If your lesson plans aren't submitted by 5 p.m., a note will be made in your file." • "We know what is best for you."
Power-with	Power-with leads to collective action and the ability to work together. It is built on respect, mutuality, and collaborative decision-making. Leaders focus on strengths and assets rather than deficits. Using power-with can build bridges within groups and across differences. The underlying belief of using power-with is that power is infinite when shared, leadership is about being in service to others, and collaboration and collective efforts enable a group to accomplish a mission or fulfill a vision. Looks/sounds like: • "Based on the feedback I got on last month's session, this time we're going to. . ." • "This activity will help us collect the knowledge that already exists in the room."

(Continued)

Table 3.3 (Continued)

Way to Use Power	Definition and Examples
Power-with *(continued)*	• "Show me on your fingers how many minutes you want for the remainder of this discussion." • "I'm asking you to sit in these groups today so that you can learn from folks you don't often meet with." • "It sounds like this prompt didn't generate the kind of thinking and sharing I'd anticipated it would. Can someone suggest a different discussion question that's still related to this topic that might be more generative?" • An email reads, "Last time many of you weren't able to make it on time at 2 p.m. I recognize you may need more transition time after school ends. Our PD session will be 75 minutes (see the attached agenda for the plans), so if there is consensus, we can start a little later. Please respond to this survey (the results are public to all), so we can determine what time we'll start and end."
Power-to	Power-to is the power to make a difference, achieve goals, and create something new, and is often combined with power-with. Power-to is generative. It is also part of what constitutes agency (the capability to make choices and act on your will). When you use power-to, you act on a belief that creativity and self-realization is a basic human right. Looks/sounds like: • "Today you'll organize yourselves into groups for this learning activity. I trust that you'll figure out what makes the most sense." • "Take a couple minutes to set an intention for how you want to show up today." • Initiating a challenging conversation. • Identifying individual professional learning goals. • Designing an advisory curriculum with a grade level team. • Reflecting on core values and striving to work from them. • Creating new thoughts and beliefs that free you from imposter syndrome.

ELENA REFLECTS:

I'm embarrassed to admit that sometimes as a facilitator I've sourced from coercive power, and I've used it to power-*over*, because I'm frustrated and anxious. For example, I remember a time when I wanted people to stop scrolling social media feeds during a small-group activity. I was irritated that their actions negatively impacted the learning of others, but I didn't know what to do. "Table four!" I said. "I'm seeing some phones out, and right now we're practicing this strategy. There's another 20 minutes before break, so could you put those away?" The folks at table four complied, and part of me felt victorious. But then I registered the expressions on their faces, and I suspected they felt hurt by my actions, felt called out. And then I noticed they were disengaging.

During the break, when I took stock of the impact I had, I recognized that this wasn't who I wanted to be. I was out of alignment with my values. I was drawing from positional and coercive power. My life's mission is to heal and transform the world: I won't do that by calling people out publicly—and I don't have to because I have other options. But before I could explore those options, I had to recognize my underlying emotions: mostly fear that I wouldn't be effective using other methods. Turning inward is a step toward exploring other options for how to source and leverage power.

An hour later, I saw someone scrolling through social media during an activity. I approached them, crouched down, and quietly said, "I'm wondering if you can wait until break because your group needs your full participation to get the most out of this learning." By doing this, I sourced from relational power and used power-*with* and power-*to* to invite collaboration. Doing this doesn't always result in compliance, but more often than not, it preserves the relationship. And I feel better about who I am being in the world. Ultimately, that's all I can truly control.

The Impact of Power

> What impact am I having? Do I truly want to have this impact? Does this impact align with my intentions, my core values, the values of my organization? What is being created by my actions? Who do I want to be?

When your actions are aligned to your values and most deeply held beliefs, you experience a sense of integrity. It's easy for us to slip out of alignment—sometimes because we're swirling and twirling to get things done, and we act without thought, at other times because we lack the skills to meet a challenging situation. Whether it's because we're overworked or under-prepared, acting in ways that are not aligned to our values will leave us frustrated and anxious—and, likely, powerless. And when we feel powerless (because other people aren't doing what we want them to do and we don't know how to make them!), it's easy to reach for *power-over* strategies.

Power-over strategies are familiar. We see people using them everywhere, and we've probably used them a great deal—so we know how to use them. In the opening story, Elena was trying to use power-over over Terry and the other teachers in her PD. And yet when we pause and look at the impact we're having by using *power-over* over others by drawing from coercive or reward power, we may experience cognitive dissonance. If we pause and notice, deep down it doesn't feel good. Sometimes it feels really bad. Although almost 15 years have passed since Elena facilitated the PD session described in the opening, she still feels icky remembering it.

Think about a time when you sourced from positional power and used *power-over*—perhaps as a classroom teacher with a student or the whole class, or as a leader. Did you get what you wanted? Perhaps you wanted the class to be quiet or turn in their homework on time. Did you get those results, and were they sustained over time? What was the cost of the way you used power? How did your actions align to your deepest beliefs about how people change, and how do we create a better world? What was created by your actions? What was destroyed? Were you being who you want to be?

These philosophical questions deserve contemplation. They are best explored with someone else—a coach or colleague or trusted supervisor who can push your thinking, ensure that you practice self-compassion, and help you shift into other ways of being. We can't say, "I don't want to be that way!" unless we can see another way of being. We have to see the possibility of another way of doing things, other ways of sourcing and using power, if we are going to abandon our coercive tendencies.

To judge whether drawing from a particular source is good or bad, ask the following questions:

- Am I consciously and intentionally drawing from this source? Or am I drawing from it because it's habit and I don't know how to draw from other sources?
- Why am I drawing from this source?
- What are the unintended and intended consequences of drawing from this source? What are the consequences for our community? For the people we are here to serve? For the present and the future?

Dr. Salazar was a professor at an Ivy League university and a national expert on English Language Development. She'd written a book based on decades of research on the usage of ELD strategies in New York City. She was contracted to provide a multiyear professional development series to site administrators and coaches in a large California district. When Dr. Salazar began this engagement, she sourced from positional power and the power of expertise: In the first PD session she led, she spoke about her experience and knowledge for almost 20 minutes. She believed that by sourcing from expertise, she would earn respect.

However, after a few sessions, the learners complained to their supervisors. They felt that the PD wasn't relevant, that Dr. Salazar didn't listen to them, and that it was sit-and-get PD. They argued for the sessions to include the sharing of best practices already in use in their district. While the learners recognized that they could benefit from Dr. Salazar's experience and knowledge, they felt that she wasn't accounting for or respecting the ground-level expertise in the room. What they were saying, through the lens of power analysis, was that she was using her expertise as a form of control to leverage status over others. The unintended consequence of sourcing from positional and expertise power sources was that the learners disengaged and didn't access the learning opportunities—of which there were many.

Can you imagine how this scenario may have played out had Dr. Salazar also sourced from relational power? Even an outside consultant in a very new context can build relationships and source from relational power. Dr. Salazar was deeply committed to providing English Learners with access to core content, but in this case, by sourcing almost entirely from positional and expertise power, she was unable to accomplish her mission.

Let's consider another situation. For several years, Washington High School had been in the news because of racist incidents both between teachers and students, and among students. Parents lobbied the school board to address the issues, which extended into the curriculum, grading policies, class assignments, and site leadership. The principal, who had been at the school for a decade, had avoided the racism and had essentially abdicated leadership. The faculty felt like there was a leadership void at the school, and the school board required that the principal be transferred to another site and a new leader hired. From the moment the new principal entered Washington High, he made it clear that racial equity would be the top priority and the primary focus of professional development.

While the new leader sourced from relational power, he also sourced power from his experience and position. He faced pushback from some teachers and community members, but he didn't waiver from his commitment—and he worked fast and hard to convene a team to engage staff in looking at what was going on at their school and interrupting toxic practices. The new principal leveraged *power-to*, *power-with*, and *power-within*: He described a vision for what the school could be and enlisted stakeholders to realize this vision; he invited collaboration and collective problem-solving; he created space for racial affinity groups and opportunities for reflection on identity experiences. At the end of the first year of his leadership, almost 40 percent of staff resigned, in great part because they disagreed with his focus on racial equity. While some school board members were concerned and questioned his leadership, many were hopeful.

And Washington was changing. Three years later, Washington was in the news for the progress it had made in terms of both experiences and outcomes for students of color. When one African American mother was interviewed by a local TV reporter, she cited the principal's leadership as the key factor: "We had a place at the table, and he listened to us, but he also didn't let up on his commitment that we were going to change things here for our black and brown students." This principal's leadership is an example of a positional leader skillfully using power in many ways to realize a vision.

Social Capital as a Form of Power

To understand the many ways power can be used, you also need to understand social capital. Social capital can be leveraged by folks at different places in a hierarchical system, and sometimes those who feel disempowered work to build their social capital as a way to exert power across the system. Social capital is value neutral, and it's not the same thing as social intelligence—which is an ability to understand and navigate the emotions of a group.

Let's return to the opening anecdote in which Elena faced resistance from Terry. To add more context, Terry was a veteran teacher who seemed to be on every school and district committee. She spoke up with strong opinions in every staff meeting. When an announcement was made, everyone waited to respond (or perhaps even form their own opinions) until Terry had spoken. Sometimes she didn't even need to speak—her influence was such that she could sway opinions with a facial expression. Almost every Friday, she left big boxes of donuts or bagels in the staff room. She seemed to be best friends with many staff members, she was the one who always took new teachers under her wing, and she knew generations of students and their caregivers.

Terry had a high degree of social capital, and she was well-networked and had built extensive relationships in the community. She didn't have much positional power, but sourced from *expertise power* (she'd been at the school for 26 years), *relational power* (she was liked by many), and *informational power* (she was on every committee). Given the combination of her social capital and multiple sources of power, she could wield power in different ways. Often she used *power-over* and was coercive, influencing her colleague's opinions or intimidating them into falling in line with her opinions because they feared her power to ostracize them if they disagreed. She had ostracized people before, denying entrance to the inner cliques in the staff.

It's important to recognize that Terry did not have high emotional intelligence. She had many unmet needs, and she was not able to effectively communicate her needs, or the emotions that she experienced, to her colleagues or supervisors.

Furthermore, she sometimes responded to other people's emotions in a way that caused harm. Terry amassed and used social capital as a way to leverage power, which was part of what made it so difficult to interrupt the unproductive dynamic she created.

Practice: Observing Power around You

You will improve your skill at navigating power by observing how others do so. Identify someone whose behavior you'd like to better understand—a supervisor, a student, or a colleague. Perhaps it's behavior that makes you feel uncomfortable or that you find inspiring. Reflect on these questions:

- What source of power do you perceive them as sourcing from?
- What source of power do you suspect they think they're drawing from? If there's a difference between your perception and what you suspect they think, why might that be?
- How does this person leverage power? Do you think they'd agree with your experience of how they leverage power?
- What's the impact of the way this person uses power? Do you think they are aware of this impact? Do you think it's their intention to cause that impact?
- Which other options for action does this person have? Do you think there are other sources of power they could source from? Are there other ways they could leverage power?

If you're brave, ask others for feedback on how they experience your use of power. You can offer them this last set of questions to guide their reflection. Their feedback might help you see your options and impact in new ways.

Possibilities for Navigating Power

If you are committed to building resilient communities and if you recognize the role that transformative PD plays in creating those, you'll need to be intentional about how you source and use power. You'll need to draw primarily from relational power and leverage power-with, power-to, and power-within. There are many ways to do this, and in doing so, you recognize the many possibilities for

> What possibilities exist for how I source and leverage my power?

navigating power. We'll explore how you navigate power before we dive into resistance, because we want you to see the many ways in which you can prevent resistance or redirect it when it first starts to appear.

15 Ways to Navigate Power

In the subsequent suggestions, you'll see how navigating power can also be understood to be sharing or distributing power. But when your intent is to create transformative learning spaces, the foundation of your power is the relationships you build. It's how you invite conversation, seek understanding, strengthen trust, and how you listen—and listen and listen. In the following 15 ways to navigate (and share, distribute, and respond to) power, see if you can identify the moves that shore up relationships as the foundation of our work.

Name the goal or objective for a session or activity and communicate the **why.** Learners want to know why they're being asked to do something, or do something in a certain way. Making this clear can build buy-in to the activities and content. This can sound like any of these:

- "This activity will allow us to unpack our beliefs about neurodiversity."
- "I am asking for two minutes of silent time while you work on this reflection. Some folks have a really hard time concentrating when there's any background noise, so let's give them those two minutes of silence. I'm going to ask that you don't move around the room during this time—let's really be silent. Two minutes, starting now."
- "We're going to hear from our students now because we value different perspectives on our discipline policy."

Cultivate connections to mission. Explain the connection between the content and the ability to meet the mission. Orienting around purpose reminds people that you are making decisions based on an organization's mission. This can sound like any of these:

- "We are committed to every child, every day in our school, and we know that our Latinx students are not thriving like our white students are. Today's session will help us explore our biases and how they might be affecting students."
- "Our mission is to create lifelong learners. To fulfill this aspiration, we need a deeper understanding of technology's role in learning, which is what our presenter today will be explaining."

Be transparent about what might seem like your personal requests. People can be sensitive about being told what to do, and if you are perceived as having ulterior motives or being nit-picky about what people do, resistance can take root. Pulling back the curtain on why you're asking people to do something builds trust. Explaining your *why* also prevents cognitive energy from being drained from the room as participants try to guess at your motives. This can sound like any of these:

- "I'm asking you to talk in pairs because we have six minutes, and this will allow each of you to have three minutes, which feels like the minimum amount of time you need for this conversation."
- "I'm asking you to work with someone you don't know well because in a few weeks you'll be collaborating on a project and this activity will help you get to know each other."
- "Please put away phones because we need everyone's full participation in this activity. It's going to go fast and be challenging! I know how easy it is to get distracted by our devices, so for the next 30 minutes, I'll ask for phones to be away."

Provide choices and differentiate learning. Offer a menu of options for activities that aren't optional. This can sound like any of the following:

- "Your small groups have two hours to do these three things. The order you choose to do them in is up to you and you can decide when to take a break."
- "For the next two months, our PD will be on meeting the needs of diverse learners. We've got five different groups that'll focus on different kinds of student needs. You'll get to pick which group you'll be in."

Invite opinions and input. This is another way to build buy-in and distribute power. This can sound like any of the following:

- "Show me on your fingers how many more minutes you'd like. I see two minutes, three, six, some of you are done. . . let's take the average and spend about three more minutes on this activity."
- "I'm hearing that some of you don't find this activity relevant to your content. Could you make an alternate suggestion?"
- "Our goal was to vertically align our core standards by March, and we haven't accomplished that. What suggestions do you have for how we can do this?"
- "We've got 15 minutes left, and we still have three agenda items left. Could we take about 5 minutes to make a decision about what to address?"

Build collective understanding and empathy. Share anonymous feedback from all the participants to illustrate how you make decisions and facilitate. This is a way to work from relational power. This can sound like any of the following:

- "Seventy-five percent of you really liked that activity last time—many of you said you wanted more time for it, but 15 percent said it wasn't helpful and you wish we'd spent much less time on it. Based on this feedback, this time we'll. . . ."
- "I really debated whether we should continue doing role-playing. Your feedback is split. Some of you love it, and others hate it. Today, you'll have two options when it comes to our practice time. . . ."
- "In your feedback from our last session, a number of you mentioned that side conversations are distracting you, and you asked me to do something about them. Although this will feel awkward, I will honor this request because it's my responsibility to ensure that this is a focused learning space. So if I hear side conversations, I'll try to subtly remind you of our community agreement."

Invite allegiance to community agreements. Rather than asking participants to follow what they could perceive as being your "rules" or accommodating your preferences, orient them to the community they are a part of and ask for commitment to that community. This can sound like any of the following:

- "One of our community agreements is to be fully present. I'm noticing a lot of coming and going from this room. Can we re-anchor in this agreement?"
- "This might be a good time to pause and consider how you're living our community agreement, remembering that we need everyone's full presence to create the optimal conditions for learning."

Honor agenda timelines. By declaring a start and stop time, and times for breaks, you've made an agreement with learners. If you honor the times you've agreed to, trust will increase. If you start late, people will arrive late. If you run over, people will feel like you've crossed a boundary and trust can break down. Honoring timelines is also a way to get people to show up on time. This can sound like any of the following:

- "I promise we'll end on time—or even one minute early! I'm asking for your partnership to keep to our timeline and asking that you return from breaks perhaps 30 seconds before we're scheduled to restart."
- "I want to apologize for running over last time we met. I'm confident that today's agenda is doable in our time, and regardless, we will end at 4 p.m."

Acknowledge the larger power structures and external systems at play.
Sometimes you might have to ask people to do something that you may have reservations about, and about which even the people who told you to do it also have reservations. What's tricky here is to acknowledge the situation without undermining other people. This can sound like any of the following:

- "I recognize that there's frustration about the superintendent's decision. I think you know she made it in response to the state's mandates. This is challenging for many of us. Although I have reservations about this new curriculum, I know we'll figure out how to make it relevant to our students."
- "I don't entirely understand all the factors at play right now, but I trust our principal's intentions and decision. She has recommended that we incorporate this approach to testing in our practice, and I want to ask that we try it out."

Understand your tendency to source from coercive power. Cultivate awareness of the first inclinations that arise in you as you encounter challenges or resistance. Notice when your instincts are to try to control people. Which kind of behaviors in others make you want to use power-over? Can you identify patterns in who or what triggers you? What fears come up when you're triggered? Which insecurities are activated?

Pick your battles and let the little things go. Don't take anything personally. And remember that people will sense your emotions—even if you think you're masking it well, participants will perceive your annoyance. Get clear for yourself on what matters most, and let little things go.

Compromise on topic, time, teammates, or task. If you get pushback on something, consider what you can let go of. Be flexible and adaptive. This can sound like any of the following:

- "I hear that you all feel like we've spent too much time on this activity. Let's do this. Take just 5 minutes to synthesize your learning, jot down a phrase that reflects that synthesis on a sticky note, and as we go to break, you can post it here."
- "I've gotten some feedback that many of you feel you need a break before digging into the next set of data. Thanks for sharing that, and let's go ahead and break for 15 minutes. I'll adjust the agenda, and we'll still be good on time."

Authentically appreciate and acknowledge individual and collective efforts.
This can sound like any of the following:

- "I know y'all are tired. It has been a long week. I'm amazed by how focused you've all been."
- "We had the highest parent and caregiver turnout at our event on Saturday, and I want us to celebrate that."
- "I know this school year has been incredibly hard. And I'm so moved by the way we're caring for each other and our students."

Reflect on and define what is within your control, within your influence, and outside of it. While you can influence a great deal, you can control little beyond your thoughts and emotional responses; you can control how you show up. Choose what to work on influencing, and let go of what you can't control. You might be frustrated with the district's decision to adopt a new curriculum; if you don't want to challenge that decision, let it go and figure out what you can and want to influence—how the new curriculum is rolled out, what kind of training is provided to teachers, how the curriculum is evaluated, and so on. You get to choose who you want to be and how you show up. That is within your control.

Ask for feedback on your facilitation. Listen to that feedback, even when it stings, and sometimes share how you're responding to it. This can sound like any of the following:

- "Last year, I got requests for our sessions to be co-facilitated with teachers here who have found novel solutions to some of the challenges we face in the district. This year, each of our sessions will include a 'bright spot' where we'll hear best practices."
- "I appreciated that during our break someone privately asked me if I was upset or annoyed. I'm grateful for that feedback. I had a hard morning at home, and I'm sorry if I brought there here. That's not how I want to be with all of you."

We've now led you through our four-part process to navigate power. Remember, you can make choices about where you draw power from and how you use that power. Make sure you take a look at the impact your choices about power have on those you interact with. If your impact doesn't align with your deepest intentions and values, consider other possibilities for how you source and leverage power.

And ask yourself frequently if what you are doing and the outcome you are having is transformative.

How to Dissolve Resistance

Now, let's finally talk about that most common question that so many educators have: the question about how to deal with resistance. Take a moment to recall your experiences with resistance:

- What are the behaviors that you associate with resistance in a PD context?
- Which of these behaviors have you enacted? When and where?
- Which of these behaviors have you seen other people take?
- Which feelings come up for you in recalling resistance?

Resistance feels challenging because strong emotions are always involved. Whoever is resisting has strong emotions, which in turn generates strong emotions in the object of their resistance. If you've ever been the object of resistance, you can probably easily recall your anger or fear or hurt.

Resistance is born when there is a power struggle. It mushrooms in hierarchical settings in which some people are unable to express their emotions, and in which those who hold power are unable to build relationships. You don't see a lot of resistance in settings in which people have high emotional intelligence and in which an organization or leader has high social intelligence. In contrast, when individuals and groups have low emotional intelligence and the organization is unresponsive to needs, has weak communication practices, and doesn't work to build a commitment to mission or vision, you see a lot of resistance. In organizations where there's healthy culture, you're less likely to see resistance. Where there's unhealthy culture, it's far more likely you'll see resistance.

Finally, remember that resistance can be overt (as it was in the opening anecdote in which Terry tried to undermine Elena's PD) or covert, even passive-aggressive, such as when people repeatedly agree to do something and don't follow through.

Recognizing Power Struggles

Resistance is the expression of a power struggle. Power struggles happen when people aren't aligned in purpose or on process, or sometimes both, and often when one person is perceived to have more authority than another. Power struggles are intensified by hierarchies. In a hierarchical system, power is constantly in negotiation. Sometimes, those who feel they have less power take actions to subvert the dominant power. Let's consider a subtle example: At a daylong district training, teachers were given 30 minutes for lunch, which was not provided. Teachers who hadn't brought food needed to leave the site to purchase lunch. When teachers said that 30 minutes wouldn't be enough time to go get food and eat it, the district leaders weren't responsive. The majority of teachers left the site for lunch and returned 20 minutes late. While this may have been the amount of time some teachers truly needed, it may also have been a passive-aggressive move to reclaim power.

Common power struggles in the context of PD fall along these lines:

- *Topic*: Participants have different opinions from the presenter on what should be focused on in PD or challenge why a focus has been selected. ("We can't do cooperative learning until our students learn to behave. We need training in classroom management," participants might say. Or, "We don't need training in coaching. We're technology specialists.")
- *Time*: Participants object to how much time is allocated to a topic, task, or activity, or they don't like when the PD is scheduled. ("We need more time to read all of this and create the tools." Or, "This PD needed to happen before school started, not at the end of an exhausting day.")
- *Teammates*: Participants object to who they are partnered with or are asked to work with or to who is present or not present at the PD. ("It would be much more useful if we could do this activity with our grade-level team." Or "Why isn't our principal made to attend this training as well as the coaches?")
- *Task*: Participants dislike what they are asked to do. ("I really don't like role-playing. I find it inauthentic. I'd rather have time to just read." Or "I know we have high staff turnover and this needs to be reintroduced, but I've done this at the start of every school year.")

Whenever a leader attempts to use coercive power or power-over in response to a power struggle, the struggle will intensify. It might go underground, or it might gain strength, but it won't go away and relationships will deteriorate. If you've ever done any of the following things as a facilitator, you've likely used power-over to respond to a power struggle:

- Defending your authority or credibility
- Issuing unenforceable consequences
- Making decisions about activities or groupings to control people

You can prevent many power struggles by sourcing from relational power and use power-to, power-with, and power-within. But sometimes power struggles grow, and then resistance intensifies. Let's explore what's at the root of resistance: unmet needs.

Resistance Indicates Unmet Needs

When someone is resistant, they are expressing anger, fear, or sadness. They may not be aware that these emotions are present for them or why these emotions are arising. Emotions that feel uncomfortable, such as anger, fear, and sadness, are often a reflection of unmet needs (see Appendix B). *Needs* is a term and concept used in *nonviolent communication* (NVC), a conflict-resolution approach created by Marshall Rosenberg in the 1960s. According to NVC, human beings have common needs that drive our actions. Needs are universal and cross-cultural, and there is nothing wrong with having them. Unmet needs give rise to anger, apathy, fragility, anxiety, or animosity, and we can resort to harmful behavior, violence, or other ineffective tactics in an effort to meet our own needs. Resistance is the expression of emotions that arise from unmet needs.

In the anecdote that opens this chapter, it's likely that Terry and many of her colleagues had unmet needs for choice, freedom, contribution, participation, belonging, consideration, and more. The emotions they expressed (frustration, irritation, annoyance) and their behavior (disengaging, opting out, pushing back on the activity) were a result of these unmet needs.

It is not necessarily an organization's or an individual's responsibility to meet everyone's needs all the time. Let's say a ninth-grade English department chair is angry because the district is requiring that the core texts are diversified. *The Great Gatsby* has been removed from the approved texts and replaced with *The Bluest Eye*. The English chair feels that her need for autonomy is blocked; she challenges district leaders and begins organizing parents in protest. In this case, district leaders or the site principal can use an understanding of needs and emotions to open up conversations with the chair, to unpack the beliefs that surround her commitment to *The Great Gatsby*, and to explore ways to bring her aboard the new curriculum. It's possible that the department chair may be able to meet her need for autonomy in some other way. But it's also possible that the need will no longer be met in the way she wants.

Whenever changes are underway, it's common for people to have more needs or feel an intensification of needs. Change is hard. It implies loss, and we're not very good at saying goodbye, grieving, or dealing with loss. PD providers are often on the front lines of change—bringing in new initiatives, approaches, ideas, and strategies—which is why we need to learn how to facilitate change and all the emotions that arise when we're in the midst of it.

Sometimes when a need feels unmet at work, it is also unmet in other sectors of our lives. If, for example, you often feel your need for appreciation at work is unmet, you might ask yourself if you also feel unappreciated at home, among friends or with family. We carry our emotional lives with us, and frequently patterns emerge in how we set ourselves up to get our needs met and how we experience and express our emotions.

Recognizing other people's unmet needs doesn't mean you have to figure out how to meet all of them. But beginning with this understanding—that resistance is the expression of unmet needs—is an entry point to conversation, connection, and a path forward. Figure 3.1 depicts this concept and can help you remember that when you encounter resistance, you need to dive below to surface behaviors to understand the full extent of unmet needs.

What to Do When You Encounter Resistance

So what do you do when you encounter resistance? First, apply all the knowledge and understanding you've gleaned from this chapter about power and how you use it. Make sure you've scrutinized how you've sourced and used power and the impact you've had. Then try the following:

- Get curious about emotions. Ask about feelings. Create opportunities for people to understand, explore, express, and release emotions. In a PD session, this could sound like, "I'm hearing a lot of rumbling about the activity I just asked

Figure 3.1   Diving into Resistance

you all to do. I didn't anticipate that response. Can you help me understanding what's coming up for you?" (See Aguilar [2016] for more on how to build the emotional intelligence of a team.)

- Explore unmet needs. Consider whether you can meet these needs and, if so, how. You may be able to leverage power-with and power-to. In a PD session, this could sound like, "I'm hearing a lot of frustration about the activity I just introduced. It seems like many of you are wanting more autonomy in how you learn this content. Does anyone have a suggestion for what this could look like?"

- Step back and take a hard look at the social intelligence in your organization. How are relationships built and valued? What's the state of trust in the organization? Scrutinize communication. How do leaders listen? (Also see Aguilar [2016] for more on how to build trust in a team.)

- Slow down and look inward. Reflect on how you are understanding, experiencing, and expressing your emotions and unmet needs. What comes up for you in response to other people's resistance?

- Stay firm or change course. Remember, just because you encounter resistance doesn't mean you need to do something different. Sometimes resistance indicates

---

Navigating Power in Virtual Settings

In a virtual setting, your power is both amplified and limited. As the master of the virtual platform, you have more control over who speaks and when they speak, you can close down breakout rooms when you decide time is up, and you have the ability to ignore a question in a private chat. To some extent, in some programs, you can also control how much the chat box is used. However, you have little control over what is publicly shared in the chat box or how much private text messaging is going on or what's being discussed in breakout rooms—or if people even show up to those breakout spaces. In a virtual setting, it's more difficult to access coercive power, which can be hard for PD facilitators who are used to relying on it.

The opportunity in virtual facilitation is in leaning into relational power and in leveraging power-with, power-to, and power-within. Give people choices, as well as opportunities to connect to the content and with each other. As you release control and explore new ways to build relationships, you create more authentic learning experiences.

that a leader has taken a stance—perhaps declaring that student testing data will no longer be publicly displayed—and people don't like it. Maybe there's a need to cultivate group emotional intelligence or strengthen commitment to the mission, but you may not need to back off from your stance or change course.

If you work with a group of people regularly (whether you are a site leader or an external partner), it can be useful to introduce the NVC concept of needs to build a shared understanding and vocabulary. Similarly, using a tool such as the Core Emotions (Appendix A) is helpful. Providing professional development on emotions and communication contributes to an emotionally intelligent organization and creates the conditions in which people can learn. Ultimately, if organizations want to reduce the amount of resistance they experience, they need to attend to emotions.

Start and End with Relationships

Your task as a PD facilitator is to create the conditions in which people can learn. Relationships among learners, and between learners and the facilitator, create the conditions in which we learn. Navigating power is not just about being reactive when power dynamics are counterproductive; it's not just about dealing with resistance; it's about creating the optimal conditions for productive relationships. The essence of this habit is about learning how to engage power, work with it, and shape its flow so that people can develop healthy relationships, take risks in their learning journey, and grow.

Often resistance captures our attention because it generates many strong emotions. We can focus on one person who seems to lead the resistance or whose behaviors we find most triggering. In the anecdote that opens this chapter, Terry's behaviors are emphasized. However, Terry was not the problem: She was certainly part of the problem, but there were many complex dynamics that created a situation that was unpleasant for many adults and children. When we see resistance, it's an invitation to look at all the relationships and factors involved.

Because we live in a hierarchical society and world and because so many of our institutions are inherently inequitable, it's imperative that we attend closely to power dynamics—so that people can learn. Our PD sessions are a microcosm for what happens in the larger world. As we work to interrupt inequitable power dynamics, to move away from our habitual and conditioned tendency to use coercive power and power-over, we create the schools we want to work in, the classrooms we want children to learn in, and the world that we want to live in.

Have you ever surfed or boogie-boarded? Can you imagine the energy and the thrill of surging across powerful waves? Navigating power effectively keeps you riding the wave, and as a facilitator, it's your job to learn how to do just that: how to source from relational power; how to use it to cultivate agency, learning, collaboration, and community; how to engage emotions; and how to respond when others draw power from destructive sources. Navigating power is the facilitator's work—through every moment of every PD. Embrace this work. Like surfing, navigating power takes skill, knowledge, and practice, but when you get it and you're effortlessly riding those waves, it's awesome.

Before You Go

Pause and Reflect:
- Re-read the opening anecdote about Terry. How has your understanding of the resistance that Elena faced in that PD session changed after reading this chapter?
- How do the ideas in this chapter better help you understand the power dynamics in your organization?
- How have your thoughts about resistance changed?
- When it comes to navigating power, based on what you've read in this chapter, what do you want to stop, start, and continue doing?

Remember:
- Power is always present. Learning to see power and to understand power dynamics is empowering.
- When it comes to how we source and leverage power, we've got options. Make sure your choices align with your deepest intentions and commitments.
- Navigating power skillfully is thrilling, and it is key to transforming our world.

CHAPTER 4

Anchor in Adult Learning

A week before school started, the district's elementary teachers convened in a cavernous auditorium. Elena waited in the dim light, her shoes sticking to the floor, for the PD on the new reading curriculum to begin. A first-year teacher, she was excited to acquire more skills; however, her enthusiasm waned as the session began. The presenter publicly shamed a couple of teachers who arrived late. The agenda didn't seem to be about understanding the new curriculum and began with a childish community-building activity. After repeatedly shushing the teachers, the presenter said, "District specialists will do unannounced visits to your classroom to ensure that you're following the pacing guide." His voice boomed through a microphone that crackled with feedback.

A teacher next to Elena leaned toward her. "You know he was a principal for something like a decade, but there were so many complaints against him that the district finally decided it was easier to give him a central office job."

The presenter adjusted his tie, advanced the slide, and motioned to a group of teachers. "I appreciate how all of you are sitting quietly and attentively," he said. "And Marcia, I see that you're taking notes," he nodded at a woman in the front row. "Good job." Marcia cringed.

The presenter proceeded to explain the next activity. Teachers would divide into groups to jigsaw-read the first portion of the implementation manual (which covered fidelity to the curriculum, not reading strategies). It took 20 minutes for the hundreds of teachers to count off and for the presenter to review the directions. *This seems inefficient*, Elena mused.

As Elena moved into a small group, she felt nervous. She didn't know any of the other teachers in her group. Because there was no time allocated for introductions, the teachers in Elena's group whispered hasty introductions. Elena began reading the portion she'd been assigned, but was stumped by some of the references and acronyms. The presenter broke the silence every few minutes to announce the remaining time. "Six minutes left!" Elena's concentration broke. "Two minutes! Start wrapping up! Be sure you've identified the key takeaways!"

The share-out with her group felt tense, an undercurrent of frustration in each teacher's words. They had all complied with the instructions, and each offered a key takeaway. They had complied with the instructions, but they hadn't learned anything.

At the end of the day, as she weaved through the parking lot to her car, Elena bumped into Grace, a teacher who had been in the district for several years. "I can't believe we have two more days of that," Elena said. "What a huge waste of time."

"Get used to it," Grace said.

"And he was so insulting! We might teach kids, but we're not little children."

"Yeah," Grace said. "We're treated like robots to be programmed. Not like we actually know anything about teaching."

"I don't get it," Elena said, exasperated. "I *wanted* to learn how to teach reading. I *needed* this PD." Grace shrugged and turned to unlock her car door.

In tenth grade, Elena had started a list titled, "What NOT to do when I'm a teacher." Don't, she noted, give surprise quizzes, use red ink to grade papers, or assign group projects where everyone gets the same grade. When she became a teacher, she referenced this list regularly. That evening, after that first terrible day of training, Elena started a list titled, "What NOT to do when I deliver PD." That night she committed to try never to

- Treat adults like children
- Make them do meaningless things
- Embarrass them in front of their peers
- Tell people they're going to get one thing and then give them another
- Treat them like they don't have any ideas of their own
- Tell them to do things they can't do
- Throw them into a group with strangers and not even give them a chance to say their names
- Make them feel like they're in jail and have no choice about what to say or do for three days

Years later, when Elena read adult learning theory, she felt validated. She hadn't simply catalogued her personal gripes—she'd identified some of the key principles of adult learning: Adults need to be able to make choices about their learning, they need psychological safety, and they need to have their knowledge and experiences validated. Adult learning didn't have to be as miserable as it was for Elena in this opening anecdote.

The purpose of a PD session is for participants *to learn* something. A so-called "Professional Development training" is not an excuse to enforce compliance. The presenter of Elena's terrible district training may have wanted teachers to learn what was expected of them in terms of fidelity to the curriculum, or what the compliance and accountability measures would be, but he didn't seem to want teachers to learn how to teach reading. It could be reasoned that he didn't even conceive of the teachers as being adult learners—as people who wanted and needed to *learn* something; it could be argued that he saw the teachers as laborers to control.

If you aspire to provide PD that changes practice, that transforms individuals and communities, then you must start with a commitment to teaching learners rather than to controlling objects. This is part of what it means to move away from a transactional approach and take instead a transformative stance. This kind of reorientation toward transformation takes work. Anchoring ourselves firmly in a transformative way of working calls for a set of principles you can act on and strategies you can use to meet the needs of adult learners. That's what we'll explore in this chapter. Establishing adult learning principles lays the foundation for delivering transformational PD, and learning the strategies in support of those principles can begin to make it a reality.

You Can't Make People Learn

During our many years teaching about coaching and facilitating PD, we've heard educators use the idiom, "You can lead a horse to water, but you can't make it drink." At times, we've nodded in agreement. Because, yes, perhaps you can lead a horse to water and talk to it kindly and encouragingly along the way; you can splash your hand in the water so that the horse sees that the water is not dangerous; you can be sure the water is clear and clean; you can sip at the water yourself and grin as the liquid dribbles down your chin; you can talk about how the water will make the horse feel good and how the horse really needs water to stay alive—*but you can't make the horse drink the water.*

But this doesn't capture the whole truth. There's more to it. You can't make a horse drink water, but you can do better: You can *create the conditions* in which the horse will choose to drink water.

That's probably about as far as we need to take the horse metaphor for now, but of course, the same is true for all human activity, including learning: The conditions for learning can and must be in place for us to learn.

Let's start by looking at the biggest part of the picture—the macro conditions that need to be in place—and then we'll hone in on what's known about the conditions in which adults learn and what this means for how we facilitate PD.

Digging into the Conditions for Learning

The phrase *conditions for learning* can feel abstract, so let's define the term. Returning to our party metaphor, consider which of the following help you to enjoy being at a social event:

- *A feeling of purpose or meaning*: There's a good reason for the event—a birthday celebration, a high school graduation, a discussion of a book, or simply a chance to unwind.
- *A feeling of comfort with the other guests*: Either you know them or meeting them is eased, perhaps through introductions or wearing name tags.
- *A thoughtful host*: The host welcomes guests on arrival, facilitates activities, responds to needs, ensures that everyone is having a good time, and so on.
- *A comfortable physical setting*: You're neither too cold nor too hot, you can move through the space easily, you find places to sit or stand.
- *Agency, a sense of choice or freedom*: You can make decisions about what you do and with whom, you don't have to talk to someone you don't like, you can eat or drink what you want.

You might consider this short list to be among the conditions for socializing—certain things need to be present and true for you to benefit socially and psychologically from coming together with other humans. The conditions for learning are similar and include: learner buy-in to the reasons for learning, a baseline of psychological safety, a skilled facilitator, an appropriate physical setting for the learning activities, and a degree of learner choice. To some extent, the way we use the term *conditions* overlaps with the way we use the term *needs*—be those Maslow's well-known hierarchy of needs or the Universal Human Needs (as put forth by in the philosophy of nonviolent communication that we explored in Chapter 2 and found in Appendix B). In this chapter we will explore how we attend to the needs of our audience—to learners—and we'll understand how principles of adult learning can guide our planning and decision-making.

To get started, take a moment to recall a positive experience as an adult in which someone guided your learning—perhaps a PD experience, an academic course, or a fun class. This could be the same experience you called to mind in the introduction. Now, reflect on these questions:

- What did you learn? Why was that learning meaningful?
- What were the conditions in which you learned? Consider the physical setting, your orientation to the learning, and the teacher's role.
- Based on that positive learning experience, what would you include on a list of things to always do when providing PD?

Consider Organizational Expectations

Many years ago Elena helped hire coaches and administrators to work in some of the most struggling middle schools in the Oakland Public Schools. The descriptions for these positions included the following language:

> This job will be hard. We don't expect you to have all the skills you need when you walk in the door, so we're committed to providing you with support, in the form of a coach, to help you grow and navigate the challenges we know you'll face. In addition, you'll participate in a professional learning community with others who share your role, and you'll attend bimonthly PD sessions. We know that the only way we can meet our students' needs is if we, the adults, engage in rigorous learning. We expect that those who join our team hold this belief and value. If this is you and you're excited about learning, we encourage you to apply.

You can't make people learn. However, an organization can communicate a value of learning and an expectation that those in the organization will be active learners. This is a necessary starting point. Mandating learning or coaching can be tricky—learners who feel like they're being coerced can resist. But when people join an organization in which expectations are clear about the value of learning, and when learning opportunities are framed by strengths-based thinking (rather than a deficit perspective), people orient positively to the requirement to learn. They are likely to be more open, engaged, and onboard from the start.

A clearly articulated, organizational value around learning can help to prevent resistance by building buy-in, creating culture, and being clear about expectations. Ideally, employees are aware of this value from the moment they consider joining an organization—and for many, this value can be an enticing draw. When such a value is sharply articulated, a superintendent or principal doesn't have to backtrack and say, "I haven't been clear about this, but in order to meet our students' needs, we've all got to be active learners, myself included, and this means. . . ." Sure, this can be done and sometimes it's what's needed, but you can understand why a teacher who was hired 12 years ago may experience some frustration if all of a sudden a principal insists that all teachers work with a coach.

So a declared commitment to learning is important, and it's not enough: A commitment to learning needs to be authentic, and it has to shape every action leaders make. Sometimes leaders say they're committed to learning because they know it's the right thing to say, but their actions contradict their statements. Often this breach is apparent in the staff culture of an organization—learning can't happen in a dysfunctional culture. Sometimes it's clear that leaders don't value learning when they make decisions about coaching, evaluation, retention, and promotions. For example, a leader may say they value learning but then reprimand a staff member who made a mistake.

In contrast, a leader who values learning will facilitate a conversation in which the staff member who made a mistake can reflect on what happened and ultimately learn and grow. The staff member may be held accountable for the mistake, but a leader who holds a value of learning will use different processes and hold different the expectations for the future. When Lori was a school leader, she worked with a new teacher who hadn't worked with high school students before. This teacher made some early mistakes in his expectations of students that hurt the classroom culture; rather than first reprimanding the teacher for his knowledge and skill gaps, Lori gave him a book on teaching adolescents and set up brief check-in sessions to discuss what he learned and what he was going to try in class. Lori also planned class observations to focus on how this teacher applied his knowledge. A leader who lives a value of learning expects growth and creates conditions to foster that growth.

So if an organization's values are brought to life in the words and actions of its leaders, why isn't transformational PD more common? Acting from values can be very hard. Staying true to an organization's values takes diligence and teamwork. If a principal and assistant principal aren't both messaging values of learning, then staff get mixed messages, trust in leadership weakens, and adult culture can become dysfunctional.

Organizational values and expectations around learning must be articulated, over and over, and they need to be acted on. Those in roles with positional power—from the superintendent to the principal to the department head—are responsible for creating the conditions for learning. Without laying down the foundations for learning to occur, a lone coach or PD leader who aspires to deliver transformative PD will face challenges. Lots and lots of them. But if this is you, don't give up hope. Here are two strategies that can help:

- *Explore and expand your sphere of influence*: We can choose how we experience and express our emotions, and we can shape our thoughts. When we're clear on what's within our control, we can make wiser and more informed choices about where we spend our energy. Beyond what's in our control, there's also a lot we can influence. If you are in an organization in which the leaders don't message a value of learning, and if you're a coach aspiring to provide transformative PD, get really clear on what you can influence. Perhaps you can influence resource allocation, for example, or perhaps you can advocate for more time for PD. Figure out who and what you can influence.
- *Coach up*: Use coaching strategies in conversation with those who supervise you. Remember that your bosses are also learners and that you can help them reflect on their behaviors and beliefs. When Elena was a site-based coach, she often found herself coaching up in discussions with her principal about hiring, curriculum, and PD. She asked reflective questions that helped her principal unpack his beliefs, analyze student data, and identify his next steps. There were times when she wanted to shake him by the shoulders and tell him what he should do; but for many reasons, she couldn't do that. When she took a coaching stance, remembered that her principal was also learning the craft of leadership, and activated her compassion and curiosity, she was far more effective at helping her principal make decisions about PD that advanced the district's commitment to equity.

Read more about the Spheres of Control in *The Art of Coaching Workbook* and *Onward*.

Know and Act on Research

Now that we've considered the big picture in which you work, which will impact the conditions in which learning happens, let's explore where you have the greatest influence on establishing the conditions in which adults learn best. There's a lot of research from the fields of psychology, sociology, neuroscience, and biology about what it takes to ensure that adults can learn. If we put this research into practice, we'd see immediate results in what happens on a Wednesday afternoon PD session: We'd see teachers learning and enjoying the process. The next day in the classroom, it's likely that we'd see an application of that learning—and then it's likely that we'd see children learning.

What follows is an overview of the research on adult learning. As you read the rest of this chapter, we hope you'll feel affirmed. We hope you'll be nodding and underlining and highlighting information that affirms your experience. We hope you'll be reminded of what works to create the conditions for learning. And, of course, we hope you'll find new information.

Adult Learning Theory 101

In *The Art of Coaching Teams*, Elena offers the following seven principles of adult learning that are compiled from the research on adult learning theory and confirmed by her experience on the ground:

1. Adults must feel safe to learn.
2. Adults come to learning experiences with histories.
3. Adults need to know why we have to learn something.
4. Adults want agency in learning.
5. Adults need practice to internalize learning.
6. Adults have a problem-centered approach to learning.
7. Adults want to learn.

These principles reflect what is known about brain science, learning theory, behavioral and cognitive psychology, and to some extent sociology. While the principles apply for learners of all ages, we reference *adults* specifically because there are some nuanced differences between teaching kids and grown-ups. Furthermore, somehow we often forget to provide adults with the conditions for learning that we often provide children. Let's explore each principle.

One: Adults Must Feel Safe to Learn

This is a fact: When we feel afraid, our brains shut down to learning, and new information can't be absorbed. Our ability to receive new information is directly tied to our emotional state. There are volumes of research studies about what happens in our bodies and minds when someone cuts us off in a discussion, when we are threatened with punitive consequences, or when we perceive that our teacher doesn't have our best interests at heart. This research says, essentially, that in such situations we fight, take flight, freeze, or appease. While our physical and cognitive energy focuses on survival, our ability to learn shrinks.

On that first day of required PD years ago, when Elena wanted to learn how to teach kids to read and instead was asked to read about compliance with a new initiative, she didn't feel safe enough to learn. She was intimidated by the presenter, and she'd never met the teachers assigned to her small group. During those days of training (which didn't get any better than the first day that's described at the beginning of this chapter), Elena focused on avoiding being called out in front of the group, she made sure she understood the accountability measures, and she never revealed to her new colleagues that she wasn't confident she knew enough to teach reading well.

Because this principle is so important in creating the conditions in which people learn, we give it an entire chapter—feel free to return to Chapter 2 to dig back in to the complexities of emotional safety.

Two: Adults Come to Learning Experiences with Histories

Adults show up at PD with a wide range of previous experiences, knowledge, interests, and competencies. Making explicit connections between new learning and that which we already know makes learning deeper and more permanent.

Let's explore an example. Imagine a PD session on classroom management. Here are some ways to invite adults to activate their prior knowledge and use those experiences to deepen their learning:

- *Ask reflection questions about participants' experiences as children in schools*: When you were a child, what motivated you to follow the rules? Which rules felt unfair or arbitrary?
- *Ask reflection questions about participants' experiences as teachers*: When you first started teaching, which strategies did you use that were effective at managing students? Which were ineffective? If you could go back in time and give yourself advice around classroom management as a new teacher, what would you suggest?
- *Ask learners to apply new learning to past experience*: How does this strategy you've just learned about help you understand your past experiences

managing students? What does it affirm? What new insights do you get into past experiences?

- *Ask learners to connect the past and future*: Based on what you've learned today, what do you want to stop, start, and continue doing when it comes to classroom management?

This principle is particularly relevant to working with adult learners. While children have rich experiences to draw from, adults simply have more depth, breadth, and variation in the quality of previous life experiences than do younger people. When you acknowledge the experiences of adult learners, you communicate value in what they bring to the table. You're saying that you don't see them as empty vessels into which you'll pour information.

Acknowledging participants' perspectives doesn't require you to condone anything they've done or said. For example, in a session on classroom management, a teacher could share that she uses a timeout corner and that students have to face the wall. While you may understand that this kind of shaming of students is harmful, and your PD session may intend to help the teacher develop other strategies to respond to student behavior, you can still appreciate her for sharing. Furthermore, understanding this kind of information about your learners will help you be more strategic and effective.

To be seen is a basic human need. When you acknowledge what adult learners bring to a learning experience, you say: *I see you. I respect you. You bring something to the table.*

Three: Adults Need to Know Why We Have to Learn Something

Imagine a class of seventh graders. A teacher stands in front of them and tells the 30 tweens that they're starting a new unit today, and a collective groan echoes through the room. A hand shoots up: "Why do we have to learn this?" As children grow up and internalize social norms, some stop asking *why*; but most of us adults still *think* about this every time we're asked to learn something new. For many of us, the answer (or lack of an answer) may be the moment when we either embrace learning or check out and start grading papers, browsing social media, or daydreaming.

Many adult learners commit to learning when the *why* is answered and the objectives seem to meet personal and professional needs. PD facilitators can communicate the *why* for a session by writing objectives on the agenda, by including the objectives in their introduction to an activity, and by inviting learners to make connections between the content and the participants' lived realities.

Let's go back to the example of the classroom management PD session. Imagine a veteran teacher in that session who has attended dozens of such PDs in the course of her career. You might quickly wonder if she'd be annoyed by having to attend yet another training on redirecting student behavior or following through with consequences. But imagine how she might feel if she received the following email from her principal a week before that session:

> Many of us experienced 2020 as the hardest year of our careers. Our students faced tremendous challenges during the year of distance learning, and they struggled to readjust to school. I know that so many of you felt ill-equipped to respond to their needs and the management strategies we'd long used didn't seem to work anymore. I've heard your fatigue and frustration, and I'm concerned about everyone's well-being.
>
> Last spring, I learned that Sunny Valley District is using a new approach to management and their principals are seeing a remarkable positive impact on teachers and students. When our leadership team visited their sites, we were inspired by what we witnessed and believe we could adopt many of these approaches at our school. As a team, we agreed that we wanted to try out this management model.
>
> Next Monday, we'll begin PD on this new program. I'd like to ask you to come to this meeting ready to talk to others about these questions: How have my management approaches been working? What hasn't been working? What might be possible if we had some additional management strategies to use?

Can you identify the ways in which this email makes the *why* clear and paves the way for buy-in to the purpose of the PD? Articulating the *why* prevents resistance, creates opportunity to learners to find authentic points of connection, increases trust in the facilitator, and primes learners to be receptive to new ideas.

Four: Adults Want Agency in Learning

Adults crave autonomy and want some control over the what, who, how, why, when, and where of our learning—the key word here being *some*. To get the most out of a learning situation, adult learners need to be empowered to make some decisions.

There are endless ways to offer choice when you provide PD. For example, you might offer a few prompts for reflection and say, "You can answer all of these, some of these, or none of them. The purpose is for them to get you thinking about____."

And then you can add, "You're welcome to write about them if you'd like or just think." That's another choice point. After the reflection time ends, you can say, "Now you'll share your thoughts with your partner. If you want to share what you wrote, that's fine, or you can share the general thoughts that came up." And you've provided another choice.

Whether in a single session or across the course of a PD experience, there are almost endless ways to provide choice. This doesn't mean you always need to do so. And it doesn't mean that there aren't times when you say something like, "I know that role-playing is scary, and it's normal that you feel nervous. And I know that some of you feel like role-playing fictitious scenarios feels inauthentic. And yet, I'm going to ask you to try it—just for 10 minutes, because. . . ." You can mandate an activity if you provide rationale, but make sure you're also giving people lots of other opportunities for choice.

Ultimately, folks who really, really don't want to do an activity won't. They make a choice. But there are times when it's important for you to nudge and insist and encourage. When mandates are balanced with choices, there's a greater likelihood that participants will follow your instructions, heed your nudges, accept your invitations—and learn. When Lori and Elena insist on role-playing to practice coaching strategies, the feedback they receive affirms their insistence. "I didn't want to role-play, and I'm so glad you made me," participants write. "It was a great experience, and I learned so much." Although we "make them" role-play, we give them a number of choice points: which scenario to role-play, what to get feedback on, and how long to role-play. We also provide structures for preparation and a protocol. Those contribute to the conditions in which people learn.

Honoring adult agency is about trusting the folks you're teaching. It's about recognizing that they know themselves and their students and that they can make decisions to guide their learning. When you act from this principle as a PD facilitator, you demonstrate humility, acknowledging and shifting the balance of power.

Five: Adults Need Practice to Internalize Learning

According to professor Linda Darling-Hammond (2009), teachers will learn a new skill *well enough that it will positively impact student learning* after approximately 50 hours of professional development. Read that again: *50 hours of PD*. But these aren't 50 hours of being lectured at in a dimly lit training hall—these must comprise hours and hours of practice. Professional development could be transformed if we simply acted on this 50-hour rule, and perhaps as a result, the experience of children in schools could be transformed.

How many PD sessions have you attended during which you thought, *this is interesting and useful*—but then weeks or months later, you couldn't really remember what you'd learned? And then you realized that the ideas you'd been exposed to in that session hadn't actually made their way into the classroom?

As a new teacher, Elena attended many trainings. Sometimes she'd recognize a gap between what she'd heard in the session and what she was actually doing in her classroom, and she felt ashamed. But it wasn't surprising that she wasn't able to apply the learning. She'd been in sessions where teaching strategies were described and explained and where she'd watched videos of teachers using them and listened to explanations of the research behind the strategies, but she hadn't been given an opportunity to *practice* the strategies.

One of the top reasons why "one-shot PD" is ineffective is because it rarely includes enough time for learners both to understand the new skills or knowledge and to practice. To internalize learning—to build fluency in a new skill or in putting new knowledge to use—we need to apply it. And so concepts and strategies we're exposed to in PD will become daily habits only when we practice them. In a PD session, practice can look like role-playing, scripting the opening of a lesson, using a set of criteria to make choices about instructional design, and analyzing student work.

Engaging in reflection through thinking, writing, and talking is a form of practice. When we reflect, we make connections between previous experiences and the present; we identify the *why* for which we're engaging in learning; we connect learning components and uncover solutions to our problems (Garvin, 1993). To internalize learning, the special kind of practice called *reflection* needs to be interwoven with other kinds of practice.

Another key element of practice is feedback. When we're trying out new strategies—whether those are strategies to build relationships with students, to manage our response to a frustrated parent, to analyze disaggregated data, or to scaffold lessons—we need feedback from people we trust. When we're practicing new strategies we hope to internalize, we have to practice right. The feedback can come from colleagues or other participants in a PD session, or from coaches or supervisors, but for the feedback to be received, the learner has to trust the person giving it. This takes us back to the principle of safety.

Six: Adults Have a Problem-Centered Approach to Learning

Adults can be highly motivated to acquire new skills if we think these will help us solve an issue we're struggling with. When PD focuses on problem solving, learners grapple with content more deeply. *I can actually use this!* participants think.

Because we're problem-centered and have limited time, we want to feel like we are getting something useful out of PD.

Among any group of learners, there will be some who are more eager for activities, tools, and strategies that they can use the next day, and there will be others who relish contemplative activities that may not have immediate application. This range of needs sometimes correlates to a learner's level of experience in a field or with content. For example, as a brand new coach, Elena was desperate for sentence stems and technical tips for organizing her notebooks. A few years later, however, she was eager to analyze how dominant culture impacts levels of trust between coaches and coachees. While facilitators must be responsive to this desire for immediate takeaways, we also need to be mindful of the danger in offering PD full of tools and quick fixes. A "do this!" PD can be superficial.

When activities do not seem to have direct relevance to a learner's immediate situation, it's the facilitator's responsibility to make those connections. Here are a couple examples of what this can sound like:

- "I'm asking you to participate in this silly community-building activity because we'll boost our endorphins and this will help create the connections between us that will allow us to have a more honest, meaningful discussion about educational inequity."
- "I'm asking you to recall what discipline approaches worked for you as a child so that you can better understand the decisions you make in the classroom now. Sometimes we are not consciously aware of how our past experiences influence our decisions, and this reflection activity will help."

When PD addresses what educators feel are pressing issues, it builds trust, creates the potential for buy-in, and makes it far more likely that the learners will remember the PD session and apply their learnings.

"Humans are the learning organism par excellence. The drive to learn is as strong as the sexual drive—it begins earlier and it lasts longer."

—Edward T. Hall

Seven: Adults Want to Learn

Human beings want to learn from the time we are born, and even though we don't always show it, we love to learn. When that cranky veteran teacher stomps into your PD session mumbling, "this too shall pass," it can be hard to see them as someone who loves to learn. But once, perhaps many years ago, they did love learning, and maybe the learner that's been dormant for decades could emerge again. At our core, adults want to learn—and we will engage in learning when conditions are right.

When you stand in front of a group of adult learners, assume that they want to learn. Speak to the part of them that loves learning (even if that part is hibernating). Remember that they come to the learning experience with history—including history of being a learner. If some of their prior learning experiences were negative, then they may not be open to new learning. Regardless, it's your responsibility as the PD provider to do everything possible to create a safe environment, to articulate purpose, to invite in past experience and already existing knowledge, to offer choices, to make the learning relevant, and to provide opportunities for practice and feedback so that the learning can be internalized. All human beings at some level really do want to learn. And if you hold this as a truth, it makes delivering PD much easier—and more effective.

From Principles to Practice

Let's look at some more examples of what it looks and sounds like to act on the principles of adult learning. Table 4.1 provides a handful of immediate implications for working from these theories. If you're a newer PD provider, think about your own experience as a learner in PD as you read these. Which ones have you experienced? How have those supported your learning? If you're a more experienced PD facilitator, we encourage you to create a table with these same column headings so that you can expand on these ideas and add your own.

Pause and Process

Before moving onto the next section, take a moment to look back through Table 4.1 and see if you can identify anything that you want to stop doing as a facilitator, start doing, and continue doing. This will help you process this information and retain what might be most useful to you.

The Stages of Learning

Let's consider how we actually learn a new skill. Do you remember learning to ride a bike or drive? Can you remember those early stages of skill acquisition when you felt awkward and uncertain? Do you remember when you began to feel comfortable and competent at riding a bike or driving? Those tasks might now feel like second nature to you, but at one time they were made up of many challenging elements.

Table 4.1 From Theory to Practice

Adult Learning Principle	Example: Looks Like, Sounds Like. . .	Nonexample: Doesn't Look Like, Doesn't Sound Like. . .
Adults must feel safe to learn	• Providing time for learners to introduce themselves and connect with each other at the start of a PD session. • Establishing community agreements and structures to uphold those agreements. • Clearly communicating expectations. • Using open body language and a welcoming, inviting tone of voice. • Quickly and explicitly addressing any threats to safety. • Correctly saying names.	• Making thinly veiled threats about what will happen if anyone leaves early. • Using strategies commonly associated with teaching (especially teaching younger grades) to silence a group or call everyone to attention such as "I'm going to wait until all eyes are on me before I continue." • Being disorganized, not attending to details. • Cold calling and not saying names correctly.
Adults come to learning experiences with histories	• Doing a "Learner Survey" prior to the PD experience to ask what learners already know about a topic. • Activating prior schema and offering learners opportunities to share their background knowledge with each other. • Validating past experiences. • Asking, "What have you done in similar situations?" "That's a good question, and I know that there are folks here who have addressed that issue. Is there someone who might share what you've done in that kind of a situation?"	• Presuming to have all the knowledge and expertise. • Providing new content without any knowledge of the learners' previous experience with that content.

(Continued)

Table 4.1 (Continued)

Adult Learning Principle	Example: Looks Like, Sounds Like. . .	Nonexample: Doesn't Look Like, Doesn't Sound Like. . .
Adults need to know why we have to learn something	• Clearly stating objectives, outcomes, or learning targets for a session. • Including a "why" column on agendas. • Framing an activity with the *why*: "This next activity will help us better understand our triggers so that we can more quickly regulate our emotions when a student's behavior gets on our nerves."	• Asking learners to engage in seemingly random activities. • Not explaining the reasoning or rationale for a session or PD initiative.
Adults want agency in our learning	• Offering opportunities for learners to select whom to work with in a PD session, what activity to do, what to read, and how to share their knowledge. • Doing a "Learner Survey" and inviting participants to select a learning track. • Offering affinity groups, role-alike groups, or experience-alike groups in a PD session. • Being flexible: "I'm hearing that many of you feel like this activity would be more useful if you work with your departments. That makes sense. If you'd prefer that, go ahead and reorganize yourselves."	• Having agendas that feel rigid, jam-packed, and controlling. • Not offering learners time to think. • Directing and controlling every moment and movement. • Violating implicit agreements such as start and end times.
Adults need practice to internalize learning	• Writing, pair-sharing, small-group discussions. • Role-playing and receiving feedback. • Observing and deconstructing demonstrations of strategies. • Analyzing student work. • Creating lessons and assessments. • Receiving peer feedback on lessons.	• Lectures. • Lengthy whole-group discussions. • Reading long texts without opportunities to discuss.

(Continued)

Table 4.1   (Continued)

Adult Learning Principle	Example: Looks Like, Sounds Like. . .	Nonexample: Doesn't Look Like, Doesn't Sound Like. . .
Adults have a problem-centered approach to learning	• Identifying content that is relevant to learners' current needs. • Making connections between the PD content and the challenges faced by students and teachers. For example, "Our student survey data shows that our multilingual students feel anxious about speaking up in class. In this session, we'll learn three strategies to increase the verbal participation of all of our students." • Inviting learners to identify a problem of practice within the content of the PD session. For example, by saying, "Given our agenda for today, can you anticipate where you might be able to use the skills you'll learn?"	• Explanations of sessions that don't include a connection to a relevant issue. Such as, "Every teacher needs to understand Vygotsky's theory on. . ." or "This approach is successfully used in many Japanese schools. . ."
Adults want to learn	• Assuming that everyone wants to learn. • Expressing curiosity if a learner questions the content or learning activities. • Understanding that people express enthusiasm for learning differently. • Remembering that you may not see immediate evidence of behavior or belief change, but that doesn't mean it hasn't happened or won't happen. • Authentically saying something like, "I'm really excited that you're here today and I'm looking forward to learning together."	• Assuming a learner isn't willing if they push back or disagree about a learning activity. • Adopting an *us vs. them* mentality when facilitating. • Taking it personally if a learner seems disengaged.

When you guide people in learning, it's useful to recall your own experiences learning, at least in part to activate your humility. It's also helpful to understand the concept known as the Conscious Competence Ladder. This framework, laid out in Figure 4.1, helps us recognize the four stages of learning.

The model highlights the factors that affect our thinking and our emotions as we learn a new skill: consciousness (awareness) and competence (skill level). It identifies four levels that learners move through as they build first consciousness and then competence in a new skill:

- *Unconscious incompetence*: At this stage, we don't know that we don't have a skill or that we need to learn it. We are blissfully ignorant, and our confidence exceeds our abilities. Our task on this rung is to figure out what skills we need to learn.

Figure 4.1   Conscious Competence Ladder

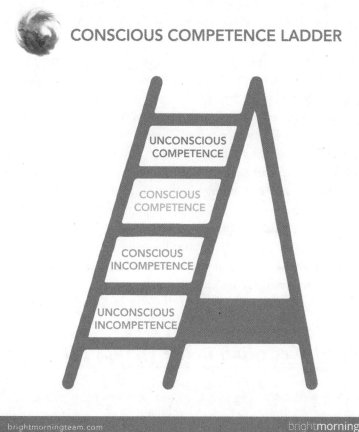

- *Conscious incompetence*: At this stage, we know we don't have the skills we're trying to acquire. We realize that others are much more competent and that they can easily do things with which we struggle. We can lose confidence at this stage or give up on our learning. This is when we most need to manage discomfort, fear, and anxiety, and to boost our confidence.
- *Conscious competence*: On this rung, we know that we have the skills we have worked to attain. As we put our knowledge and skill set into regular practice, we gain even more confidence. We still may need to concentrate when we perform these skills, but, as we get more practice and experience, these activities become increasingly automatic. We need to use these skills as often as possible in order to move into the next stage.
- *Unconscious competence*: At this level, we have likely achieved a level of mastery in a skill set, and we use our new skills effortlessly and perform tasks without conscious effort. We are confident of success. To keep growing, we need to teach these newly acquired skills to others. This deepens our understanding of the material and keeps our skills finely tuned; teaching the skills also can be rewarding. Be warned: We can go backwards down the ladder if we don't regularly use our skills.

Before we consider how you can use this concept in your work to deliver transformative PD, take a moment to think about yourself as a PD provider. Where on the ladder would you place yourself?

Now think about yourself as a teacher or administrator—or in any area in which you feel skilled. Can you recall when you were at the unconscious incompetence stage in developing that set of skills? Do you remember moments that allowed you to step up the ladder? Again, understanding your own experience will allow you to have more empathy for others and also to guide them in learning.

This framework can be helpful for you in planning and facilitating PD. When you plan PD, you can assess or guess the level of development for those who will attend your training. This can help you determine which activities might help learners meet the objectives. It can also be helpful to share this ladder with learners so that they can develop self-awareness about their learning process. Learners can feel relieved by the normalization of the process that this ladder suggests.

Adult Learning in the Virtual PD World

When designing and delivering virtual PD, most of the principles of adult learning transfer easily. While there are some technical tricks to consider around creating practice spaces, or providing agency, how you create psychological safety deserves greatest consideration. Some learners say they feel safer in a virtual PD setting. They can keep their cameras off if they want, there's a general reduction in noise and activity, and there can be less performance anxiety. Both synchronous and asynchronous virtual PD require different kinds of engagement than being in person together, and for some learners, this contributes to safety.

But some adult learners say they feel more vulnerable in virtual settings. Without a facilitator quietly circulating through a big space and keeping a kind eye on small groups, what happens in a virtual breakout relies entirely on how a group manages itself. Sometimes people don't even show up to a virtual breakout, leaving a group member or members unsure what to do. Here are a few ways to address this:

- Provide explicit instructions about what will happen in a breakout space. For example, you might say, "You will have 12 minutes total. The person whose first name starts with the letter closest to N is the facilitator who keeps track of time and ensures that everyone has a chance to share. Take about 90 seconds to do introductions. Then shift into discussing these questions. . . ."
- Give instructions about what to do if participants can't attend a breakout space (so that their group members aren't abandoned), and be clear about what to do if you end up in a breakout space and no one shows up.
- Remind people that on some virtual platforms (like Zoom) they can send you a private message to get assistance. Say something like, "If your group is struggling to stay on task or ensure that everyone gets a chance to talk, feel free to message me so I can help out."

While a chat feature can be a powerful tool to facilitate virtual PDs, it can also, when misused, contribute to participants' feelings of vulnerability. When a chat allows a few people to debate or when it is used for folks to talk about each other during a session, it can undermine our efforts to create psychological safety. Ideally a group comes to some agreements about chat feature usage. But a facilitator can also speak directly to the chat feature and how and when it's used. At its best, the chat feature can be a space where folks can contribute and be "heard" more than they might be in a whole-staff PD session. A facilitator can invite learners to respond to a prompt in the chat box or ask a question.

When delivering virtual PD, it's especially important to gather feedback about participants' experiences and feelings around safety. Because you can't scan the room and see the facial expressions of folks as they're walking out, you need data to understand their experience. This is also a time to be transparent about your concerns and say something like, "I recognize that I can't gauge what's going on in your breakout spaces. This makes me feel uncertain about how I can best support you. I really want to invite you to connect with me if there's anything going on in your breakouts that makes you feel unsafe so that I can figure out what to do."

What goes on in virtual PD sessions, including in the chat box and in breakout spaces, will reflect both the larger culture in the organization and the culture the PD provider creates. Just because a community only meets virtually doesn't mean that you aren't also responsible for creating culture there: Yes, sometimes it feels harder, but it can be done.

You Can Create the Conditions for Learning

After consulting with equine expert Jeanne Carlson (who is Elena's aunt), we have concluded that maybe you can make a horse drink water. If you lead a horse to water and it seems reluctant to drink, you might try the following:

- Talk to it nicely; share your intentions.
- Make sure there aren't any cranky horses around that might kick it while it's drinking.
- Let the horse know that you're going to watch out for mountain lions while it's got its head in the trough and that you'll scare them away if they approach.
- Understand the horse's recent drinking history. Horses often don't drink if they're not thirsty—maybe it's been doing a lot of drinking lately and you don't realize that and it just needs a break from drinking.
- Add salt to their feed to make them thirsty. This will encourage them to drink.
- Add some sort of sweetener to the water. Horses don't drink if the water doesn't taste like the water they're used to. This can happen if they've been relocated or are being hauled somewhere.
- Stick your face in the water and drink. Show the horse that the water is good.

Now, we know that people are not horses, and we're aware of the limits of using this idiom. And at the same time, symbolism can help us think differently.

We have had a handful of experiences in which, in spite of using all their best tricks and strategies, we've faced folks who seemed to refuse to learn. The truth is, because we can't see inside others' minds, we don't really know whether those folks learned. But we are committed to modeling an openness to new things, kindness and curiosity, and the courage to take risks. We know that it's our responsibility to create the conditions in which people can learn and that our attitude makes a big difference. Even when we don't see evidence of learning right in front of us, we don't abandon the ways of being that we're committed to.

Ultimately, you can control only what you think and believe—and to some extent, what you feel. Although we shared the Principles of Transformative PD in the introduction, we're sharing them again to remind you of our core beliefs:

- Humans are bursting with untapped resilience, strength, and abilities.
- Teachers create the conditions in which transformative learning happens; we embrace this responsibility.
- Learning is a basic human need.
- Learning is a social process.
- Learning is the pathway to justice, healing, and liberation.
- PD can be a party.

So, no, you can't *make* people learn, but you can do a whole lot to create the conditions in which people can learn, and you can stand firmly in your core beliefs.

Before You Go

Pause and Process:
- Think back on PD that you provided in the recent past. How did you make space for learners to bring their background knowledge to the session?
- If you could design the PD session of your dreams that would meet your own current learning needs, what would it be? What's the problem that you'd want help to solve?
- Think back on PD that you provided in which you presented new content. How did you give learners an opportunity to digest the material? To practice skills? How did they get feedback? How did learners reflect on the new content?
- Imagine the titles for a few PD sessions you could deliver that would engage learners immediately because they'd get answers to questions they're dealing with or challenges they're facing. For example, "How to Get Kids to Stop Looking at Their Phones" or "How to Dissolve Resistance." Come up with some titles given the needs of an actual audience.

Remember:

- People want to learn.
- Less is more.
- We need to make time and create structures for practice.
- Adults need choice.
- You can't make people learn, but you can create the conditions for learning.

CHAPTER 5

Design Intentionally

LORI REFLECTS:

I opened my laptop. My job was to design a Bright Morning workshop called *Artful Design and Facilitation*, a six-session virtual series on creating and facilitating transformative PD. I set conditions for planning. First, my comforts: mug of steaming coffee, comfy sweatshirt and favorite slippers, my dog Buster curled up and snoring in his bed beside my chair. Next, my planning tools: a blank What-Why-How Agenda template on my screen, a blank slide deck (my design playground), a web browser open to access online tools, and my biggest necessity—a stack of fluorescent orange sticky notes.

Closing my eyes, I envisioned what I hoped to hear and see at the end of the workshop: I imagined participants coming off mute or sharing comments in the chat like, "I'm going to try these activities right away" and "As an adult learner, I felt seen and respected in this space" and "The design was so intentional!" I imagined them leaving the Zoom room invigorated. When I opened my eyes, I wrote these phrases on sticky notes, placing each little note at the base of my computer monitor so I could see them as I planned.

Today I was going to work on the first session: Principles of Adult Learning. I had 150 participants to consider, 90 minutes to design for, and two intended outcomes to address:

- Design learning structures and agendas aligned with the principles of adult learning.
- Cultivate optimal conditions for learning.

Ninety minutes wasn't a lot of time. Eventually I would remind myself that less is best. But for now, I wanted to give myself the freedom to consider all the possible ways to meet the intended outcomes. I set my timer for 10 minutes (timers help me stay focused) and brainstormed one idea per sticky note. After time was up and my desk was covered in orange notes, I reviewed what I generated, which included some of the following:

- Storytelling about adult learning principles
- Padlet community builder
- Small-group sharing to process readings
- Lightning round design challenge
- Collaboration board idea-sharing
- Save the Last Word discussion protocol
- Dance party

I couldn't stop looking at "dance party." Something about the idea was sitting with me. But I hate to dance (at least when people are watching). Rather than ditch the dance party idea just yet, I pictured what a virtual dance party might look like. As I imagined music playing and people dancing in their tiny Zoom screens, I thought, *Yes. This is one way we might build community and create conditions for learning. We might dance a little and have fun. And through this activity, we'll build connection.*

I then let my mind wander a bit more: Since this is Session 1, the first half could be about fostering connection and belonging; maybe we'll do a couple of different community builders. I'll design these with adult learning principles in mind. In the second half of the session, maybe participants could collectively reflect on which principles were used in the opening activity.

I immediately thought about some pre-readings that would align with the intended outcomes and sequence of this session. I pulled Elena Aguilar's

The Art of Coaching Teams off my shelf and thumbed through the pages to Chapter 9, "Supporting Adult Learners." I grabbed a second book from Buddhist teacher Sebene Selassie, *You Belong: A Call for Connection* (2020); the first chapter contained excerpts on belonging and connection that would be perfect for this session. I also thought of a blog post I wrote about how play is good for adult learners and opened that blog post on my web browser.

As I considered these ideas and readings, I could picture the arc of the workshop, from the pre-work to the final feedback form. I was energized and ready to geek out on intentional design.

Think about an upcoming PD session you'd like to design—perhaps your next PLC, a workshop for all staff, a do-over PD you want to re-imagine, or perhaps even your dream PD (the workshop you've always wanted to lead). Imagine you're just about to plan it. What would you want participants to know and be able to do by the end? What would you want participants to say and feel? What can you picture about the experience?

In the opening anecdote, Lori reflected on some of the components that contributed to her planning: her conditions for design (comforts and tools), the outcomes, and the possible activities. She also envisioned what participants would say and feel by the end of the first session. This visualization primed her for the rest of the design process and got her excited about how she might create and sequence learning that would be meaningful, rigorous, and transformative.

In this chapter, we'll explore the habit of designing intentionally and pull back the curtain on the design process. We'll begin with the tools and then guide you through a process for intentional design: considering everything you know about participants and infusing your plans with the kinds of routines, topics, and activities that allow participants to learn at their best. You'll also consider planning for virtual PD as well as how to mitigate the forces of dominant culture in design.

Throughout this chapter, you'll revisit Lori's process so you can see how her initial vision came together in her final design. As you read this chapter, think about that upcoming PD, the do-over PD, or the dream PD, and apply what you learn to your design.

Tools for Intentional Design

After years of delivering PD, Bright Morning presenters have come to rely on three core design tools, no matter what kind of PD we're creating. The following three tools will help you to create learning conditions that allow for all participants to feel seen, heard, represented, and valued:

- *Participant data* informs decisions about every aspect of PD design, especially as we create learning outcomes.
- *Planning questions* focus our design to include what's essential and what best meets our outcomes.
- *The agenda* captures everything in one place and communicates outcomes, topics, activities, and materials.

Let's look at how each of these tools can support your design.

Participant Data: Feedback and Surveys

The number-one issue we see in PDs we observe is that facilitators don't have enough time to get through their planned agenda. Or they run out of time because their intended outcomes didn't match up with participant needs—they underestimated how long something would take or they didn't understand what their participants knew or could do in relation to the content. Participant data helps you understand where learners are in their knowledge and skills, gauge their learning gaps, and make informed decisions about design. Later, this data will also give you a reference point as you measure the impact of your PD

The two most useful types of data are feedback forms from previous sessions and learner surveys. If you work at the site where you lead PD, you most likely have access to feedback from previous sessions. If you're an external provider, you may not have access to feedback, but you can get information about your participants through creating a learner survey.

Feedback from Previous Experiences

If you have access to feedback surveys from previous PD sessions, review them and identify themes. Look for what participants learned, what they still need to learn, and their suggestions for improving PD.

After Ridgeway Middle School's summer PD sessions, Vanessa, the assistant principal, shared a feedback form with staff. Her feedback forms consisted of a balance between quantitative (rating scales of 1–5) and qualitative questions (What did you learn? How will you apply your learning to your classes this year?). When staff submitted feedback forms, she quickly scanned the rating scales to gauge participant reactions; she reviewed qualitative responses for patterns. When she saw three or more comments that zeroed in on the same topic, she considered that a pattern. While she appreciated comments like, "I loved the lunch outside" and "The connecting activities were fun," she also assessed for learning. For example, when several participants wondered about the relevance of the connecting activities, Vanessa made a note to be more purposeful in selecting connecting activities when designing PD.

The Learner Survey

If you don't have the benefit of previous feedback to draw on, either because you're an external provider or because you're new to your site, that's okay. A learner survey can provide data about participants' knowledge and skills and other design considerations. The following are questions you could ask:

- What do you already know about this topic?
- What skills do you already possess as related to this topic?
- What would you most like to know about this topic?
- Among the terms listed here_____, which ones are you most familiar with/least familiar with?
- What do you hope to be true by the end of the workshop? What will you hope to learn or be able to do?
- What is a question you're hoping to have answered by the end of this workshop?

  Let's consider an example. Jamilah, a new assistant principal, was designing PD for the first time. Since she was responsible for designing PD all year, she wanted to learn more about topics her staff was interested in and how they learned best. Figure 5.1 is a sample of the survey she shared at the beginning of the year.

Imagine Future Feedback

Before diving into planning a PD, imagine participants filling out the feedback form at the end of PD. Imagine what their big takeaways will be and how will apply their learning. As you envision your future feedback, ask yourself what you hope participants will say. What would meet your expectations? What would exceed them? Write down what you hope to read. Keep those notes nearby and refer to them as you plan.

Figure 5.1   Eagle River High School PD learner survey

Please take about 10 minutes to fill out the following survey. This will give me insight into what you want to learn and ways you learn best. While I can't guarantee we'll address all the topics you'll share, I'll do my best to prioritize the most pressing topics.

What you want to learn: This year's content focus will be on academic literacy.

• What do you already know about this topic?
• What do hope to learn about this topic?

How you learn: What methods help you learn best? For each statement, place an "x" closest to the phrase that's most true for you.

Seeing a model	↔	Experimenting myself
Reading and writing	↔	Listening and speaking
Learning theory and then practicing	↔	Practicing and then learning the theory
Being guided by a facilitator	↔	Being self-guided
Learning alone	↔	Learning with others
Doing linear-sequential activities	↔	Doing nonlinear, creative activities
Practicing in hands-on ways	↔	Reflecting about what I'm learning

---

How you gain and lose energy:
Mark the statement that best describes you:

☐ I am an introvert. I like to think before I speak, and I gain energy through small-group interactions.

☐ I am an extrovert. I like to speak as a form of thinking, and I gain energy through large-group interactions and mingling activities.

☐ I am an ambivert. I am either a verbal or internal processor, and I prefer a range of interactions.

Wishes and Aspirations:

• How do you want to feel as a result of this year's PD? How will this feeling result in change for your students?

Tips and Tricks:

To gather participant data, consider the KWL method to gauge what your participants Know (K) about the PD topic, Want to know (W), and after the PD, what they Learned (L). This is a practice we use with students that can easily be transferred to working with adults.

When designing feedback surveys for the end of PD, consider some of these samples of questions you might ask:

- Quantitative: On a scale of 1–5 (1 = strongly disagree and 5 = strongly agree)
  - This PD met or exceeded your expectations.
  - This PD was relevant to your role.
  - You would recommend this PD to others.

- Qualitative:
  - Share a big takeaway from the PD and explain how you will apply this learning.
  - Identify a tool, exercise, or activity from today that most contributed to your learning.
  - Share something from the session you are still wondering about.
  - Share something about the session that could be improved.

After you collect and review feedback, summarize the feedback and share highlights with feedback, including a handful of comments that represent different experiences. This practice reveals your facilitator moves, which helps further trust and psychological safety. When Lori presented Bright Morning's two-day *Art of Coaching Teams* workshop with Birmingham Academy, she gathered feedback after the first day and shared the results at the beginning of the second day. When sharing which activities were most helpful on the first day, Lori noted that 37 percent of participants indicated individual reflection time. When sharing which activities were least helpful to learning, Lori shared that 40 percent of participants indicated individual reflection time. Lori recognized that she needed to remind participants about the purpose of individual reflection time: to balance introverted and extroverted ways of processing the material.

Planning Questions: 21 Questions That Will Make PD Awesome

The series of questions that follows will guide your design and take into account the habits you have learned so far. In Chapter 6, "Attend to Details," you'll receive additional questions to enhance your planning. But first, it's important to lay the groundwork for your agenda. Taking time to engage with the questions in "21 Planning Questions That Will Make PD Awesome" will allow you to think broadly about all facets of your PD and specifically about what will work best for participants as you craft your plans. We recommend you write out your responses to some of these questions—you need to be clear on the answers for yourself. While the questions are categorized by theme, they don't need to be addressed in sequence.

21 PLANNING QUESTIONS THAT WILL MAKE YOUR PD AWESOME

Purpose
- What is the purpose of this session?
- What makes this purpose compelling?

Intended Outcomes
- What are the intended outcomes for this session(s)?
- How do these intended outcomes support participants in building knowledge and skill?

Audience and Context
- What do you know about participants' attitudes and beliefs about the content you're presenting?
- Where are participants currently in their knowledge and skill development?
- How will you create an environment in which adults feel psychologically safe and challenged to grow?
- What strengths and growth areas can you identify in relation to participants' knowledge and skill?
- How are you ensuring that people from all backgrounds, races, and abilities (physical and neurological)—particularly historically marginalized populations—are considered in your design?
- How will you establish authority and credibility, and how will you source and leverage power as a facilitator and in group activities?

Topics
- Which specific areas of knowledge and skill development will be addressed in this session, and why are these the priorities?
- How are you offering opportunities for choice and differentiation within activities?

Structures/Activities
- How will participants learn this content?
- What will engagement look and sound like?
- How will learning be sequenced?

- What is the suggested length of each activity, and how will that timing allow for learning, processing, synthesizing, interpreting, applying, and/or creating?
- How will adult learning principles be reflected in your activities?
- Where might there be opportunities for risk-taking, cognitive dissonance, play, and joy?
- Where and when are you inviting a range of voices to engage, either through the interactions in the learning or through the resources you use?

Measuring Learning
- Which measurement tool or rubric will be used to evaluate learning and growth?
- What kind of growth or development is expected from participants, and how will participants demonstrate their learning?

When you're a new PD provider, these questions can be a useful starting point to design intentionally. When you're more experienced, identify the questions you might consider when planning. Which ones might enhance the PD you design? And whether you're newer to facilitating PD or more veteran, if you're short on time, focus on these four questions to guide your planning:

- What is the purpose of this session, and how is purpose infused throughout?
- Who is the audience, and how will you create the conditions for psychological safety?
- How will people learn?
- How will you know people learned?

The What-Why-How Agenda

If you have ever attended a Bright Morning workshop, you've received the signature What-Why-How Agenda. This agenda is a game-changer for PD because it lays out the topics clearly and makes every element transparent for participants. The What-Why-How Agenda helps you see how the sequence of topics fit together. Appendix C contains a template you can use when you create your own agendas (with instructions built into the template). You can also download this template from www.brightmorningteam.com.

Agendas will take different forms, and we advocate for a comprehensive agenda whenever possible—something that is a guide for the whole learning experience and includes the following elements:

- *Title of the workshop/session*: The name of the workshop/learning experience. The more concrete and specific to the topic, the better.
- *Facilitator(s)*: Name(s) of any presenters and their pronouns.
- *Intended outcomes*: Include what participants will know, understand, and be able to do as a result of their learning.
- *Agreements/norms*: If you have community agreements or any norms that guide your organization, it can be helpful to include them at the top of the agenda.
- *Time*: Include either how long a segment might take and/or the time frame of the session.
- *What*: Briefly state the topics and subtopics you'll address.
- *Why*: Provide a brief phrase that describes the purpose of each overarching topic.
- *How*: Share how participants will learn—facilitator guided, group discussions, games, role-plays, reflection, or any other mode of learning.
- *Materials*: Include what participants will need to access—relevant tools, handouts, readings, links.

Figure 5.2 is a sample participant What-Why-How Agenda for the first session of Lori's *Artful Design and Facilitation* workshop.

Figure 5.2   Sample participant agenda for Lori's *Artful Design and Facilitation* workshop, session 1

Artful Design and Facilitation

Session 1| Facilitated by Lori Cohen (she/her)

INTENDED OUTCOMES *Participants in this series will:*
- HONE your leadership identity, grounded in your core values.
- DESIGN learning structures and agendas aligned with principles of adult learning.
- CULTIVATE optimal conditions for learning.
- CHOOSE and BUILD buy-in for effective professional learning goals.
- REFINE your communication skills.
- DEVELOP skills to encourage productive conversation and healthy conflict.
- IDENTIFY ways to gather data and reflect on the effectiveness of professional development.

(Continued)

Figure 5.2 (Continued)

AGENDA			
Time	**What**	**Why**	**How** **Materials**
15 min	**Opening** • Welcome • Outcomes and Purpose • Community Agreements • Inquiry Question • Setting Intentions	*To center ourselves, our needs, and our dispositions as we transition into the learning space.*	Facilitator sharing Group introductions/breakouts • Participant agenda • Note-taking tools
30 min	**Principles in Practice: Community Building** • Introverted Introductions • Extroverted Introductions	*To engage with adult learning principles through community building activities.*	Individual sharing Breakout groups • Padlet • Note-taking tools
30 min	**Principles Applied** • Reflecting on Experience • Making Sense of Pre-Work and Synthesizing Learning in Community	*To process our learning experience so far and make connections to the pre-work. To practice with discussion protocols as we synthesize content.*	Individual reflection Breakout group Gallery glance • Pre-work: Excerpts from *You Belong* and *The Art of Coaching Teams* • Discussion protocol using Google Docs • Padlet to post notes
15 min	**Pulling Back the Curtain and Closing** • Q&A • Revisit Intentions and Inquiry • Appreciations • For next time. . .	*To address questions or insights that emerged from today's learning. To reflect on learning; to bring our session to a close.*	Whole-group question and answer Individual reflection • Note-taking tools

Using a learner survey, working with the planning questions, and creating a What-Why-How Agenda will set you well on your way to planning transformative PD. In the next segment of this chapter, we'll dig into some of the activities on this agenda to better understand what it looks like to bring this agenda to life. Before we move on, take a few minutes to reflect on which tools are already part of your toolkit and which ones you might add.

A Process for Intentional Design

What is your process when designing a session, whether a single workshop, PLC session, or a multiday experience? How do you select activities? How do you ensure that people from historically marginalized populations are considered in your design? These are the kinds of questions we'll address in this section as you'll learn to design using five steps.

Step 1: Assess the Amount of Time You Have

There's an idiom when someone overindulges in a meal: *Their eyes were bigger than their stomach.* When it comes to planning PD in the allotted time frame, many PD leaders' eyes are bigger than their stomachs, which is why assessing the time you have and planning appropriately (what we call *portion control*) is an important skill to learn. Let's explore an example.

Vinh was responsible for leading a weekly 45-minute PLC with his instructional coaching team. Each week, Vinh planned for coaches to connect with each other, learn new content, practice coaching skills, and identify a next step in their practice. In Table 5.1, you'll see how Vinh intended to spend his time compared to what actually happened. In the left column you'll see how much time Vinh allotted for each agenda item. The right side of this table reflects the amount of time actually spent.

Like many PD leaders, Vinh had a portion-control challenge: Vinh packed his agenda with too many activities and found himself pressed for time. We would love to talk about how schools in general pack too much into their schedules and how harmful this is for students and adults, but for our purposes here, we'll just say that no matter the time frame you're working in, less is best.

With time and practice at designing, you will have enough experience to know how much is too much for your agenda and what feels manageable in the time frame you have. In the meantime, it can be helpful to have some parameters to

Table 5.1   Weekly PLC Time Allocated Versus Actual

Agenda Item	Time Allocated	Actual Time Spent
Community builder	**5 minutes** (All will respond to check-in prompt.)	**12 minutes** (Learners were really into the activity.)
New content (e.g., using the ladder of inference to coach beliefs)	**15 minutes** (Coaches will jigsaw read and share.)	**25 minutes** (Coaches had a lot of questions.)
Coaching (quick rounds or whole-group demonstration)	**25 minutes** (Coaches will complete three rounds of coaching.)	**10 minutes** (One round of coaching, with one member of the pair getting to be the coach.)
Closing and next steps	**5 minutes** (Whole-group debrief and individuals choose individual next steps.)	**No time** for closing

work within. Table 5.2 provides examples of how to spend the time you have. This table includes considerations for both virtual and in-person learning.

Overall, regardless of how much time you have, we suggest the following as part of any agenda:

Table 5.2   Time Allocations for Pacing Professional Development

Time	Format	Structures for Allocating Time

One hour* *for less than one hour, cut down the time on review or meaning-making	Virtual or In-Person	Consider the following structure:
		• 5–8 min: Brief opener + connecting activity
		• 10–15 min: Review prior learning or introduce new content
		  • Process new content and ask questions
		  • Small-group discussion or protocol for synthesis or idea generation
		• 30 min: Make meaning and create something (action plan, decision, etc.)
		• 5 min: Closing (one big takeaway or action step)

(Continued)

Table 5.2 (Continued)

Time	Format	Structures for Allocating Time

Half Day	Virtual	• A virtual half day is 3–4 hours. Consider learning blocks no more than two hours long.
		• A 2-hour learning block might look like the following:
		  • 5–10 min: Opener + connecting activity
		  • 75–95 min: A deep dive into one topic OR a 35–45 minute two-topic agenda. Activities might include the following (shorten for a two-topic agenda):
		    • 10–15 min: Process new learning, ask questions, synthesize
		    • 10–20 min: Discussion, activity, movement breaks
		    • 5–10 min: Whole-group check for understanding
		    • 30 min: Role-play practice
		    • 15–20 min: Make meaning and create something (action plan, decision, etc.)
		  • 5–10 min: Closing (one big takeaway or action step; opportunity for accountability)

Half Day	In-Person	• An in-person half day is around 3–5 hours.
		• Consider about one topic per hour to 90 minutes, unless you're doing a deep dive into a single process; then consider varying the ways you engage with the task in 30–45 minute increments
		• For any task, consider the following sequence of activities:
		  • Individual reflection
		  • Group sharing, meaning-making (pair share, trio share, some sort of small-group team configuration)
		  • Whole group (depending on size):
		    • For groups with fewer than 30 people, a whole-group discussion, fishbowl discussion, or debrief is possible.
		    • For groups of more than 30 people, consider using tools like a backchannel chat, Padlet, posters around the room (like a "chalk talk"), or make slightly larger "small" groups for processing information.

(Continued)

Table 5.2 (Continued)

Time	Format	Structures for Allocating Time
Full Day	Virtual	• Consider 5–6 hours as the absolute maximum for screen time. • Consider learning blocks no more than two hours long. • Take breaks every 60–90 minutes (stretch, hydrate). Get people moving if possible. • Consider the previous 1-hour or 2-hour plan for the breakdown of activities per learning block.
Full Day	In-Person	• 6–8 hours (including meals and breaks) is typically a full day. • Consider including a variety of activities: individual and whole-group; reading, reflecting, discussing, synthesizing, evaluating, creating. • Build movement into the day: strolls around the room (or outside if possible), energizers (stretching or games) + discussion opportunities (walk and talks) • Start the day with a community builder and do "energizers" after breaks and lunch to re-engage people.
Multiple Days	Virtual or In-Person	• Consider selecting one theme for each day of a multiday experience, and/or work on just a couple of outcomes per day. Link the theme of each day to the overarching purpose so participants can see the connection. • Avoid packing too much in; multiday doesn't always have to mean multifaceted. • Determine if there is any work people can do asynchronously. • Even though you have lots more time in a large-scale, multiday PDs, less is still best to give people time to think and process. Consider one core subject per learning block and vary instruction or discussion/learning method every 20–30 minutes.

- *Make time for opening and closing routines* of some sort (at least 5–10 minutes on each end). These opening and closing routines help participants transition in and out of the learning (and provide a buffer at the end if you run short on time).
- *Plan for more time than you think you need* for each activity, which means planning for fewer activities. It's easy to forget about time for giving clear directions or checking for understanding, and few presenters allow enough time for participants to process their learning.
- *Design for multiple types of engagement* to meet the needs of a range of learners; engage as many senses as you can throughout your PD.
- When possible, *invite different kinds of participation beyond talking* (chat, polls, collaboration boards, protocols like "Chalk Talk").
- *Make time for breaks and movement.* Whether in-person or virtual, people can't stay in one mode for too long, and shifting energy every 20–30 minutes is optimal. Include a few energizers to get participants moving, and draw on the strategies you learned to engage emotions in Chapter 2.

When Lori planned her first *Artful Design and Facilitation* workshop, she had 90 minutes to work with. After making time for opening and closing routines, she had about 60–70 minutes, which she allocated to two 30-minute activities. Later in this section, we'll see how she designed each of these activities.

Step 2: Generate Intended Outcomes

In the design process, intended outcomes are the essential link between your overarching purpose and the topics and activities in your PD. Intended outcomes are a balance of the aspirational (ideal) and the practical (doable). Specific, actionable outcomes make ideals possible. Consider using the following criteria when generating and articulating intended outcomes:

- *Aim for three to five intended outcomes.* Yes, you can try to accomplish more than five intended outcomes (especially for multiday PD), but you will maximize your impact if you limit intended outcomes.
- *Use strong, active verbs that link to clear actions.* Think about what you want participants to understand, know, and be able to do by the end of your learning experience. Put an emphasis on the "do" part. PD leaders are better able to measure impact when participants leave PD with something actionable. Verbs like *examine*, *create*, or *practice* are actionable.

- *Be specific.* Specific intended outcomes allow participants to connect the activities they are engaging in with the overarching goals of the session. An intended outcome such as "Participants will connect with one another" is broad. An intended outcome such as "Participants will connect in whole-and small-group communities and build empathy across roles and responsibilities" is more specific and action-oriented.

Kolby and Raquel were assistant superintendents who designed a workshop on transformational leadership with site principals. As they considered their ideal outcomes, they hoped principals would increase their emotional intelligence and resilience so they had the skill and capacity to support all staff at their sites. To meet their aspirations, Kolby and Raquel created three intended outcomes for their workshop:

- Cultivate emotional intelligence through community and trust-building.
- Explore resilience through reflective activities.
- Practice emotional intelligence and resilience through role-play practice and case study analysis.

Each outcome contained a strong verb and specific actions that supported principals throughout the workshop.

To learn more about articulating outcomes, both for PD and for meetings, read *The Art of Coaching Teams* (Aguilar, 2016).

Step 3: Select Topics and Activities

The next phase of PD design is building activities in a meaningful learning sequence. Our experience suggests that every hour of an agenda can take two hours to plan. While the planning process can feel lengthy, especially for newer PD leaders, it gets easier and more intuitive over time—and it can be a joyful process.

In this section you'll decide how to open and close PD as participants transition in and out of their busy days, how to select the activities that align with your PD's purpose and outcomes, and how to build a sequence that allows participants to practice and transfer their learning.

Openings and Closings

Opening and closing routines support participants to transition into and out of the PD, and we suggest you design these routines first. Let's start at the beginning.

In the first 10 minutes, as participants are settling into the learning space, rituals help people get centered. In Bright Morning workshops, our opening routines are comprised of the following:

- *Land acknowledgment*: A minute or two of acknowledging and honoring Indigenous communities on whose land we are learning. The facilitator names the Indigenous people on whose land they stand. If the learning is virtual, participants are also invited to share the names of the people whose lands they are on. (To learn more about land acknowledgments, see "Appendix F: Resources. for Further Learning")
- *Facilitator introduction (if applicable)*: For facilitators who are new to the group, this is an opportunity to share some brief details to establish credibility and presence.
- *Agenda preview*: Two minutes for participants to scan the agenda and identify something they are looking forward to learning. This activity primes the mind for learning.
- *Intention setting*: This two-minute activity invites participants to check in with how they are doing, what will help them make most of the learning experience, and how they want to show up. Examples of intentions might include "I want to be fully present" or "I want to take risks." Participants can share their intentions in a brief pair share.
- *Community agreements*: These are agreements that allow people to learn together. The facilitator reviews agreements (or norms, if your site has those) and gives people a chance to reflect on how they might be able to live into these agreements.

If you find yourself short on time and can do only a couple of these activities, we suggest an agenda preview and intention-setting. These two activities will prime participants for learning.

Closing routines matter as much as opening ones do. Our brains are hardwired to remember first and last impressions, so a strong final impression can be a powerful capstone to PD. Just as Bright Morning workshops have opening routines, the 10- to 15-minute closing routines help usher participants out of a learning space. They include the following:

- *Big takeaways*: Participants take a few minutes to identify their biggest insights or takeaways. When in person, they may turn and talk to a neighbor as well. Virtually, participants might share takeaways in the chat or on a collaboration board.

- *Revisit intentions*: Participants take a minute or two to check how they met their intention. Here, too, they may turn and talk to a partner if they are in person. They can share whether they were aware of their intention throughout the PD and what it was like to set an intention for their learning.
- *Feedback*: Save five minutes to solicit feedback at the end. Details to consider as you plan feedback include decisions about anonymity (to collect names or not?), format of questions (rating scales or qualitative questions?), and medium (online forms or index cards?). If you build time for participants to complete feedback before they leave, your rate of return will be much higher.
- *Appreciations*: Appreciations are good for the brain and the soul and connect us to one another. People may leave the PD more energized after a round of appreciations.

Depending on time, even one or two routines allow for participants to transition out of a learning space. We suggest giving participants a chance to share their big takeaways so you can best determine if participant learning was aligned with what you envisioned participants saying by the end.

Selecting Activities

While reviewing intended outcomes and participant survey data, begin a list of possible activities. When choosing among those activities, think about participant demographics (role, experience, and identity markers such as race, gender, and physical abilities) and how to differentiate activities to meet the needs of the group. For example, how might you generate activities that are accessible for people of all abilities or for neurodiverse learners? How might you consider protocols that allow for a range of voices to be heard and affirmed?

The 20/80 Rule

PD provides greater opportunities for learning when it's not filled with all new content. We advocate for sticking to the 20/80 rule: There should be about 20 percent new content compared and 80 percent processing time. While the new content portion typically involves direct instruction or some kind of "text" (a reading or video), the processing portion largely varies and depends on the purpose and outcomes of your PD.

When selecting learning activities, it's helpful to have frameworks for the kinds of activities you do. The 20/80 model draws on a range of learning frameworks, but mostly Revised Bloom's Taxonomy (2001), a process that invites participants to learn through knowing (or understanding), remembering, applying,

Table 5.3 Using the 20/80 Rule: A Breakdown of Sample Activities

Percentage Breakdown	Type of Learning	Sample Activities
~20%	Knowing, understanding, and remembering (This type of learning is typically frontloaded in pre-work and when facilitators are introducing a topic.)	• Pre-work (handouts, readings, reflection questions) • Direct instruction • Texts related to the topic • Reflection questions or surveys to gauge prior knowledge
~80%	Applying, analyzing, evaluating, and creating (Select a variety of activities to ensure a rigorous experience and multiple entry points for differentiation and engagement.)	• Discussion protocols (for pairs or small groups) • Reflection on new learning and understandings (individual or collaborative) • Checks for understanding: "thumbometers," "exit tickets," "triangle, circle, square" feedback • Polling tools • Developing action steps and implementation plans • Role-playing • Case studies • Scenario analysis • Drafting new policies • Creating curriculum • Developing rubrics

analyzing, evaluating, and creating. The activities in Table 5.3 provide possible approaches based on the 20/80 rule, and Table 5.4 provides sample activities for whole groups, small groups, and individuals.

Make Space for Risk-Taking, Energy-Shifting, and Play

Halfway through an event on cultivating resilience, Elena brought out canisters of tennis balls, placed a couple balls at each table, and asked participants to stand and throw them around as a way to engage and get to know one another. Participants were awkward at first. They'd signed up for what they thought was a talk about resilience, and they likely expected that they'd gain some wisdom from Elena and participate in some meaningful table conversation. Eventually, awkwardness gave way to laughter, connection happened, and the energy in the room shifted. Play, whether intentional or purposeless, is good for the brain and body—and for group dynamics.

Table 5.4 Sample Activities Based on Group Size

Sample whole-group, small-group, and individual activities

Whole Group	• Movement activities that get people mingling and connecting • Poster sessions that showcase participant learning • Gallery walks • Chalk Talk protocol (or an equivalent) • Polls and surveys to check for understanding • Video and image analysis • Depending on the group size, you might invite people to build something together, such as an index card tower Resources: • Project Zero's thinking routines offer ways to make thinking visible; they are just as useful for adults as they are for youth (see Appendix F: Resources for Further Learning). • *Gamestorming* (Gray, Brown, Macanufo, 2010) also has a variety of activities for whole- and small-group interaction. • *Creative Acts for Curious People* (Greenberg, 2021) includes assignments from Stanford's d.school that inspire creative thinking.
Small Group	• Discussion protocols • Small-group and pair-share conversations (affinity groups, role-alike groups, cross-role groups) • Walk and talks • Video and image analysis • Drawing and sculpting • Games to build community and trust • Role-play practice • Storytelling • Case studies and scenario analysis Resources: • National School Reform Faculty and School Reform Initiative offer excellent protocols (see Appendix F: "Resources for Further Learning")
Individual	• Short reflection questions • Brief readings and texts • Polls and surveys • Drawing and sculpting • Visualization • Mindfulness and meditative activities • Solo walks

LORI REFLECTS:

I think about choosing activities much like I think about selecting cheese for a dinner party. There needs to be a variety of flavor profiles that can meet everyone's needs: something that is familiar or reliable and some kinds that might challenge people's taste buds. Sometimes I'll throw in a cheese that no one was expecting, something tangy or tart to shift people's expectations. I approach design in a similar fashion: a combination of familiar and reliable, something more challenging, and unexpected activities that promote a shift in practice.

As I narrowed possible activities for *Artful Design and Facilitation*, I ended up designing two activities to demonstrate adult learning principles in practice: the Introverted Introduction and the Extroverted Introduction. I thought about how in Western, dominant cultures, extroverts tend to be regarded more highly than introverts, so I wanted to shift this paradigm by doing a more introverted type of introduction first. I also wanted to create psychological safety by easing participants into the learning and giving people choice in the ways they engaged, particularly for the Introverted Introduction.

For the Introverted Introduction, I decided I would use a tool called Padlet and its "mapping" feature: Participants would introduce themselves to one another by dropping a pin of their location on a map and typing some information about themselves. Participants then would read others' introductions, click the "like" button to indicate they had read their peers' posts, and write a brief comment to their new virtual colleagues. I also knew that tech tools might not work for everyone, so I decided to create an alternative to the Padlet: Participants could interact using the chat feature on Zoom. If participants weren't up for that, I'd let them know they were welcome to write responses in their notes and share later in breakout rooms.

For the Extroverted Introduction, I decided on a dance party. To do so, I mimicked an in-person activity I often use called "The Bump." The in-person version of The Bump has participants move around the room while the facilitator plays a song. When the music stops, participants group with two or three people closest to them and answer a prompt on the screen (e.g., "What brings you to this workshop?"). In the virtual space, I wanted to create the same level of energy and interaction. I decided to do three rounds of The Bump. I would play a series of three music videos and invite people to dance along if they wanted. After a minute of playing each video, I would project a prompt on the screen, open breakout rooms, and set a timer for three minutes. Participants would then introduce themselves and share responses to the prompt. The pace would be quick to generate some fast connections and offer participants a chance to meet several different people in each round. The size of the breakouts (two to three people) could create intimacy.

I considered additional factors in designing the Extroverted Introduction, particularly around representation in each music video. I didn't want to make assumptions about participants' mobility (and I imagined, like me, some participants might not want to dance while on camera). I would give participants the option to keep their cameras on or off. I decided I'd play music videos on the screen so participants who didn't want to dance could at least enjoy people moving on the screen. I selected videos that represented people of different races, international backgrounds, and physical abilities, and I chose music from different places in the world. For each breakout round, I would pose prompting questions that were "low lift" enough for an opening session: questions about why people chose the workshop and what they hoped to learn.

At the end of this activity, I decided to throw in a bonus video: Michelle Obama doing some "mom dance moves," a popular video that participants might enjoy. My hope was that participants would begin feel psychologically safe(ish), energized by this opener, perhaps laugh a little, and feel a little more connected to their peers, regardless of their introversion or extroversion.

When selecting activities, make space for play where appropriate. Just as our students need play, we adults do, too. We need play to balance the hard work of learning with opportunities to recharge. We need play because it fosters our resilience in times of stress—and education is a stressful profession. We need play because it's good for our health and well-being, and our students are looking to us as models for how to be in the world. We offer a series of playful activities in Chapter 2 for you to draw on in your planning.

Whether you love play (like Elena) or are play averse (like Lori), invite opportunities to play when you need to shift energy, when people come back from a break, or when you've done something difficult. Even more importantly, explain why you're asking everyone to play. You'll foster trust when the purpose is clear, and you'll engage more folks in whole-hearted play. Along the way, you also might have fun.

Step 4: Design for Gradual Release

In Bright Morning's *Art of Coaching 101* workshop, participants engage in a blended learning experience: They complete eight hours of asynchronous learning modules to learn about the tools and practices of Transformational Coaching. These portions are largely facilitator-led with some opportunities for independent reflection and practice. The learning culminates in a four-hour synchronous, virtual processing session where participants share insights and plan and practice for a coaching conversation of their own. By the end of the workshop, participants are working predominantly in small groups—transferring what they learned throughout the course and practicing their skills without facilitator guidance. This process follows the gradual release of responsibility model (GRR) (Duke and Pearson, 2004).

In the GRR model, facilitator-directed activities are included earlier in the PD, and more participant-led activities (either small-group or independent work) are built in later so that participants can apply, transfer, and/or demonstrate their learning. Table 5.5 offers questions to determine where your activities fall along the GRR spectrum—from facilitator-led at one end to independent practice on the other.

Table 5.5 Guiding Questions for Designing Gradual Release of Responsibility (GRR)

Facilitator-Directed Activities	Facilitator-Guided or Group-Guided	Independent Practice and Integration
Guiding Questions	Guiding Questions	Guiding Questions
• What do I need to research, create, share, and model for participants so they can build knowledge, skill, and capacity in this area?	• What will we all do together so we can build knowledge, skill, and capacity? • How might I differentiate learning to meet the diverse backgrounds and needs of this group? • At what points will I check for understanding to see what participants have learned?	• What will participants be able to do on their own? • How will they demonstrate their knowledge, skill, and capacity in this area? • What kinds of reflective questions will create a little cognitive dissonance and invite people to investigate beliefs and how they show up? • What new practices will allow participants to be transformed?

Identifying where activities fall along on the GRR continuum helps PD leaders determine where to place them in their learning sequence.

Let's return to Lori's *Artful Design* workshop to see how she shifted the learning from facilitator-led in the first activity to group-guided in the next one.

LORI REFLECTS:

After designing the Introverted and Extroverted Introductions, I then planned how participants will process and synthesize their learning. My intention was to gradually release participants from facilitator-guided activities to group-led synthesis and discussion.

I decided to shift the energy from the buzz of the dance party to individual reflection. Participants (especially introverts) would benefit from five minutes of quiet individual time to process the experience. Drawing from their pre-work readings and the experience they just had with the Introverted and Extroverted Introductions, participants would be invited to reflect on the following questions:

- Where do you see connections between our opening activities and the readings for today?
- If you didn't complete the pre-work, how do these opening activities relate to what you know about adult learning?
- What conditions do you need to learn at your best?

Participants would then be grouped randomly in breakout spaces for 20 minutes (groups of three to four people, so everyone had time to share). I designed a protocol for the discussion and participants would receive a writable copy of the protocol on which to take notes. Regardless of expertise or completion of the pre-work, everyone could participate in the discussion. This activity would honor the adult learning principle that adults come with histories; when honoring the expertise of participants in the room, they typically have greater buy-in to what they are learning.

Finally, this activity invites accountability; as the last step of the protocol, each group will be asked to post notes from their discussion on a virtual collaboration board. This accountability step would hopefully ensure that groups stay focused on the protocol. Using protocols and then inviting participants into a whole-group share-out helps keep groups on track.

If PD were in person, participants might be asked to post their notes around the room, and everyone would be invited to do a "gallery walk" to view one another's responses. In the virtual space, I decided to create a "gallery glance" using Padlet. Participants would be assigned one other group (e.g., group #1 will be paired with group #25, group #2 with group #24, and so on) and click their pair group's notes to review.

When we come back together as a whole group, I would then invite participants to share in the chat the themes they noticed from one another's notes. I also will invite a couple of participants to share by saying, "We have time for one or two people to come off mute and share with the whole group." Saying this as a precursor to the discussion will allow me to stay on pace with my agenda without the discussion becoming a free-for-all.

Tips and Tricks:

Keep whole-group debriefs brief. You might want to hear how an experience worked for people, but whole-group debriefs can be alienating to introverts and, often, draw out the same few extroverts. Furthermore, whole-group debriefs don't often result in whole-group learning, unless you also include time for processing what was shared in small groups. To invite more representative participation, consider small-group conversations with representatives sharing out, using backchannel chats, or taking advantage of crowdsourcing tools instead. Keep whole-group debriefs to five to seven minutes.

Step 5: Finalize the Plan

After you've determined activities and created a learning sequence, it's time to add notes and considerations to your facilitator's agenda. Lori calls this part "telling a story" with your design. This part of the planning brings everything together so you can frame activities, identify what's essential about each one, and build transitions from one activity to the next. Within each portion of the agenda, it's critical to write facilitator notes on the following:

- *Timing*: How long will each topic/subtopic take?
- *Key points*: What ideas are most important to share? Some facilitators script every word they'll say, while others note a few key points. If you tend to ramble, scripting your key points will help you communicate ideas more tightly and

concisely. Scripting key points also helps you to internalize the content. It's helpful to consider how you'll link one topic to the next throughout the workshop.

- *Facilitator considerations*: This section may be used as needed. For example, if you're about to raise a more controversial topic, you may write something like, "be mindful of how you frame this portion," or if you aren't sure about pacing, you might write "cut this portion if short on time."

Table 5.6 contains a segment of the facilitator's agenda from Bright Morning's *The Art of Coaching Teams* workshop. Take a look at what kinds of notes we include

Table 5.6   Sample Portion of Facilitator's Agenda: What's the Purpose of Your Meeting?

30 min	**What's the Purpose of your Meeting?**
	 • (3) Direct Instruction: Introduce the core questions about the purpose of a meeting.
	  • Why should we meet?
	  • What can we do together that we can't do alone?
	 • (10) Six Reasons to Meet + Agenda
	 • (13) Practice opening a meeting and stating the purpose for it.

Timing: 30 minutes

Key Framing Points:

- *Transition from Previous Topic*: In our last segment, we discussed how we need clarity on the purpose of our teams; just as we need that clarity, we also need clarity on the purpose of each meeting.
- *Direct Instruction and Six Reasons to Meet*:
  - Start with these two questions. If there's no clear answer to either of the first two questions, there's no reason for a meeting. Trust erodes quickly when we call people to meetings for which there is no clear purpose. Honoring people's time builds trust.
  - Recall what Elena writes about this: "Learning is the primary work of all teams." The only way we'll make a dent in the mountain of challenges we face in schools is if we, the educators, keep learning. Therefore, our work as team leaders is to create optimal conditions for adults to learn.
- *Practice*: You'll now have three minutes to think and write about how you might share the purpose of your meeting. You'll have nine minutes to practice in the same trios as earlier.

Facilitator Considerations:
- Reinforce the key points on the slides for the six reasons. Increase energy with each reason. Share agenda with examples of meeting outcomes connected to purpose to see how the six reasons show up in an agenda.
- If time is tight, cut the practice and get feedback with partners only (saves a few minutes).

on a facilitator's agenda. The top portion includes the topic "What's the Purpose of Your Meeting?" as well as estimated times in parentheses for each subtopic. The bottom portion contains facilitator key points and considerations.

It can be satisfying to bring all your ideas together in your facilitator's agenda, kind of like when you cook an elaborate meal with many courses—all the ingredients, flavors, and aromas—and you're ready to enjoy what you've prepared. Like an elaborate, multicourse meal, you might find your facilitator agenda is quite long, which is okay—it means that you've considered all the key components of intentional design. And that level of detail, plus what you learn in the next chapter, will make all the difference for participants—and ultimately, for students.

Virtual Design Considerations

Lori's *Artful Design* workshop was designed for a virtual setting. For those leading virtual learning, here are additional factors to consider:

- *Breakout rooms for small discussions.* Setting up assigned groups in Zoom can take time. Have participants do a reflective activity while you create groups, or, if you are co-facilitating, one person can make breakouts while the teammate facilitates. Or, create breakout groups in advance, and then direct participants to self-select into their breakout rooms. Before placing participants into breakout rooms, include instructions in the chat so participants have access to them when they get whisked away into their small groups.
- *Be mindful of screen time.* In live workshops, take a 30-minute break every two hours. You might also consider which activities you could do asynchronously versus synchronously.
- *Take advantage of online tools* for discussion, crowdsourcing, drawing, or making videos to share with one another. You might still consider some of these tools for in-person learning as well.
- It's easier to facilitate on two screens, but if you have only one, *print out your facilitator's script in advance*, or get comfortable with not being able to see all the participants all the time so you can look at your script on the screen. Practice with a setup that allows you to access what you need. For example, you might stop sharing your screen every once in a while to see all the participants. When Lori presents with two screens, they look like Figure 5.3.

Figure 5.3 Sample screen setup

Screen 1

Facilitator agenda

Chat box

Participant list

Screen 2

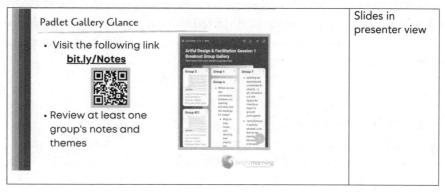

Slides in presenter view

Shift the Dominant Culture in Design

Students learn best when they feel a sense of belonging, when the learning space is inclusive, when students see themselves represented in the curriculum, and when content and activities are differentiated to meet students' learning needs. The same holds true for adults. When PD leaders approach design through the lenses of inclusion and belonging, they shift the dominant culture by acknowledging and honoring the diversity of backgrounds, experiences, and ways of learning and communicating that participants bring to PD sessions. It also means considering the role of power and authority, considering which voices we most often rely on when we're learning theory, or considering what images we typically see on presentation slides. We can diminish the forces of the dominant culture by making intentional choices about every element of our design, from the resources we select to how we design our slides to how we source and leverage power.

Resources

When selecting texts and images, consider the source and who is represented. Whose voices are you privileging with the texts you select? What images are you including on your slides? If you have images of people, what are their races, gender identities, or physical abilities? When Lori selected readings and images for *Artful Design and Facilitation*, she mitigated the effects of dominant culture by selecting texts from women and people of color who were authorities on the topics they were writing about. For example, in Session 1 Lori selected excerpts from Elena Aguilar's *The Art of Coaching Teams* (2016) and Sebene Selassie's *You Belong: A Call for Connection* (2020)—authors who are women of color and experts in their respective fields. In her reflection about the Extroverted Introduction activity, Lori shared her design choices for the slides: including people with a diversity of identity markers to create a visual sense of belonging or inclusion.

Activities

When selecting and designing activities, consider the ways to shift the dominant culture, to pause for "equity checks" where appropriate, and to strive to ensure all participants feel affirmed in their identities. One way to shift the dominant culture is through an activity called "De-Dominate the Dominant Culture," which brings awareness to who is in the room, who isn't in the room, and how to consider the needs of all learners.

When Belinda facilitated trainings for early career teachers at her nonprofit's *Teaching Fundamentals* workshop, she began with a "de-dominate the dominant culture" exercise. She shared a brief survey with questions about how people identified. These questions were anonymous and optional, and she explained why she began with this activity: "An activity like this one helps us know who is and isn't in the room so we can be attentive to the needs of this particular group. If we're making any decisions, this gives us a chance to do an equity check to be sure we're not deciding on behalf of a select few. This activity helps us broaden our awareness and attentiveness to one another. To the degree to which you feel comfortable, please fill out this anonymous form. You may skip any categories you feel uncomfortable responding to."

Categories for the survey included the following:

- Role/subject area at your school site
- Grade level(s) you work with (check all that apply): elementary, middle, high school
- Years you have been an educator
- Race
- Socioeconomic class
- Sexual orientation
- Gender identity
- Ethnicity
- Primary language spoken at home
- Age
- Religion
- Political affiliation

After the survey, Belinda shared the anonymous results. Seeing the collective data served as a powerful prompt. For example, when the data showed that the majority of participants identified as white, Belinda reminded participants to be mindful of historically marginalized groups of participants (e.g., Black, Indigenous, people of color) to ensure all voices were heard and included. She reminded participants to be aware of aspects of their identities that are more privileged or are granted more power and to consider stepping back in discussions to leave room for others. When facilitating discussions, she first called on those who were less represented if they volunteered.

Another way to shift the dominant culture in your design is through building in time for equity checks. In Bright Morning's *Team Strategy Sprint,* participants spend the day-long workshop with their site-based teams to work on meaningful, focused projects on a range of topics including curriculum development, team meeting structures, and school policy changes. Once an hour, the facilitator pauses the group's work to do an equity check. Wherever the team was at that moment, they were prompted to take 10 minutes to pause and discuss, "How does this work meet the needs of our students?" One participant is designated as note-taker, and they record their team's responses. At the end of the sprint, participants commented how the equity checks were a helpful routine to keep students at the center of their work together. One team decided to make equity checks a regular part of team meeting time.

Affinity Groups

Affinity groups can offer members of historically marginalized populations a safe-enough space to connect with one another. In affinity groups, people with similar identity markers can share their experiences without having to speak for a whole group. In Bright Morning's *Coaching for Equity* series, participants who identify as Black, Indigenous, people of color (BIPOC) are often given the option to join affinity groups for small-group discussions. In cross-racial conversations related to equity—or any conversation focused on race—BIPOC folks sometimes may be explicitly or implicitly asked to educate white colleagues about race and the impacts of racism. Taking on this role—without choosing it—can be painful and burdensome, and their own learning becomes secondary. Affinity groups can be learning and healing spaces for those who have historically been oppressed.

If you design affinity groups, make sure you understand why you're doing so. Create affinity groups when they serve a purpose—and then explain that purpose clearly to participants. Consider using language like the following when explaining the role of affinity groups in your PD:

> In order for all our participants to bring their full selves to this learning experience, we are going to offer affinity groups for our small-group conversations. These are optional for people who identify as [Black, Indigenous, people of color, and LGBTQIA+] so they can fully engage in conversations without needing to explain about their identities.

When participants share feedback at the end of a Bright Morning equity-focused workshop, they often remark about the affinity groups: "This was such a healing space for me," "It was so helpful to share with people who understood me," and "The affinity breakouts were the best part of the experience." To learn more about affinity groups, check out Appendix F: "Resources for Further Learning."

LORI REFLECTS:

In the closing segment of *Artful Design and Facilitation*, right before closing routines, I planned time to pull back the curtain and share my design choices—how I wanted participants to *experience* connection, belonging, play, and the principles of adult learning rather than just talking about it. I planned to share my design choices for the slides and how I selected the images and videos. I prepared to explain the decisions behind the sequence of the learning activities and how group-led activities honor the experiences of adult learners.

I wrote down my final key points for the closing routines, and I did one final review of all my materials. I added a couple more key points to my facilitator's agenda to make sure I was clear about the purpose of each activity. I made sure the directions on my slides were clear and that the music videos worked. I picked up the stack of orange sticky notes spread across my desk and put them into a pile. I liked saving evidence of my process. As I stood up to stretch, I felt light, energized, eager to meet participants and present this workshop.

In this chapter we pulled back the curtain on how we intentionally design PD, and we hope in doing so you find that the "wizardry" participants experience in our workshops is accessible. We also hope you'll find that this process is joyful. When we are rooted in purpose and consider the *why* for everything we design, when we take a "less is best" stance so we can be more deliberate in the activities we choose, when we honor the needs and backgrounds of participants—sharing *power-with* where possible—we can design intentionally and create the conditions for transformative learning.

Before You Go

Pause and Process:
- What is something new you learned? What is something that reinforced what you already do?
- What is something you'll now do in your design process?
- How can you design for inclusion and belonging?

Remember:
- Intentional design takes time, but it gets easier and more intuitive as it becomes a habit.

- The 21 planning questions will make your PD awesome (even if you just answer four questions when you're short on time).
- Less is best. Create more space in your agendas so participants don't feel rushed.
- Mitigate the dominant culture in your design by choosing resources, designing activities, and creating spaces that affirm all your participants.

CHAPTER 6

Attend to Details

Josué checked his email a third time—an updated message with the subject heading "CORRECTION ON WORKSHOP LOCATION." This was Josué's first professional development as a new teacher, and he was anxious. The last email he received about the workshop was a "Thank you for registering" email two months ago.

Arriving 30 minutes before start time, Josué wasn't sure if he was at the right place. There were three different entrances, so he circled the building until he saw somebody. He pulled at the door. Locked. Someone with a stack of papers under their arm ran toward the doors. "I'm so sorry. Are you here for the equity-centered design workshop?" they asked. Josué nodded.

"Follow me." Josué jogged a little to match the host's pace. He was led down a long hallway and then around two turns. *Would I remember how to get out of here?* Josué wondered.

When they arrived at the meeting room, the host said, "I don't have the check-in table set up and Kimmie isn't here yet, but tell me your name, and I'll make sure get you checked in."

Josué wondered, *Should I know who Kimmie is?*

The host continued, "Here, take these sheets. You can put an 'x' next to your name when you find it. That will ensure you get your PD hours. You can find your name tag and welcome folder in that box." They pointed to a table with three cardboard boxes. "Oh, the caterer isn't here yet. The address correction may have caused confusion. I hope you're not too hungry."

"Um, that's fine," Josué said. He was hungry.

Josué found the box with the name tags. There was a *José* Silva, but not a *Josué* (people always forgot the *u*). He checked again, no blank name tags. With his pen, he crossed out José on the name tag he received and re-wrote his name. Josué took a folder from the welcome box and made his way into the meeting room, a large multipurpose room where half the chairs were folded on a cart near the entrance. He found a table with chairs already set up.

Josué opened the folder to find his learning packet. As he thumbed through the pages, he noticed the text was cut off the right side of each page. Returning to the entrance, he grabbed another folder and found the same issue with another packet. And another. *That's annoying*, he thought. He went back to his table where two others were now sitting, engrossed in conversation. They ignored Josué.

Kimmie arrived. She rushed toward the front of the room, her face flushed. *Oh, Kimmie's the presenter,* Josué thought. He looked at his watch. Fifteen minutes until start time.

"Nat!" Kimmie yelled toward the entrance.

The host popped their head into the door. "What's up?" Nat asked.

"I have the wrong hookup for the projector. Do you have an extra dongle?" Kimmie sounded stressed.

Distracted, Nat offered an indifferent response, "Let me check. Do you know who our tech support is supposed to be?"

"I have a dongle," one of the participants shared. Kimmie smiled in relief. "You're a lifesaver."

Kimmie cursed again. "This is the wrong slide deck. This is not going to be a good day, is it?" she said to no one in particular.

Do so many things always go wrong? Josué wondered as started to lose faith in this PD.

"Hello, everyone!" Kimmie yelled to the meeting room large enough to hold 100 people. There were 25 in attendance so far. "We're going to delay our start time by 30 minutes. The address change confused people, so the caterer and most participants went to the wrong location."

An audible sigh could be heard throughout the room. Another said, "I hope this still ends on time. I'm driving carpool today."

Nat, the host, entered the presentation room and started setting up the remaining tables and chairs. "What a disaster," Nat said, looking directly at Josué.

Details Matter to Learning

Hit pause on this story. While it doesn't predict what comes next, this was a rough start—for everyone in this situation. If Josué's PD were a televised sporting event, this might be the moment when the commentators press the replay button, scan the scene, and use their electronic implements to circle all the missed opportunities—in this case, for learners like Josué to feel welcomed, valued, and cared for—all before the session begins. What would you identify as the missed opportunities?

Here are some possible responses:

- The location was listed wrong; participants received an email with a last-minute correction.
- The entrance was unmarked.
- There was no signage to direct people to the right room.
- The host didn't introduce themself.
- Josué checked himself in.
- Materials were still in boxes.
- Josué's name was spelled wrong.
- The room was only partially set up.
- The presenter was late and seemed flustered.
- The presenter had the wrong dongle and the wrong slides.
- The location change impacted the start time and those in attendance.
- The host called the day a disaster before it began, and they looked right at Josué when saying it.

Details matter to learning. Attending to details is key to creating the conditions for adults to feel welcome, affirmed, valued, and psychologically safe. In well-planned professional development, the details say, "You've made the commitment to be here, and we value you. We will focus on the little things so you can focus on the learning."

Here are some examples of what this might look and sound like:

- A recent incident on campus has teachers feeling more stressed than usual, so the presenter makes time to attend to the emotions of the group.
- Participants receive an email a week in advance to remind them where they are meeting, what they need to bring, and what pre-work to complete.
- The technology is set up in advance, and the facilitators have everything they need for a smooth presentation.

- Materials are printed, proofread, and ready to share, so when participants walk into the library at the end of a long teaching day, they can take a learning packet, sit down, and preview its contents.
- The presenter warmly greets participants at the door. Participants feel affirmed in their identities because their names are spelled and pronounced correctly.
- Tables are easy to find, because they are marked with a number. Tables also include supply boxes that contain pens, highlighters, sticky notes, and individually wrapped snacks.
- There are handouts on each table that include a series reflection prompts so participants have something to connect with one another about before the learning begins.
- The presenter works the room during small-group activities so they can be attentive to questions, listen for themes in the conversation, and gauge energy levels.
- At the end of the workshop, the presenter shares a protocol for cleanup—where to recycle items and leave unused learning packets—and how to leave the space better than participants found it.

Paying attention to details like these allows the learning to feel like a seamless sequence of intentional moments from start to finish, conditions that foster learning and growth.

In the opening story, the host and presenter could have arrived early enough to be ready to welcome Josué. At the least, the doors could have been unlocked, and the signage could have directed him to the workshop location. Josué could have received a name tag with his name spelled correctly. The host could have been more welcoming to Josué, perhaps knowing he was a new teacher in the district who might not be sure about the protocols—so the host would help Josué feel welcome and cared for. Kimmie could have checked her technology to make sure she had the right equipment and slides, perhaps not cursing about the missteps she made or borrowing a dongle from a participant. Perhaps Josué would have been able to settle in rather than hearing the day was a disaster before it even started.

Instead, before the program even began, Josué was annoyed. Can we blame him? Kimmie and Nat's missteps increased Josué's frustration. He was a new teacher attending a workshop to support his skills. He was anxious because this was his first PD, and its beginning set a negative tone that may impact the rest of the day and, possibly, Josué's opportunity to learn.

Supporting the Conditions for Transformation

Recall a time when someone hosted an event, professional or personal, at which you felt well taken care of and where you felt welcome, cared for, and valued. This might be a class you took, a wedding you attended, a visit to an acupuncturist—or it might have been a well-run PD. Recall as many details from the event as possible and how you felt.

What does it feel like to recall these details?

Now think about an upcoming PD that you're leading, perhaps the same one you thought of from the previous chapter. How will you attend to details? How might you create the conditions that allow participants to feel as welcomed, cared for, and valued?

This chapter lays out ways to attend to the details that matter the most for transformative PD. In the coming pages, we'll lay out what you need to address in the long term, in the short term, and on day of your PD. In each section, we'll provide you with a checklist and guidance about what details to consider in seven categories:

- *Context*: Who the PD is for and what you need to know about them
- *Partnership*: Who your partners are (co-facilitators, site administrators, technology coordinators, meal providers)
- *Location*: What you can do with the space
- *Resources*: The materials you and participants need to engage in the learning
- *Communication*: The reminders, updates, and follow-up participants receive before and after the PD
- *Presentation*: What you do (the routines, messages, and actions) to meet participants' needs before, during, and after the learning experience
- *Closing*: How you will leave the space better than you found it

Depending on whether you're internal to your site or an external provider, the degree to which you address details will differ, but all of us will attend to some level of detail to create—and enhance—the conditions for learning.

Timeline to Transformation

Depending on when the PD takes place and whether it stretches over several days and sessions, is embedded within a conference, or stands alone during a Wednesday staff meeting, a timeline helps organize your planning into manageable segments.

The rest of this chapter is organized along such a timeline. We'll consider what you and participants need long term (anywhere from several months to a month before your PD), short term (within a few weeks of your PD), the day of the event, and after the experience. Each section begins with brief checklist to guide your planning. We recognize these time frames won't work precisely as laid out for everyone—some of you are planning larger events that require a longer on-ramp in your planning timelines, some of you run more frequent PD sessions, while others of you are solo practitioners or have people who help you with logistics. We trust that you'll take what's here and adapt it to your context.

Throughout this chapter we'll also revisit Josué's story to imagine what's possible when Kimmie and Nat attend to details.

Long-Term Planning: Get Ready

Long-term planning can take place anywhere between several months to one month before your PD. Within this time frame, a PD leader learns about context, establishes relationships with partners, confirms the details of the location, prepares resources, plans the session(s), and communicates with participants about what to expect. Table 6.1 offers considerations for your planning (you can find the full checklist for attending to details in Appendix E).

Context

Understanding the context for your PD is about knowing your audience, the region and site where they work, the culture in their organization, the students they serve. It's about participant attitudes about the PD, what they know and can do already, what skills they need to build, and what is happening within and around their community.

In Chapter 5 we gave you 21 planning questions that will make your PD awesome, and the questions about audience and context are applicable to your long-term planning. Internal PD providers, especially on-site providers, usually know their contexts well, and they can use the answers to the audience and context questions to guide their planning. External PD providers may need to spend more time getting to know the context in which they're presenting. The following questions can support greater understanding about context:

- Who is this PD for? What are participants' roles (e.g., teacher, site leader)?
- What are the demographics of the group?

Table 6.1 Long-Term Planning Checklist

Long-Term Planning Checklist	
☑ **Context**	✓ Know your audience: understand demographics, roles, needs of the group, and larger contextual factors that can support the planning phase.
☑ **Partnership**	✓ Identify all the partners necessary to execute PD: site leaders, hosts, co-facilitators, technology coordinators, custodial staff or security who might be on-site, meal service providers, or caterers. ✓ Clarify roles and responsibilities to ensure everyone is clear about what they need to accomplish and by when. ✓ If co-facilitating, build relationships through understanding core values, strengths, identities, roles, and responsibilities for planning.
☑ **Location**	✓ Confirm details of the location, the size and capacity of the space, seating arrangements, technology, accessibility for those with mobility needs. ✓ Determine how you (if applicable) and participants can access the location (transportation and parking, if applicable). ✓ Determine whether signage is needed to direct participants. ✓ Identify what setup is needed to get the space ready.
☑ **Resources**	✓ Prepare materials: pre-work, packets, or handouts. ✓ Consider tools and supplies participants will need to supplement their learning.
☑ **Communication**	✓ Send a message to participants with all the essential details of your PD.

- What is happening in the world or in the community that may be pertinent to this site?
- What populations do these practitioners serve?
- What are terms or concepts is this site/organization used to hearing?
- What additional professional development has been done?
- If this PD is for practitioners who work in the same school or district, where does this PD fit into a larger PD sequence?

When Lori was invited to present Bright Morning's *Art of Coaching Teams* workshop to the Conexión Charter Academy, she wanted to ensure the workshop would meet the needs of new leaders in the school. Lori used the context questions listed previously to get to know her client. In a 45-minute Zoom conversation with school leaders, Lori learned that Conexión Charter Academy served predominantly Hispanic/Latinx students (80 percent of whom were heritage Spanish speakers) with a smaller percentage of Black and white students as well. She learned that statewide content standards for language acquisition were shifting, which was causing anxiety among site and grade-level leaders. The implementation of these standards posed a cultural shift for schools, especially for educators who have been at the site for a long time. New leaders needed support to manage this change, to build skills as leaders, and to grow in their emotional intelligence.

Network leaders' responses to her questions helped Lori consider how to deliver the workshop in a way that would support deep change. Lori used their answers to inform how she would frame each activity, and she added examples to her slide deck that would help leaders think about how to foster change in their context. She built in additional time for coaching conversations and created a segment in which participants would create agendas for PD and get feedback on their design.

The questions Lori asked the leaders of Conexión Academy provided her the necessary details to learn about their context. You may have some of your own questions to add, and you may also consider asking, "What is a question you think I should ask you?" The responses may give you insights you hadn't considered before.

Partnership

Relationships are central to transformational professional development, not just in the workshop, but among partners prior to the workshop. Partnerships can run the gamut from two people co-facilitating to several different entities working together—such as the partnerships we make with administrative support staff, technology coordinators, meal providers, and hosting organizations. In Chapter 1, Lori's partner was her principal, Dr. Deal. When Lori led *The Art of Coaching Teams* workshop at Conexión Academy, her partners were the charter network leaders, their technology coordinator, and on-site meal providers. Working out the details of partnership as early as possible—determining responsibilities and what needs to be accomplished and by when—can allow for effective planning.

Joanna and Arden are the principal and vice principal, respectively, at Sojourner Truth Elementary School. They work closely together, and yet they don't get along very well. When they meet each summer to plan their year-long PD sequence, they often argue about what works best, and each person spends time defending their respective perspectives. Instead of planning collaboratively, they end up dividing the PD sessions, each one taking responsibility for designing and leading their assigned workshops. Staff feedback indicates that the PD has been disjointed and inconsistent and that the "leaders seem to be at odds with each other."

Last summer Arden decided to try "coaching up," sharing with Joanna her a desire for more consistency and better collaboration. Arden introduced a new process into their PD planning: collaboration agreements. Each person shared what they needed to be effective partners as they worked collaboratively, and together they generated the following series of agreements:

- Be a good steward of time—dedicate the last 15 minutes of meetings to action items and next steps.
- Be curious rather than defensive—engage in "active listening" practices and hold one another accountable for our words and actions.
- Be conscientious about following through with what we agree to accomplish.
- Be honest and thoughtful communicators, whether verbally or through email or texting.
- Center the needs of students throughout the process.

These agreements, they both knew, would work only if they were "living agreements," if they were each committed to upholding what they decided on. So at the beginning of each meeting planning for the first-days PD, Arden and Joanna reviewed their agreements and also identified goals for meeting. At the end of each planning meeting, they chose tasks to accomplish before they met again. While the two didn't become best friends, their agreements allowed them to work together in partnership, which better supported PD at their site.

Establishing agreements for working together can allow planning partners to stay on track and support one another in the months and weeks and days leading up to PD. But this kind of agreement may not make sense for some kinds of partnerships. You may not work as closely with technology coordinators, meal providers, and on-site hosts or security who will let you into the building where you'll lead PD, so these partnerships will require a different kind of attention. Establishing relationships early on will allow you to know whom to contact, when to contact one another, and for what purpose. For example, it's important to know how long in advance you need to connect with a caterer or a technology support person; it's useful to know what time security arrives at the PD site so you can be sure the building will be open when the caterers arrive. Working out these details in advance, and determining what people will do and by when, can preclude last-minute scrambling.

Location

While some space considerations are within a PD leader's sphere of control, many PD leaders may not have a say about the space in which they are presenting. Elena and Lori have presented in windowless conference rooms with dim lighting, cavernous multipurpose rooms, and classrooms where the chairs are meant for elementary-age students. If you will be leading PD in a space you've never seen and can't visit ahead of time, it's helpful to see a photo of the space and, if possible, to know how furniture will be arranged. It's also helpful to think about the spaces where breaks might happen and the amenities nearby (bathrooms, vending machines, or cafés) so breaks can be relaxing and learning time can be more focused.

Consider this example: Have you had to attend an after-school PD and had only 10 minutes between the end of your school day and the beginning of the PD, and you needed to use the restroom, get more coffee, and get a good seat in the back because you knew everyone would be filling those seats first? Getting across campus from your classroom to the library (where the PD was held) takes seven minutes, so perhaps you decided to forego the bathroom break and the coffee, and you made a beeline for the PD, only to find you really needed to go to the bathroom now and you were sleepy because it had been a long day already. When PD leaders attend to details, they take these factors into account and build these considerations into their plans.

In Lori's pre-meeting with network leaders at Conexión Charter Academy, she learned that the projector and screen were far from the electrical outlets, that adult bathrooms were about a three-minute walk away, that most water bottles wouldn't fit under the water fountain spout, and that the workshop was taking place on the first floor (one participant needed wheelchair access). Based on this knowledge about the site, Lori asked for the long extension cords and planned for 15-minute breaks, so all participants had time to get to the restrooms with time for a snack and some mingling with colleagues. She had carafes of water set up in the meeting room so participants wouldn't have to fiddle with the water fountains, and she considered which type of movement activities would be accessible for everyone. Each of these details matter—they center the participants so they could focus on the learning.

A Remedy for Missed Opportunities

In Josué's story, Nat and Kimmie could have considered the following to improve the participant experience:

- *Context*: Did Nat and Kimmie consider the experience level of their participants? Were they all new teachers like Josué, or was there a range of experience levels? Perhaps a pre-session survey could help them learn who would be in attendance (and how people pronounce and spell their names). Knowing these details could determine what kind of support participants would receive.

- *Partnership*: Kimmie and Nat seemed to be operating independently of one another. Nat seemed to be setting everything up on her own. Kimmie didn't have what she needed for setup, no technology support was on-site to help her, and a participant ended up loaning her a dongle. While this is a generous gesture on the part of the participant, this person now has to worry about getting their dongle back at the end of the day.

- *Location*: It's not clear when Nat and Kimmie secured the location, but they communicated the wrong location. Confirming this detail and communicating it accurately would have allowed the session to start on time. Doors could be unlocked earlier, and signage could guide participants to the conference room. The presentation room would be set up before participants arrived, materials would be ready, and a greeter at the check-in table would welcome people to the PD and help them get what they needed to prepare for the day.

If you don't have the time to address all these details in your long-term planning, at least consider these two questions about your context: Who is your audience, and what might you do to best meet the needs of the group? You can then design experience to center the needs of your participants.

Resources

We love the process of gathering resources for our workshops—the readings, videos, and images that best support participant learning—and we begin this process at least a month prior to our workshops. In Chapter 5, you learned about the facilitator's agenda, which provides PD leaders with a tool to pin down details such as timing, key points, and other facilitator considerations. In this section, we'll focus on the additional materials that support facilitation: pre-work, workshop handouts, slides, supporting materials like supply boxes, and virtual considerations that can make remote learning feel more personal.

Pre-work

Pre-work primes participants for what they're about to learn—and hopefully builds excitement for the PD they are about to experience. Whatever you choose to assign, consider sending the pre-work one month in advance, and give participants a sense of how long it might take. For Bright Morning workshops, we typically assign pre-readings and surveys that take a total of half an hour to a couple of hours to complete. There is no specific rule for how much to assign, but since PD happens in addition to an educator's daily responsibilities, we need to be realistic about what we can ask people to complete.

Facilitators also need to prepare for when participants don't do the pre-work. It's a bummer, but it happens. They need to consider how to balance holding people accountable for the pre-work while still offering alternatives for those who didn't complete it. For example, in Bright Morning's *Artful Design and Facilitation* workshop, participants are asked to complete about 45 minutes of pre-reading. Some participants, however, register at the last minute and don't get a chance to finish the pre-work before the PD begins. To address this, Lori included some reflection questions that anyone could respond to, even if they hadn't completed the reading—this way, everyone was able to participate in their first conversation.

Workshop Handouts

Participants need an efficient and convenient way to access PD resources. As you plan what learners will see and read, it's helpful to create the links and handouts you will actually use in the PD. This way, session resources can be compiled in the same sequence as the agenda. Consider these possible ways to organize resources for participants:

- Compile handouts into a single PDF to share with participants in print or online.
- Create an online folder and share materials virtually.
- Share copyable slides or a learning packet (and share a link that automatically generates a copy of these materials).
- Share a hyperlinked agenda.
- Create a website where all the resources live.

For websites, you may need to look into any security or firewalls that make accessing the site a challenge. Printed packets are the most convenient way to share materials without technology barriers, but printed copies are not the most ecologically friendly. If you do create a packet of resources, add a table of contents or number the pages.

Considerations for Slide Design

Slides are a nice-to-have detail (we love creating slides!), and well-designed slides can enrich a presentation. When creating slides, use these tips:

- *Use simple templates or designs.* If you don't want to spend hours on your design or if slide design is not your forte, use a template. Simple designs are better (no weird animations or clutter) and allow your content to be the focus.

- *Choose appropriate fonts and colors.* Go for fonts that are simple and readable. You can choose a recommended color palette in most software programs so that the colors are consistent throughout the presentation. Make fonts big enough (none smaller than 30-point) so that participants easily see what's on the screen.
- *Write less text.* Keep text concise and bullet points short. Make key points in a few simple words. There should be no more than six lines of text (and less if possible) on each slide.
- *Use high-quality photos and graphics.* Use free stock photos to enhance the design. Keep the images simple but high resolution. One image per slide is typically enough. If you include images of people, ensure there is representation across identity markers such as race, gender, and physical ability.
- *Use accurate, relevant, clear charts and graphs.* If you're presenting data of any kind, make sure the graphics you have included (tables, charts) are clear enough for the audience to decipher without explanation.
- *Brand your slides with your logo and social media handles.* If you are representing a school or organization, put your logo on at least the first slide. Include social media handles if you want people to find you on social media or tag you in their posts.
- *Include page numbers from your learning packet.* If you're working from a learning packet, include the page numbers on your slides as well.

Figures 6.1 and 6.2 provide examples of slides from Bright Morning's *Coaching for Equity 101* workshop.

Here are additional considerations for slide decks:

- To shift energy, it can be fun to share a short video (you can even go silly and cute with puppies and kittens playing) to lighten the mood when appropriate.

Figure 6.1 Sample title slide
Source: Bright Morning

Figure 6.2 Sample content slide
Source: Bright Morning

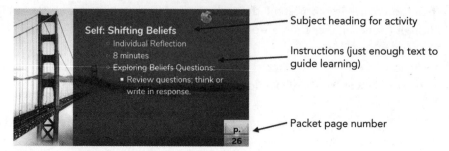

- In some virtual platforms, there is an annotation feature that allows participants to choose a stamp or draw on the screen the presenter is sharing. Or there are software platforms that offer a virtual whiteboard function. Inviting participants to annotate or draw on the screen often adds levity and play to a learning experience.

Supporting Materials

When presenting in person, we number the tables so participants can easily find where they are supposed to sit. When they arrive at each table, they find a placard that contains some connecting questions; this way participants can get to know one another before the workshop begins. We also provide table supply boxes, such as bins on each table with useful desk supplies. Include whatever participants might need, as well as hand sanitizer and fun additions such as snacks, thinking putty, or small fidget toys. Of course, your budget may determine what you can offer, but here are some options:

- Pens (gel or ball point)
- Sticky notes of a couple different sizes
- Thinking putty or fidget toys such as pipe cleaners
- Felt tip markers
- 3 × 5 notecards
- Highlighters
- Snacks in individually packed portions (such as chocolate, almonds, or jelly beans)
- Mini tins of mints

You may also consider adding life to tables with low-cost plants. Tablecloths are a nice touch as well. These small additions take a bit more effort, but they show the learners that you thought about ways to enhance their learning.

Virtual Learning Considerations

Virtual learning requires a different level of attending to details than in-person PD. While the remote experience may feel different from an in-person session, we can do a lot to make it feel as three-dimensional, accessible, and equitable as possible. In planning for a virtual setting, we often start by thinking about what we might do if we were meeting in person—considering everything from how people are welcomed to ways participants will interact with one another. Drawing from the work of Lipmanowicz and McCandless's *The Surprising Power of Liberating Structures* (2014) and their own lessons learned from virtual facilitation, we have compiled Appendix D: "Structures for Virtual Learning," which offers a series of structures to facilitate PD on virtual platforms.

To manage the virtual directions, links, and tools for Bright Morning virtual workshops, facilitators add an "Operations Box," or "Ops Box," to their facilitator's agenda. The Ops Box allows a presenter to store all the directions, links, and resources in one place and may include the following:

- Breakout room instructions
- Links for the learning packet and session resources
- Link to the final feedback form at the end of the session

Table 6.2 shows a portion of what an Ops Box might look like and the details it might include.

> **Tips and Tricks:**
> Sharing links. When sharing links with your participants, you can create a "live link" within your participant agenda or shorten your links using sites like bit.ly or tiny.url (or any other link shortener). When possible, consider renaming links with a memorable name (e.g., bit.ly/LoriFeedback).

Communication

Once the context, partnership, location, and materials are addressed, PD leaders have all the information they need to share a pre-workshop message with participants. This is especially important when leading larger workshops. An email sent around the one-month out mark offers participants all the essential details about the workshop in one place. This message tends to be long, so it helps to think about how to sound as human as possible—even while communicating logistics—as if messages were personally written for each participant.

Table 6.2   Portion of the Ops Box for *Coaching for Equity 101*

OPS SUPPORT for Coaching for Equity 101
(times written in PT/ET)
Day 1
Block 1 8:30-10:30/11:30-1:30
Links

- Post in the chat box in the opening:
  - CFE 101 Learning Packet: bit.ly/CFE101packet2021
- Post during explanation of Land Acknowledgment:
  - https://usdac.us/nativeland
  - www.native-land.ca
- Poll: https://www.sli.do/ and enter code 71839. You must first submit your response to see our group's answers populate live!
- End of session feedback form: bit.ly/CFE101feedbck

Breakout Groups

- *Breakout session 1:*
  - Groups of 3-4 (with BIPOC affinity groups)
  - When: Around 1 hour into the session, at 9 a.m./12 p.m.
  - Duration: 12 minutes
  - Chat instructions:
    - 12 minutes
    - Person with last name closest to *F* goes first
    - Share the story of one of your values (~2 minutes a person)
    - Group members: Practice expansive listening; think about having this conversation in your context.
- *Breakout session 2:*
  - Same groups as before
  - When: Around 1 hour, 20 minutes into the session, at 9:20 a.m./12:20 p.m.
  - Duration: 12 minutes
  - Chat instructions:
    - 12 minutes
    - Person with last name closest to *Z* goes first
    - Share a term that you're most unsure of
    - Add to your definitions: How will you explain these terms in your own words?
    - Group members: Practice expansive listening and anchor in curiosity

---

Thanks to tools like mail merge, PD leaders can personalize certain text fields of their messages, such as the subject heading or the first line. Whether you personalize the message or not, you'll want to communicate care and excitement for your upcoming PD. The following are some tips for crafting a one-month out communication:

- *Opening paragraph*: Offer a warm greeting that communicates enthusiasm. If your message contains a lot of details, give participants a heads-up that they may want to read the message when they have enough time to do so.
- *Sections*: Divide the message into sections with headers. This will make reading easier on the eyes and brains, particularly for longer emails.
  - Possible sections to include:
    - *Overview*: Provide a brief overview of what people will learn or focus on and who the presenters are.
    - *Location and times*: Share the start and end times. Include links to maps and any information related to public transportation and parking. For virtual presentations, include a link to access the session.
    - *Attire*: Let participants know the dress code (e.g., to wear layers, particularly because the temperature may be hard to control). Also, you might want to ask people to avoid heavy perfumes and heavy scents as some people may be allergic.
    - *Meals*: Share when food and beverage items will be available (e.g., lunch will served; coffee and tea available all day). You might also want to encourage people to bring a water bottle they can fill up, and if dietary accommodations are available (e.g., vegetarian lunches, nondairy options), let participants know that as well.
    - *Supplies and materials*: Share what participants need to bring, especially whether electronic devices will be optional or required and be explicit about their use.
    - *Pre-work*: Share links, handouts, and relevant details to prepare people for their learning.
- *Closing paragraph*: End with a short message reiterating your excitement and an invitation to reach out to you (or the relevant support people) with questions about the contents of the email. This may open you up to grumpy participants who aren't sure why they need to participate in the PD or are upset that you may not be able to accommodate their dietary preferences. Take those questions in stride, knowing you may not be able to meet all requests.

Let's now imagine that Nat and Kimmie completed all their preparation for the workshop and sent a welcome email to participants. Imagine that Josué received this kind of communication one month in advance. He might have opened his email to find the following:

To: Josué Silva
From: Nat McIlwraith
Date: August 30, 2019

Subject: ECD Workshop Sept 30: Everything You Need to Know

Dear Josué,

We are excited to have you join us for the Equity-Centered Design (ECD) workshop on September 30. This program will allow you space for reflection, connection, conversation, goal-setting, and concrete work tasks as you think about student-centered curriculum and lesson design with an equity lens. The following email is long, so please read when you can take the time to review all these details.

Program Themes and Presenter

Our workshop will address the following themes:
- Identity and Culture: Strategies for identity safety
- Representation: Three considerations for curriculum design
- Multimodality: Multiple paths to demonstrate their learning

You presenter is Kimmie Lowry, a consultant with the Equity for Learning group. She has been a classroom teacher for more than 20 years, and she has worked with districts and schools across the United States. **Click here** to learn more about Kimmie.

Location and Times

We will be meeting at Great Falls Community School 8:30 a.m. to 2:30 p.m. on Monday, September 30. **Click here** for directions to the location. Parking is free in the south lot. Carpooling is encouraged.

The workshop will take place in the multipurpose room. We'll post signs in the parking lot, on the main entrance of the building, and in the hallways to guide you to the check-in table and meeting room. Please look for the EFL logo.

Attire

Please dress comfortably. We may be doing activities outdoors, some of which involve movement, so wear something you can move comfortably in. Bring layers for indoors, as we may not be able to control the air conditioning units in the building. We want to respect that some people are sensitive to strong scents or have environmental allergies, so please refrain from wearing products with strong scents.

Meals

Breakfast will be available from 8 a.m. to 8:30 a.m., and lunch will be provided. Thank you to those of you who shared your dietary needs when you registered. If you haven't yet, please click here to include dietary restrictions (gluten-free, vegetarian, vegan, allergies). Please bring your own snacks or lunch if you believe your dietary needs cannot be met. Coffee, tea, water, and snacks will be available throughout the workshop. To be as ecologically friendly as possible during our workshop, please consider bringing your own travel mugs and water bottles.

What You Need

We'll strive to balance tech-related needs with pen/pencil-to-paper tasks. Please bring any note-taking tools you like. Bring an electronic device (tablet, laptop) for online work. Great Falls Community School can loan a limited number of iPads for those who need them.

Materials

All workshop materials will be shared electronically via a shared drive. We'll populate our shared folder with agendas and relevant handouts. If you prefer hard copies, print these handouts beforehand. To save paper, we will print only a few copies of handouts for those who need them. We'll share these materials a week in advance of the workshop. We do not share our slides.

Pre-work

To best meet the needs of the group and honor the diversity of our participants, we would like you to complete some pre-work and preview a couple of the activities for our sessions. This pre-work will take you about an hour to complete.

- **Time Sensitive: Please complete by September 7.**
  - 10 minutes. Please fill out this Google Form that asks for some basic information (name, school, grade level, years teaching, learning preferences, and a response to the statement regarding bringing our identities to our work). Responses to these questions will help us design the learning in a way that best meets your needs.
- **Read**
  - 30 minutes: Excerpts from Dr. Bridge, "What Equity-Centered Design Looks Like."
  - Be prepared to share which passages most resonate with you and which ones you want to know about. We'll be discussing this article in the first learning block.
- **Reflect**
  - 20 minutes: *Identity Story Activity.* Review the identity markers handout and mark which identity markers you think about the most. Respond to the reflection questions and be prepared to share what you feel most comfortable sharing with small-group members.

If you have any questions or needs in advance of the workshop, feel free to email our program assistant, Nat, at nat@efllearners.org.
We look forward to meeting you on September 30!

Nat McIlwraith (they/them), host
Kimmie Lowry (she/her), presenter

With this message, Josué now has all the details he needs to allay his worries. He knows who he can email if he has questions. He knows what to expect for the two days of learning. He knows how to find the location. He knows how he needs to prepare. He knows who Kimmie and Nat are. He has everything he needs in advance.

Reflect on your own long-term planning process. Which of these details do you already include? Which of these details are new to you? What else might you add to your long-term planning checklist?

Short-Term Planning: Finalize the Details

In the theater world, the week or two before the performance is considered "tech week." It's the time when the director, stage crew, and actors do a careful run-through of each scene to ensure that the lighting, stage directions, and acting convey the director's vision. For party planners, this time frame is about gathering necessities and connecting with caterers, musicians, and guests to remind them of the event. For PD leaders, this time frame is somewhere between "tech week" and party planning, and for our purposes, we'll call it *short-term planning*.

The week or two leading up to the PD is the time to check final contextual details, connect with partners, preview the space (if possible), review and finalize resources, communicate with participants, and complete all the final touches. Depending on the scale of the PD, short-term planning may involve all these details, or just a few. For our purposes, we'll include all the details; you can apply what best works for your role and context. Table 6.3 provides you with items to consider.

Table 6.3 Short-Term Planning Checklist

Context	✓ Check site website and local news for any events that might have an impact on participants.
Partnership	✓ Connect with host/site leaders and co-facilitators (if applicable), technology support, and meal providers. ✓ Confirm final details and do a run-through of the PD.
Location	✓ Arrive the day before if you're traveling. ✓ Preview the space if you are able to.
Resources	✓ Review and proofread agendas, slides, handouts, and any additional resources. ✓ Make sure any web links work. ✓ Get supplies you need. ✓ Print any materials.
Communication	✓ Send a brief reminder message with key details (pre-work, accessing location).

Context

Drea led a training for teachers in Northern California in October—the height of fire season. The day before the workshop, a brushfire started to spread about 60 miles from the workshop site. Because some participants lived close to the fire, she created asynchronous options for those who couldn't attend. As the workshop date approached (about one week out), Drea started checking the weather at her workshop location. She also started reading the local news for that region. The morning of the workshop Drea opened her session by acknowledging the local fires and the impact they may be having on the school community; she communicated compassion for those most affected, and participants felt cared for as a result.

While we may be leading a single workshop or even a series, local, national, and global events also have an impact on school communities. Racism and injustice, elections, wars, climate change, and good and horrible local news all matter when preparing for PD. Even a few words of acknowledgment can go a long way in caring for participants.

Partnership

A week or two before the workshop is a good time to finalize details with any partners. With hosts, this means confirming the workshop location, participant needs, and the division of responsibilities. With co-facilitators, this is the time for one or two more rehearsals before the workshop, each facilitator increasing their confidence and refining their portions of the presentation. It also helps to connect with technology support people to confirm the audiovisual setup. Additionally, one final call to the meal provider will ensure that meals are ready and people's dietary needs are taken into account. If you're leading PD at your own site and you are in charge of meals or snacks, then a week away is an optimal time to create a list of items to bring to the workshop, order anything to be picked up/delivered the day of the PD, or check on items you ordered a month before.

Location

By now your location is set, so you can turn your attention to the setup you need: screens, tables, chairs, a place for check-in (if applicable), and a place for any supplies. If you have access to the space beforehand, visit it and visualize yourself as you run through each component of your PD. If you don't have access, see if you can get a photograph of the space, even if just to picture how the day's events will unfold.

What might the leaders of Josue's PD be attending to in the last week before the PD? Nat can use this time to confirm that they have the right number of tables and chairs at the workshop location. They can make a plan to visit the location in advance to determine where signage needs to go. They also can determine what time to arrive to finalize the setup and be ready for participants.

Resources

Completing presentation slides and other materials at least a few days in advance provides more time for the following:

- *You can refine your presentation and practice your facilitator moves.* Spend those final days rehearsing key points, making sure that your communication is crisp and clear. You can perfect your pacing. You can make sure your slides and materials are accurate. The more time you have to refine, the better.
- *You can send learning materials in advance.* Having everything complete and ready to go might allow participants to preview session materials.
- *You can rest.* Stressed presenters bring that energy into a learning space. Similarly, calm, confident presenters allow participants to feel more ease. When Kimmie came into the presentation room on the day of the workshop, she was frazzled. What might have been possible if Kimmie had all her details sorted the day prior to the workshop? Even if the workshop start time was delayed, participants like Josué may have trusted the facilitator's calm confidence.
- *You can take care of additional details.* You can gather your supplies, make supply boxes for participants, and finalize seating charts. If you have pre-printed name tags, you can cross-check names on registration forms—and fix any errors. Having additional time might also mean you also can attend to details such as making playlists, buying some plants, or getting some snacks for participants.

Tips and Tricks:

Music can be subjective and tricky, and music can also be a powerful community builder. If you're going to play music before and during your workshop, consider taking song requests from your participants, and choose songs that are universally appealing. Think about tempo for different points of the day. When choosing songs with lyrics, make sure songs have a "radio edit" version if there are explicit lyrics. Add enough songs so you don't have to hear any twice.

Do a Final Round of Proofreading

In the opening story, Josué looked at his learning packet and noticed that one side of each page was cut off. The same was the case for additional packets he looked at. Before sharing or printing any materials, proofread, proofread, proofread. If Nat and Kimmie had proofread in advance and printed a test copy, they would not have wasted paper, and participants wouldn't have to do the extra work of deciphering the end of each line. Or better yet, all resources could have been shared electronically. Then, Josué could have a choice between using digital materials, printing out his own copy, or asking for a hard copy at the workshop.

Many PD leaders share their resources electronically to be more ecologically friendly, but you also may have participants who prefer to write by hand. If you need hard copies of materials for your presentation, print only what you need. Invite participants to bring their own print copies if that's available for them. What matters most is that participants can access resources with relative ease.

Communication

Short-term communications tend to be far less voluminous than long-term communication. Within a week or two of the PD, a brief email message ("We're looking forward to seeing you; here are some quick reminders!") serves as a friendly reminder about the workshop, location, and pre-work. These messages can also build excitement or accountability for the upcoming learning experience.

In Josué's case, the one-week away reminder might calm his nerves. He can double-check the location. He can set aside time to complete the pre-work. When he clicks the materials link and downloads the handouts, he may get excited because he already can see so many strategies that will support his teaching. This kind of proactive communication could bolster Josué's enthusiasm and ease his anxiety further.

The Final Touches

Let's look at the day before the PD through Josué's, Nat's, and Kimmie's perspective to see how attending to the details prepared them for the workshop.

Josué: The day before the workshop Josué receives one brief, final reminder. He decides to print a hard copy of his materials so he can write directly on his own handouts. The night before the workshop, Josué puts his school-issued laptop and workshop handouts in his backpack, and he places his water bottle and travel mug next to the door so he doesn't forget to bring them. He adds the workshop location on his phone and double-checks the directions. *Travel time: 15 minutes.* He decides he'll arrive 30 minutes before start time. Josué is excited.

Nat: At the workshop location, Nat checks with the school's custodial staff to see if it's okay to set up tables and place signage along the walls. Nat asks what time the building opens (7 a.m.) and lets the staff and security know she will arrive at that time. She pictures where the check-in table will be, where the food will go, and where to put the supplies. Nat stores boxes of name tags, sign-in sheets, seating charts, and workshop materials in the back of the presentation room. Nat is prepared.

Kimmie: Kimmie meets with the technology coordinator and does a tech check to make sure she has the right cords. She does not have the right dongle, so the technology coordinator gets an HDMI cord for her to use and places it next to the projector. Kimmie makes sure her technology works and projects her slides (it's the right deck). She tests her microphone; with 100 people in the room, she wants to make sure everyone can hear her. When the technology coordinator leaves, and Kimmie and Nat are alone in the presentation room, Kimmie turns to Nat. "I'm going to do some visualization right now." Kimmie then does a moment-to-moment visualization of the following day, beginning with where she is standing, what she is wearing, and what song is playing when participants arrive. She imagines herself circulating while participants are in pair and small-group conversations. She imagines the end of the workshop, seeing feedback about the experience—she hears words like *transformative* and *empowering*. As she goes to the parking lot, she feels energized and excited to meet participants. Kimmie is ready.

It's go time.

The Day Of: Go Time

While Chapter 7 will focus on the skills of adaptive facilitation, this section will support you to be a kick-ass presenter before, during, and after the event. Table 6.4 can serve as a guide for the day of your PD.

Before
Before You Leave Home
Details not only matter for the workshop itself, but for you, too. Consider what you need to feel prepared and whether rituals such as visualizations, meditation, or exercise help you. For newer PD leaders, you also may wonder about your attire. Whatever you choose, consider shoes that are comfortable and quiet (especially

Table 6.4   The Day-Of Checklist: Presentation

The Day-Of Checklist: Presentation	
☑ **Before**	✓ Mentally prepare yourself for the day through visualization and personal getting-ready rituals. ✓ Gather your materials. ✓ Arrive early and do one final rehearsal. ✓ Greet participants and build relationships.
☑ **During**	✓ Use opening routines to usher participants into the learning. ✓ Project confidence and care for the group. ✓ Foster and nurture relationships. ✓ Circulate during small-group time. ✓ Model leadership and learning.
☑ **After**	✓ Use closing routines to transition participants out of the learning. ✓ Share appreciations. ✓ Ask for feedback. ✓ Plan for next steps.

for hard floors), clothing that isn't too fussy, and layers that will be comfortable no matter the temperature.

Your checklist of items to pack for the day might include the following:

- Computer, cords (including charger and dongle)
- Clicker for advancing slides
- The facilitator's agenda
- A copy of the workshop packet
- Supplies for the group if you can't access the space beforehand
  - Large sticky note paper
  - Markers for the sticky note paper
  - Learning packets if they are printed out
  - Supply boxes for tables
- Food for the group, if you are providing it
- Snacks for yourself so you can stay energized
- Water bottle and/or travel mug
- Layers for different temperatures

60–90 Minutes Before Start

If possible, it helps to have a lot of time for setup, ideally 60–90 minutes or whatever you need to build in a time cushion. We suggest setting up from "the outside in," especially if PD leaders are facilitating solo. Start with posting any signage outside, and work your way into the tables to set up packets, the check-in table, snacks, and your presentation materials.

Then it's game on: a time to be calm, organized, ready, and excited to build relationships with participants. When people arrive, a presenter who mingles and chats with people communicates ease. Presenters establish credibility (or lose it) from the very start of the workshop, so little details such as noticing participants' names and pronouncing them correctly help people to feel welcome. If you're an internal provider, consider making small talk as people enter the presentation room; while you may not need to build relationships, it helps to nurture the ones you have.

Let's imagine as Josué arrives at the workshop location, he sees signs in the parking lot directing him to the entrance. He pulls open the door to see more signs guiding him to the check-in table. Nat greets him and asks for his name. "Josué Silva," he says.

"So great to meet you, Josué. I'm Nat, the host who sent those long emails." They smile. "I see you're new to this district. We're so glad you're here. So when I check this box on this sheet here, this means that you'll get a certificate of attendance; this will count toward your PD hours. Sometimes you'll have to do this yourself at some PDs, so I want to alert you to that. And here is your name tag and welcome packet." Josué's name is spelled correctly. "You'll be at table six on the far side of the room."

"I don't need the packet, thanks," Josué says, "I already downloaded the materials at home."

Josue walks into the presentation room; he hears Motown music playing on the speakers, and he easily finds table six. His table has a supply box with sticky notes, markers, and thinking putty. He puts his stuff down and goes to the coffee station. *That coffee smells good,* he thinks.

Kimmie is circulating the room, introducing herself to participants. Five minutes before the start she projects a countdown timer on her slides and reminds participants the workshop is beginning soon.

Before Virtual Learning

In virtual learning, presenters also want to give themselves time before participants arrive, but 30 minutes is typically enough. When sharing screens or any video or audio, it helps to do a test run. All the tabs one needs are opened; notifications and unnecessary programs are closed. It can also help for a presenter to rehearse their navigation patterns—such as how they'll review the chat and where the script is (on the screen or printed out)—so that facilitation looks seamless.

PD leaders may not be able to see everyone on their screen in virtual learning, but that doesn't mean they can't communicate enthusiasm for all participants.

As people enter the virtual space, it's nice when there is music playing or when a check-in question or poll is waiting. Some facilitators give participants a quick overview of the virtual platform so they can rename themselves and access the content. In Bright Morning workshops, presenters ask participants to make sure their name is written as they want to be addressed; participants are given the option to share pronouns if they like as well. Sometimes presenters also ask participants to share their location and a bright spot in the chat. These little details build community before the workshop begins.

During

Opening

The first 15–20 minutes of a workshop are everything. As discussed in Chapter 5, opening routines help usher participants into the learning experience; the facilitator can introduce themselves and build credibility, and they can establish the conditions for learning: for participants to orient toward learning, to set aside distractions, and to consider what will allow them to make the most of their experience.

Let's imagine Kimmie uses opening routines in the first 15 minutes of her workshop. She presents a slide that contains her photo and core values. She shares a little bit about herself and then invites participants to do the same through a turn-and-talk. Josué meets another new teacher, Ingrid—when they realize they teach at rival schools, they joke about how it's a good thing they're on neutral territory. Josué then previews his agenda and puts a check mark next to what he is looking forward to: the segment on building classroom culture. He is excited to learn some new tools. When Josué sets his intention, he writes, "I want to take risks by speaking up in group discussions." These details allow Josué to focus more intently on what he is going to learn and how he is going to show up in his interactions.

Middle

During the workshop, a presenter wants to balance being in front to establish authority and "working the room" to build relationships and share power-with—circulating to subtly communicate accountability, to answer clarifying questions about activities, and to gently address any funky group dynamics that may be forming. When presenters circulate, they let participants know they're around, available, and accessible.

Just as it is important to circulate, it's also important not to hover. No one likes a creepy facilitator. If people are sharing personal stories, a presenter can sit or stand where they can scan the room without being intrusive.

When leading from the front of the room, presenters can still hold space. Presenters' voices are especially important at the front of the room: clear and crisp communication and variation in the pitch, pace, and volume of one's voice keeps folks engaged. When a facilitator talks too long or when they ramble, they can suck the energy out of a space.

Another way to hold space is through modeling. When the facilitator completes the same activities as the participants—such as readings and individual reflections—or when they do a role-play demonstration of what they expect participants to practice on their own, the facilitator becomes a learner alongside the other participants, setting a learning tone for the entire workshop experience.

If we return to Josué's workshop, we might see participants doing small-group work. When they are looking at case studies of identity-safe classrooms, Josué and his tablemates discuss the approaches the teacher uses, and they share some of their own approaches. Kimmie walks by as Josué shares about one of his activities; she nods her head to show she is listening, briefly smiles at Josué, and circulates to the next table. During the break, Kimmie approaches Josué. "Can you tell me how you pronounce your name? I want to make sure I get it right," she asks.

"Ho-sway," he says.

"Josué, that was a great comment you made in your small group. I just wanted to share that with you."

"Thank you. I'm new, and I don't know a lot of techniques yet, but that was a strategy that has worked so far."

"I'm sure your students appreciate it."

Kimmie smiles as she walks away. Josué feels affirmed.

Tips and Tricks:

Use a microphone if there are more than 25 people in your workshop, both for what you say, as well as for equity and access when participants share out to the whole group. Articulate and enunciate more than you think you need to. Soften your voice a bit, too; microphones can make our voices sound harsh. Insist on using a microphone, even when people say, "I don't need it." If there's no way to give people a microphone for sharing, then after each person shares their question/comment, paraphrase the key ideas for the whole group.

At the End: Closing

A strong final closing can help usher participants out of the learning and back into their busy days. We discussed closing routines in Chapter 5, and here's a quick reminder of what presenters can do in their closing: identify big takeaways, revisit their intentions, complete feedback, and share appreciations.

As Josué reflects on his big takeaways, he realizes he has so many. He and Ingrid are asked to do one final pair share and discuss their takeaways and their intentions. "I was so nervous about today," Josué shares. "But this experience made me feel like it was okay to take risks. I don't talk much usually, but today I felt like I couldn't shut up." Josué then fills out his feedback form, giving high ratings for the experience. *I felt like I could be myself. I'm a new teacher, and I didn't feel embarrassed about that. I learned so many new strategies. I feel empowered by this workshop*, he writes. Josué thanks Nat and Kimmie, both of whom say his name correctly as they say goodbye. Josué is energized as he exits to the parking lot.

Closing: Leave Things Better Than You Found Them

You may be feeling lots of things by the end of a workshop: exhausted, relieved, energized. Before celebrating, take care of closing rituals to leave the space better than you found it. Table 6.5 provides you with just a few more details to take care of to bring the experience to a thoughtful close.

Clean Up, Celebrate, and Reflect

Before folks leave you might need to attend to a few additional details, such as identifying where to recycle items, packing up, and deciding what to do with unused workshop materials and packets. Build in a minute or two for participants to tidy the space so your closing practices can be more efficient and you don't have to do it all on your own.

Table 6.5 Closing Checklist

✓ Clean up and leave the space better than you found it.
✓ Celebrate and appreciate your hard work.
✓ Reflect on the experience and review feedback.
✓ Send your final message to participants to close out the experience and identify next steps.

Once the room is clear and as clean as it can be, celebrate. It's easy to dive right into participant feedback and focus on all the things that went wrong; it's a natural tendency. Instead, pause to recognize your hard work and think of workshop highlights. Then, perhaps 30 minutes later, or some time that evening when you have time to be present, read all the feedback to identify what went well, what could be improved, what you learned, and what you want to keep in mind for future workshops. If you keep a journal or have other forms of reflection, consider reflecting on your work as one of your post-event rituals. If you co-facilitated your workshop, share some appreciations and feedback with one another as well.

Imagine Kimmie again. After everyone leaves the workshop room, Kimmie lets out a deep, satisfied sigh. "That was a great group! And I am exhausted."

"I bet," says Nat as they stack a few final packets and place them in a box to drop off at the district. "Let's get go to the café across the street and process the experience."

Over coffee, Kimmie and Nat share appreciations. Kimmie appreciates how Nat helped participants feel welcome and cared for. "You made newer teachers feel welcome. I overheard you welcoming one participant, Josué. He seemed nervous. The way you took some time with him made a difference. I hope this will support him as a new teacher."

Nat appreciates the way Kimmie engaged with participants. "I appreciated the way you really pushed participant thinking. When the world language teacher wondered about applications for their classroom, you shared an awesome strategy; lots of people were taking notes."

"Thanks! I always create an FAQ as part of my facilitator agenda so I can anticipate what people might ask. It helps a lot," Kimmie responded.

They each shared three highlights about the workshop before they reviewed participant feedback. Kimmie divided up the feedback forms with participants' "glows and grows" and shared half with Nat. Each reviewed their stack and identified themes—what went well, what to be improved. After swapping stacks of feedback forms and silently reviewing their second batch, they compiled notes and discussed what went well, what could be improved, and some next steps for further learning and implementation. With these notes in hand, they started drafting their final communication for participants.

Bring It Home

Your final communication allows you to address your participants' needs one last time. In this communication, you can share a link to the feedback form for those who didn't complete it, any final thoughts or pieces of wisdom from the session, session resources, and recommendations for further learning. It might look something like the following:

To: Josué Silva

From: Kimmie Lowry and Nat McIlwraith

Date: October 2, 2019

Subject: ECD Workshop: Thank You and Next Steps

Dear Josué,

Thank you so much for attending the Equity-Centered Design workshop. We completed powerful learning in a community of 100 participants, and the experience was inspiring. We are so appreciative you were a part of it.

If you didn't get a chance to fill out the feedback form at the end, you can find it by clicking here. We are always striving to learn and grow. Your feedback will support that growth.

As we think back to the workshop, we want to share two pieces of advice as you prepare to implement your learning:

1) Center relationships. Students will learn at their best if they feel seen, cared for, valued. Build relationships as a starting point. You may consider getting feedback from students a couple times a term to check in on how they're doing, too.
2) Do one thing differently a week. Sometimes we think that to change a system means to overhaul it in its entirety. Not true. We can do one equity-centered practice a week and measure the results of that one thing. Building our practice incrementally will keep us committed to this work long term.

Finally, in case you weren't able to download resources before the event, you can access them by clicking here; this link takes you to your own zip file of all the program materials.

We hope you will continue your learning and share the impact with us. We also hope to continue this partnership. Equity work is better in community, and we would like to be on the journey with you. Feel free to reach out if you would like to continue learning more equity-centered practices that benefit your students.

With gratitude,

Kimmie Lowry (she/her), presenter

Nat McIlwraith (they/them), host

As Josué reads this final message, he reflects on his learning experience the day after the workshop. He thinks about all he learned and what he is ready to implement in class. He is inspired. He opens up the planner on his computer and begins designing his next lesson with an emphasis on relationships and classroom culture building. He is going to try a new activity he learned in the workshop. All

Kimmie and Nat's carefully planned details supported Josué's learning; his teaching will be changed by the new strategies he learned, and his students' experience will be better for it.

Before You Go

Pause and Process:
- In addition to your usual PD preparation, what details do you want to make sure to attend to when planning PD in the future?
- What additional questions might you add to the Checklist for Attending to Details?

Remember:

This quick guide for attending to details:

- *Context*: Who the PD is for and what you need to know about them
- *Partnership*: Who your partners are (co-facilitators, site administrators, technology coordinators, meal providers)
- *Location*: What you know and will be able to do with the space you have
- *Resources*: The materials you and participants need to engage in the learning
- *Communication*: The reminders, updates, and follow-up participants will receive before and after the PD
- *Presentation*: What you will do (the routines, messages, actions) to meet participant needs before, during, and after the learning experience
- *Closing*: How you will leave the space better than you found it

CHAPTER 7

Facilitate Adaptively

Roger, Foghorn Elementary's instructional coach, was one hour into his Thinking Routines workshop for early-Wednesday PD. Participants were highly engaged and practicing protocols they would implement in their classrooms.

Roger's intentional design was paying off. His instructions were clear, his communication crisp. He felt confident, and that confidence emanated throughout the room.

Roger led participants through a See, Think, Wonder protocol using a provocative photograph from a recent article. Participants had just moved into the Wonder phase of the process, asking questions about what they observed and starting their responses with the phrase "I wonder. . . ."

"I wonder what future generations of students would say about this image?" Howard asked.

Mari responded sarcastically, "They'd say, 'I wonder why all the older folks messed up the world.'" A cascade of commentary followed, as participants shared agreements and disagreements. The energy in the room buzzed with rich debate. Roger monitored who spoke, calling on those who had not shared their views to ensure there was equity of participation.

Soon, the 10-minute discussion Roger planned evolved into 20 minutes, straying from the agenda. No longer raising their hands, participants blurted out responses, the extroverts garnering the most attention. Roger started to worry that he was losing control of the group. He felt his chest tightening. Time was running short before school started. His smile morphed into a look of distress as Irma was in the middle of her comment. Irma noticed the look on Roger's face and abruptly stopped sharing. "Did I say something wrong?" she asked.

Unaware of his body language, Roger was confused by the question. He responded tersely, "No. We're short on time now. We have a lot to do still, so let's get to the next thing."

Once buzzing with energy, the room was now silent.

Flustered, Roger explained the next protocol, not noticing that his pace had increased.

"Could you please slow down? I can't write everything you're saying," Thalia requested.

"Maybe you can get notes from a partner," Roger said.

"Which page of the handout are we on? What is this protocol called?" Mari asked, her tone communicating frustration. Roger ignored the question and continued to disregard requests to slow down.

The school bell rang in the middle of Roger's explanation. Participants got up to leave before Roger was done speaking.

"I guess that's it," Roger said sharply as people left the room.

"We should have stuck to the first protocol. That last bit was a total waste of time," Thalia said to Howard as they left the room. Howard nodded in agreement. Roger overheard.

Roger ripped up his agenda and tossed it in the recycling bin, his chest tight from stress. He replayed the moment things went awry. *They don't get how hard it is to lead adults*, he thought.

"I have come to the frightening conclusion that I am the decisive element. It is my personal approach that creates the climate. It is my daily mood that makes the weather."

—Haim G. Ginott

Have you experienced a situation like Roger's—as PD leader, site leader, teacher, or coach—replaying the moment when things went awry, wishing things were different? We've been there. It's no party.

Let's briefly unpack what happened with Roger. He had a purposeful and well-planned agenda that engaged participants. The conditions for learning were in place: Participants felt psychologically safe enough to freely to share opinions, and the content was engaging and high interest. While Roger was the one guiding the discussion, participants were empowered to take shared ownership of the experience. Until Roger looked at the clock. He was elated when things went well, but as soon as the conversation took longer than anticipated, his dismay was on display, and he wasn't aware of how his words and actions were shaping participant responses. He was being reactive instead of adaptive.

This chapter is about how you hone and practice this final habit: facilitate adaptively. To facilitate adaptively means you hold lightly to your agenda so you can be responsive to what happens. Whether it's a question the facilitator didn't anticipate, an unforeseen conflict among participants, harm that happened, or resistance, detours happen. Accepting this fact is critical to becoming an adaptive facilitator—and to leading transformational PDs.

In this chapter we'll unpack what we mean by *detour*. We'll address how self-awareness is at the root of adaptive facilitation, and then we'll turn our focus to the skills: emotional intelligence, cultural humility, clear communication, and reflection. While we won't return to this opening anecdote, we'll tell you the story of another school leader who used the strategies we're recommending that had a very different outcome.

Detours Happen

Even when we have done what we can to foster psychological safety, build trust, and skillfully use power, we still can find ourselves facing an unexpected detour. A detour, like running short on time or addressing strong emotions, is what happens when our hopes clash with reality. Our hopes reside in our well-planned agenda and all the details we attend to when things go as we imagine. But the reality is this: Detours happen. When detours happen, we facilitate adaptively. Adaptive facilitation can look like the following:

- The slides aren't loading for a presentation because there's an outage on the host site. The facilitator develops a workaround and says, "Looks like our tech isn't working. I'll do my best to share key ideas verbally. Would someone be willing to be note-taker for this segment and project those notes onto the screen? We can check later to see if the slides are working. If not, I'd love another volunteer note-taker for the next segment."

- The fire alarm goes off in the middle of a workshop, and participants need to evacuate the building. Twenty minutes pass before the firetrucks arrive, and another 10 minutes pass before everyone is let back in the building. When participants return to their seats, the facilitator notices some participants are flustered (the facilitator is flustered, too). The facilitator makes a corny joke, "Who knew that we generated so much heat in this workshop?" and then offers an energizer called "shake it off," where participants wiggle their bodies to transition back to the learning. "It seems cheesy, I know, but it's a way to shift our energy. Let's try it."

- It's 15 minutes before the workshop ends and the facilitator has one more activity—an action planning process—before the closing routines. To do the activity in a haphazard way would undermine its purpose. The facilitator loves this activity and sees it as crucial but decides to cut it and go straight to closing routines, knowing it's better to ease participants out of the learning than to barrel forward with a rushed activity.

- The site leadership team worked hard on a new protocol to navigate conflict, and they are excited to try it. But when the protocol falls flat in the workshop and staff aren't clear about the purpose, one of the leaders facilitating starts to feel defensive. His co-facilitator notices a shift in body language; calmly, she addresses the group, "It looks like that activity didn't have the intended effect. Let's take five minutes right now and reflect on when you've been able to successfully navigate conflict. We'll share our responses and brainstorm some ways we might create a protocol that better meets the needs of the group." During reflection time, the two co-facilitators briefly chat about the adjustment to their plans.

- The vice principal is leading an all-staff PD on immersive learning, and it's a stressful time in the school year. Half the group doesn't buy into the activity because they didn't read the pre-work. The vice principal says, "I'm going to make an adjustment to the plan right now. Immersive learning is a new initiative at our site, and I want to ensure we're all on the same page about its purpose. I know we've got a lot going on right now. So let's proceed with the small-group activity for those who completed the pre-work. If you didn't complete the pre-work, let's take time in the cafeteria to read it now; it will take about 15 minutes. I'll be on hand to answer any questions you have. Once you're done with the pre-reading, you will still have plenty of time to join your small group and proceed with the activity. When we all come back together, we'll synthesize our learning."

Each of these examples offers a look at the qualities of adaptive facilitation. Adaptive facilitators are self-aware: They know their strengths, values, and identities, and they understand how these elements shape their work. They can sense when things are going well or poorly. Often this sensing manifests physically in their bodies—in the way facilitators carry themselves, in their voice, or pulse—even before they are consciously aware of what is happening. Adaptive facilitators are also group-aware: They know what is in their spheres of control and influence, and they hone their skills of emotional intelligence, cultural humility, skilled communication, and reflection so they can address whatever happens intentionally.

Roger's Detour

Because Roger worked at Foghorn Elementary and the participants were his colleagues, he knew a lot about the context. We'll circle back to Roger throughout the chapter to understand how his knowledge of the context could be put to use in this scenario. But first, let's make sure we understand what happened in Roger's PD: His workshop took a detour when the discussion became especially lively and stretched beyond the time he'd allotted for it. Because he perceived this moment as a problem rather than a possibility, his body language shifted. In response, his participants read his energy and, in Irma's case, thought there was something wrong; the room fell silent when Roger told the group they were short on time. When the bell rang, people got up to leave even though Roger wasn't done speaking. After the participants left, Roger replayed Thalia's parting comment in his head: "We should have stuck to the first protocol. That last bit was a waste of time." Ouch. Roger left what had begun as a powerful PD demoralized.

The consequences of Roger's facilitation now have a longer-term impact. Participants may have lost trust in Roger as a facilitator and might be hesitant to engage the next time he leads PD. Roger may also have less trust in himself or his confidence might be diminished. Roger may need to remind himself of his strengths, core values, and who he wants to be: the confident and compassionate facilitator. He will have to consider these conditions the next time he leads a workshop.

Where Roger experienced a detour that required some course correction in his planning, other detours can reveal deep, underlying problems in a community. The more you understand your context, the better you'll be able to adapt your facilitation. Toxic cultures often perpetuate unhealthy behaviors and communication practices, and in those circumstances, detours emerge in resistance, unmanageable conflict between participants, or words and actions that perpetuate harm. The PD facilitator then needs to consider all the circumstances and dynamics at play, consider what is within and outside their spheres of control, and adapt thoughtfully.

When Harm Happens

The most challenging detours in PD are when harm happens: when a facilitator or participant says or does something that undermines psychological safety. Familiar instances of harm include when a facilitator snaps at a participant out of frustration, when participants who struggle to work together erupt in conflict, and when a participant is resistant to what the facilitator is saying and lashes out with a hurtful comment. There are other forms of harm we may be less aware of: when someone shares an inappropriate joke in moments of levity or when the facilitator shares a video clip, an image, or a text that perpetuates stereotypes. Increasing our awareness of what's harmful is an evolving process.

People who have experienced harm will have varying perceptions of when it happens. Sometimes you become aware of harm in the moment, or you may become aware of it when a participant pulls you aside during a break or you read the final feedback form and someone writes about a hurtful comment in small-group discussion. Those who experienced harm may write it off as no big deal, while others will become overwhelmed and triggered. Most of those who cause harm don't set out to do so to begin with; that's not their intention. But even with the best intentions, harm is harm. The impact of harm needs to be addressed. Those who have experienced the impact of harm need to be listened to and attended to.

Our commitment to educational equity requires us to explore harm related to identity. In these instances, harm often happens to those who have the least social power or authority. The most common form of identity-related harm are microaggressions. According to Sue and Spanierman (2020), *microaggressions* refer to the everyday insults, putdowns, and slights that members of marginalized groups experience in their day-to-day interactions. Those who often commit microaggressions are often unaware they have said something offensive. Microaggressions can span the gamut from

- Colorblindness ("I don't see race")
- To ascribing intelligence to people based on race or ethnicity ("You're so articulate")
- To making assumptions that people are not born in the United States ("Where are you really from?")
- To making assumptions about a person's gender or sexual orientation ("I couldn't tell you were gay")

The term *micro* is a misnomer, because the accumulated effect of microaggressions (hearing or experiencing them frequently) has had a significant, harmful impact to those on the receiving end.

Let's consider an example of identity-related harm that we may not always be aware of, and we'll share how the facilitator responds. At a local nonprofit leadership conference, Jeanine, a white female nonprofit director, presented a session on how to become a thought leader in education. Her first slide contained an inspirational quote attributed to a white woman whose image was included on the slide. Shortly after the slide was projected, a Black female participant, Marsha, raised her hand. "Sorry for the interruption, but that quote is actually attributed to a Black woman." There was silence before the participant continued, "It's demeaning to misattribute it."

In this moment, harm has been done, not by anything Jeanine said, but from her content, an image on a slide that's misattributed. In this instance, the way social power is operating (a white woman misattributing a quote) has a harmful impact on the Black female participant. When Marsha says, "It's demeaning," she is signaling harm and a potential rupture in trust. Marsha clearly understands the slide as erasing a Black woman's contributions and crediting those contributions to a white woman. This matters because while women have been historically marginalized, whiteness signals power, and in colonial cultures, white women have typically been conferred more power than Black women.

How to Repair Harm When It Happens

Repairing harm depends on a range of factors: the context of the PD, whether you work within a site or organization or if you are external to it, the quality of relationship between you and the participants, the ability to take time to address harm in the moment or at another juncture, and the levels of trust and psychological safety. As you learned in Chapter 2, it's crucial to understand and embrace emotions, to know your own triggers, and to attend to them to the degree you are able before and after the PD. It's also critical to recognize what's most important to address in the moment and what's in your sphere of influence.

To repair harm when it happens, facilitators can borrow from restorative practices (Costello et al., 2019). The roots of these practices draw from Indigenous peacemaking (NARF, 2021): a community-based process that addresses the concerns of all interested parties. This approach supports those who have been harmed and creates opportunities for accountability and repair when a transgression has occurred. If PD leaders work at the site where they are delivering PD, they may be able to set aside time at a later date to bring the parties involved to engage in conversation. External providers may need to address harm in the moment and will need to consider what follow-up might be needed after the PD. To repair harm, the following questions can support PD leaders—either if they bring parties together or if they address harm in their communication as they facilitate:

1. What happened?
2. Who has been affected by what happened?
3. In what way have they been affected?
4. What are the emotions involved?
5. What might need to be done to make things right?

How to Apologize If You've Caused Harm

Unfortunately, sometimes facilitators cause harm; it can feel uncomfortable, but it's important to address it. The following are some considerations for when you need to apologize:

- *Apologize as close to the moment of harm as possible.* It's okay to take a little time to re-center yourself and consider what you want to say. But the closer to the moment a transgression happened, the more the apology can repair harm or reduce further harm.
- *Be sincere and genuine.* It's important to mean what you say and communicate sincerity through your words and body language.
- *Center the needs of the those who have been harmed.* Do this by taking ownership for what happened. Say: "I'm sorry I caused harm," not "I'm sorry you feel that way."
- *Own your part in it, but don't make it about you.* Some people who apologize center themselves by saying, "I'm sorry, it wasn't my intention to cause you harm; I really didn't mean it." It's enough to say, "I take responsibility for my words/actions."
- *Be specific and concise.* Say: "I'm sorry the comment I made caused harm; it's a microaggression, and it's wrong."
- *Don't expect things to go back to normal or for the person to accept your apology.* Repairing harm is not always a tidy or conclusive process. But it's a step toward healing.

Let's now return to our first example. The facilitator, Jeanine, who has had some training in restorative practices, immediately recognized her misstep. Recognizing the impact of her actions, she paused, took a breath, and said: "I apologize for my misstep. Thank you for correcting me. I also recognize that it's more than the misattribution of the quote; it's also an erasure of people's identities and contributions. Because of the way people with more historically marginalized identities have been affected by systems of oppression—namely, racism—something like this may have differing impacts on participants in this space, depending on how they identify. I own my part in this and will change this quote during break; I'll review my sources and make sure they are attributed accurately. Marsha, if you or anyone else would like to talk further, I'd welcome a conversation during break."

Not only was this facilitator aware of power, identity, and systems of oppression, she was adaptive and skillful in how she chose to respond. Marsha still may not have trusted her, and Jeanine may have lost some credibility. But she addressed harm when it happened, and she did what she could to reduce further harm.

Addressing harm related to identity can feel challenging at times, uncomfortable at others. We may be afraid of saying the wrong thing or making things worse. We might still cause harm even when we don't intend to. We all have work to do, and our awareness of identity will continue to evolve over time. If we're committed to ensuring every child gets what they need every day to thrive, then it's worth taking the necessary steps to learn how to repair harm when it happens.

Pause and Process:

- What's one new idea you're taking from this section on harm?
- What's one thing you might do to deepen your understanding of how identity-harm happens?
- What's one thing you might try when you recognize that harm has happened?

The Roots of Adaptive Facilitation: Know Yourself

"We teach who we are."

—Parker Palmer

Reflecting on ourselves can feel like a luxury when the work waiting for us is urgent. But self-knowledge is at the root of adaptive facilitation. When we facilitate with self-knowledge, we have greater awareness about why something feels easy or challenging, what we're best at, who we are, and how we show up. We also can be aware of what triggers us and how we might take care of ourselves while meeting the needs of the group.

Strengths, Core Values, Identity Markers as a Foundation for Self-Knowledge

The first chapter of Elena's book *Onward: Cultivating Emotional Resilience for Educators* (2018) identifies how knowledge of self—understanding our psyches, values, personalities, strengths, and sociopolitical identities—helps us build our emotional resilience. Reflecting on each of these areas will allow us to deepen our self-awareness, build better relationships, and contribute to our overall health and well-being. While all these elements of self are important, three of them—strengths, values, and sociopolitical identity—can be especially important for facilitators of adult learning.

Strengths and Core Values

It's useful to identify our strengths prior to facilitation because leading from a place of strength makes you more confident when leading PD. Perhaps you're a quick thinker or a strong verbal processor—these are strengths that can help you to respond to questions you weren't expecting. Or maybe you're a great synthesizer of information, so you can connect many threads of a conversation to some core themes. Or you're an excellent listener, and you demonstrate this strength by the ways you respond to conversations as you circulate around the room. Lori has quick wit and strong group awareness. She is able to gauge, based on group dynamics, when humor is appropriate or how to redirect people when a PD session may be going off track. Elena's strengths are her patience and trust in the process. She knows how long to let a conversation play out before intervening and how long to hold silence in a coaching demonstration before the role-play participant has a revelation.

Similarly, when we facilitate with our core values in mind, we tap into what matters most to us. When Elena is facilitating and notices what she calls "funky group dynamics," her core value of community compels her to address those dynamics. When Lori is facilitating and she notices one participant in a small group is not given a chance to share, her core value of equity calls her to go over to that group and check in to make sure everyone has contributed to the discussion. Core values are a source of energy. They keep us grounded in decision-making moments.

Awareness of Identity

Which aspects of your identity are you most aware of when leading adults? To what degree have you considered how your gender, race, or ethnic background have an impact on your facilitation? Our awareness of our identity, also known as our *sociopolitical identity*, allows us to see how the social groups to which we belong influence not only our roles in PD but how empowered we feel to lead, the ways we relate to participants, or what happens for us when we experience stress. The term *sociopolitical identity* refers to the social groups to which we belong—our race or ethnicity, gender identity, class background, and sexual orientation, among additional social identifiers. These identifiers intersect and influence the power we have in different social spaces.

Awareness of our sociopolitical identity shapes how we facilitate, what triggers us, and what our relationship is to power, privilege, and marginalization. For PD leaders with historically marginalized identities, it may feel like there is an extra layer of work involved to be considered credible and to be respected as a facilitator. To disrupt this common pattern, it's helpful for facilitators whose identities align with dominant culture to increase their awareness of power and privilege, to recognize when how power is operating, and to create conditions for learning that center the needs of more historically oppressed groups. For those whose identities don't align with the dominant culture, how might you see your identities as strengths? What might you say or do to remind yourself of these strengths?

Self-Awareness for Roger

Let's imagine Roger is reflecting on his strengths, core values, and identity markers the day after leading the PD that went awry. He is sitting at his desk in his office when he first arrives at school. In his reflection notebook, he identifies his key strengths: He is a good designer, and he is skilled at designing activities that engage and energize a group. Roger is a details person, and when he creates his agendas, he often has pages of notes—not only the key points he wants to make but many other considerations to keep in mind as he presents. Roger also is equity-minded in his approach to design, a strength related to group awareness. He is aware of who is speaking, whose voices he needs to center, and how to create structures for more equitable participation. Feedback on workshops often aligns with these strengths; Roger often receives comments such as, "I appreciate how Roger considers the needs of the whole group" and "His instructions and handouts are so clear and well detailed." Roger takes pride in these strengths.

At the same time, Roger knows his fixation on details can sometimes be his downfall. When he spends a long time designing agendas and scripting every key word, he gets flustered when the PD goes offtrack. Roger had similar challenges in his lesson plans when he taught fifth grade. Increasing his self-awareness around this area can support him when he finds himself too mired in the details.

Roger's core values are faith, family, and perseverance—each value has been a guiding force in his work and his life. Before he begins each work day, Roger prays. He looks to the day ahead and prays that all will go well, that students and adults will have what they need. He also says a short prayer before his workshops, a prayer that calls him to be confident and compassionate. Roger grew up in a large Filipino and Colombian family, and those who mean the most to him are his siblings and cousins—which is why family is his second core value. When he addresses students or participants in his workshops, he often uses the word *fam* as a term of endearment. "Okay, fam," Roger might say. "Today we're going to learn about. . . ." His colleagues love that about him. Perseverance is Roger's third core value because, as the oldest of six and the first in his family to go to college, Roger had to persevere in the mostly white honors classes he took in school, and in the face of the looks he got from teachers and classmates who would ask, "Where are you from?" Perseverance is also what helped Roger complete his teacher certification program so he could create equitable conditions for all students in the classes he taught.

As with his strength in attending to details, sometimes Roger's perseverance gets in the way of his judgment. As a details person who wants to finish everything he starts, he sometimes races through agendas rather than take time to consider what might work best in the moment. As Roger reflects about the protocol workshop he just led—and as he considers his strengths, values, and identity—he begins to see why he got so frustrated during his Wednesday PD. He realizes he needs to develop some strategies to lift himself up when he is being self-critical. Reflecting on his strengths and his areas for growth, he sees he needs to hone his emotional intelligence so he can respond well even when he gets flustered. He decides he is going to do an emotional check-in with himself before and after his PD so he can identify where he felt successful and where things felt more challenging.

To learn more about working with your strengths, core values, and identity markers, you can explore tools in *The Art of Coaching Workbook* and on the Bright Morning website.

Self-Awareness in Virtual PD

Leading virtual learning can sometimes feel like you're leading a void. We stare into a tiny dot or camera and talk into silence, often without being able to see the people we're leading. Whether you approach virtual learning as a technophile or technophobe, the following practices will allow you to tap into your strengths as you speak into the silence of the virtual space:

- *Know your technology strengths and play to those.* How we approach our use of technology is bound up in our attitudes about it. The more averse or fearful we are, the less confident we'll be in our facilitation. Consider practicing with your technology before you facilitate. Keep your use of tech tools simple; these tools are a vehicle for facilitation rather than a substitute for it.

- *Make friends with awkward silence.* Have you ever found yourself posing a question to the audience and find yourself waiting for what feels like a year? Have you ever gotten zero response to your prompts? If you struggle with silence in virtual learning, it may be time to reframe your thinking. For example, consider that silence might give introverts more processing time or that silence might be a gift for those who live or work in noisy circumstances. Enjoy it when possible.

- *Know how you look on camera.* In some virtual platforms, you can turn off your self view. Our advice: Don't. It's important to know what you look like on camera, what your nonverbal communication looks like. It's also helpful to know how you're lit and where the camera is focused. Make sure to clear out the clutter in your background. Consider using a computer stand and a ring light (or something equivalent) so you're well placed and well lit on a screen. Avoid virtual backgrounds that may detract from your facilitation or that may send mixed messages to your audience.

- *Stay chill in glitchy tech moments.* Tech will go awry. Your internet may go out. That link you posted may not work. How you respond to those moments is just as important as the content you care about. It's okay to say "oops," to ask people to pause for a moment, to take a break, or to surrender to the internet gods. No one has perished from broken internet link.

Becoming an Adaptive Facilitator: Skill Sets to Refine

LORI REFLECTS:

I had mastered the skills of adaptive facilitation by the time I had to deliver a virtual workshop on leadership and team development that almost went sideways—and I was already having a hard day.

Participants reviewed a handout that contained characteristics for emotionally intelligent teams when Susan raised her hand. "I don't agree with what's here. A lot here hasn't been true for me, and some of these items are culturally biased."

Cindy then spoke, "I agree with Susan. It says here that eye contact is a trait of high emotional intelligence, but that's not true for me. When I was growing up, I was taught that eye contact is rude."

Susan followed up on her previous comment. "Interrupting was a common form of communication in my family." A few more heads nodded.

"Yeah, this list is problematic," Randy responded.

I was nervous at first. I paused and took a breath. I thought to myself, *Yes, I can see how this list could be read as culturally biased and limiting.* I was aware of how some of my implicit biases may have shown up as I introduced the list, and I wanted to validate participants for what they were raising. I also knew that as an outside facilitator, participants might not fully trust me. I wanted to ensure this could be a learning space for people of all backgrounds. I assessed what was in my sphere of influence, tapped into my strengths, thought about how to respond, and proceeded.

"Thank you, Susan, for bringing this topic to the surface. Yes, I can see how this list is culturally biased. I own my misstep there. Here's what I propose: Since this list is reductive, let's expand it and identify some characteristics that have worked best for your teams, traits that indicate a team has high levels of trust and psychological safety. Let's spend the next three minutes reflecting individually. Then we'll talk in our table groups and identify what we have in common and what's different."

As I circulated through the room, I heard an array of traits, ones that honored participants' experiences and backgrounds. The lists participants created were more nuanced than the one I had shared. I then led a brief whole-group conversation. "Thanks, everyone. This felt like an important moment to address collectively. Before we move on, are there any additions you would make to this list?"

Cindy raised her hand. "No, but I appreciate you giving us space to talk about this." Most participants nodded in agreement.

When I read through participant feedback at the end of the workshop, I saw a comment from Susan. "I really appreciate how Lori responded to that moment. She didn't get defensive, and she gave us space to share some of our own traits. That meant a lot to me."

The workshop lifted my mood that day. This moment also reminded me that what feels challenging can also be a breakthrough for deeper learning.

Before we pull back the curtain on Lori's facilitation moves, let's identify the skills she drew on in responding.

Spheres of Control and Influence

Imagine that a site implements a new mandate from the central office and staff members are grumpy about it. You can't change the mandate, but you might be able to influence how your staff thinks about its implementation. Similarly, when a group rejects a list of characteristics of emotionally intelligent teams, you might realize that, while you can't change the materials you're sharing, you can influence how participants engage with the list. When you invite folks to add more culturally relevant characteristics, you are facilitating adaptively. Recognizing what we can control and influence gives us agency. Figure 7.1 offers a helpful visual for identifying what's within and outside our control.

Let's imagine Roger looked at this graphic before leading his Wednesday session and then made a list of what he could influence and what was out of his control, shown on the left of Figure 7.1.

Figure 7.1   Spheres of influence

I can control:
- How I show up—my attitude and disposition.
- What to keep and what to cut if time runs short.
- How I interpret what happens, and how I choose to respond to what happens

I can influence:
- Group dynamics: ensuring there is equity of voice in participation.
- The energy level in the room: if it falls flat, or if we need some time for quiet reflection
- How participants feel about the outcome

I know that some things are outside my control:
- How participants apply their learning
- What participants are going through outside this workshop

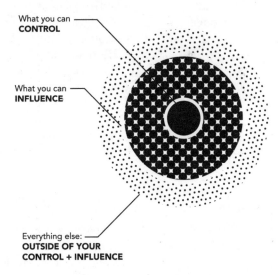

SPHERES OF **INFLUENCE**

What you can **CONTROL**

What you can **INFLUENCE**

Everything else: **OUTSIDE OF YOUR CONTROL + INFLUENCE**

Partway through Roger's workshop, when participants were mired in discussion, Roger could have determined what he could control or influence. He might have considered ways he could use his attitude to shift the room, what he could cut from the agenda, and how to respond to participant energy in the room. It's draining to focus on what we can't control. Knowing what we *can* control and influence is empowering.

Nuances of Adaptive Facilitation

Adaptive facilitation requires a level of flexibility and nuance, skills that a facilitator can refine over their career. Table 7.1 offers four necessary skill sets: emotional intelligence, cultural humility, clear communication, and reflection. Developing these skills takes time, patience, and practice. As you read, identify skills you already possess, skills you want to learn more about, and skills you want to strengthen.

Table 7.1   Skill Sets of Adaptive Facilitation

Skill sets	Examples of these skill sets
Emotional intelligence	Adaptive facilitators. . . • Are as aware of themselves as they are of group dynamics. • Recognize and navigate their own emotions—especially difficult ones—so that they can effectively address them. • Listen with curiosity and compassion and read the emotions of others; they respond in ways that honor others' needs. • Use vulnerability and transparency when appropriate—which includes being transparent about their own emotions and thought processes to deepen connection and model how they navigate emotions. • Can recognize the emotional undercurrents in a group and can identify the contributing factors; they address those contributing factors in a way that preserves the integrity of the learning space and the dignity of learners.

(Continued)

Table 7.1 (Continued)

Skill sets	Examples of these skill sets
Cultural humility	Adaptive facilitators. . . • Are invested in their own ongoing identity development. • Take intentional action to expand their perspective while acknowledging both the limitations and wisdom of their experiences. • Acknowledge and leverage dynamics of race, class, gender (among a range of social identifiers), and power in a group for deeper learning both in the moment and on reflection. • Support participants by creating brave spaces for people of all backgrounds to learn with and from each other. • Center the needs of those whose identities align with historically oppressed people and create conditions to ensure everyone's needs are addressed equitably.
Clear communication	Adaptive facilitators. . . • Recognize that words and actions matter so they rehearse key points in their facilitator's agenda. • Can speak concisely, precisely, and clearly as they articulate key points and ideas. • Plan for potential questions or resistance, and they choose their words thoughtfully as they respond. • Are aware of their nonverbal communication and how their body language can influence the energy in the room.
Reflection	Adaptive facilitators. . . • Are learners who participate in ongoing reflection to further their self-awareness. • Are able to understand their strengths, areas for growth, and key priorities for their development. • Recognize when they need additional support and take the necessary steps to seek it out. • Are eager for feedback—they actively invite it from many sources, including those that are more likely to see the world and situations differently from them. They learn from their prior experiences and incorporate feedback.

Let's see how these skill sets were evident in Lori's facilitation in workshop when participants talked about characteristics of emotionally intelligent teams. Once Lori determined what was in her sphere of control and influence (shifting participants' attitudes about an activity), Lori then practiced the skills of adaptive facilitation:

- *Emotional intelligence*: Lori remained calm and centered when her agenda took a brief detour. She also listened openly to what participants shared. She modeled leadership in the ways she sourced and leveraged power to acknowledge the experiences in the room.
- *Cultural humility*: She acknowledged her misstep and named the biases inherent in the document she shared. She also invited participants to add to the list so she could honor their backgrounds and expertise.
- *Clear communication*: Lori validated what she heard and proposed a path forward succinctly. Her plan was concrete and clear.
- *Reflection*: She was reflective both in the moment and the day after as she reviewed the feedback. In her hands, the detour fostered greater trust and didn't derail the day.

These skill sets don't only support you in difficult facilitation moments; they help you be better leaders for your teams and models for young people in your schools. Imagine what might be possible if we approached our teaching, coaching, leadership, and PD facilitation with these four core skill sets.

Adaptive Facilitation for Co-Facilitators

Shawna was a teacher on special assignment, and she was having a tough time leading her weekly PD session on measuring student engagement. This was her first time facilitating adults, and she was nervous—her voice was a little flat, she rambled, and participants had a hard time following what she was saying. When a participant asked her to clarify an engagement strategy, she got flustered and stopped talking mid-sentence.

Jaime, Shawna's co-facilitator, was circulating the room when Shawna froze, and as she stared ahead, Jaime spoke from the side of the room. "Let's consider the strategies Shawna has shared so far. In your notebooks, write down three more ways you can measure what engagement looks and sounds like."

As participants wrote reflections, Jaime passed Shawna a sticky note that read, "You've got this." Shawna smiled, and as participants finished their reflections, she proceeded to facilitate the conversation. Before the workshop, Jaime and Shawna talked about their nerves and about the kinds of encouragement they could offer each other, and Shawna had said, "a small sticky note with some encouragement would be great."

When a detour happens in co-facilitation, PD leaders have the benefit of a partner who can troubleshoot, step in, collaborate, or even offer encouragement. In Shawna and Jaime's case, Jaime was able to influence the situation by adapting on the fly and prompting participants; he also offered Shawna some encouragement. The following are some additional tips to consider for co-facilitation.

- Before you facilitate:
  - To build trust, have a conversation about strengths, core values, and identity markers. Knowing about one another in these ways can foster connection, allow facilitators to play to their strengths, and help each other when things go awry.
  - Generate a list of possible questions you might receive and delegate who might respond to each. Role-play possible responses to these questions.
  - Determine ahead of time what all facilitators are doing during each agenda item. When one facilitator is leading, determine what the other facilitator(s) will be doing to support.
- During facilitation:
  - When the facilitator leading doesn't see all the hands raised, another facilitator can draw attention to the participants: "I think we have a few more people who still would like to share."
  - If you get a tough question or a participant is resistant or you need some support, address the issue together. Ask your co-facilitator for their thoughts, "Jaime, how would you answer this question?"
  - If a bigger detour occurs, ask the group to take a 5- or10-minute break so you can regroup. Together with your co-facilitator, troubleshoot about possible next steps or divide up and address individuals who may need to process what happened one on one.
- After facilitation:
  - Reflect after the PD together. Share what went well and what still needs work. Talk about yourselves individually and as a team and identify areas to work on for the future.

As you review the following list of potential detours, which ones are familiar to you? Which ones cause you the most worry?

- The facilitator runs out of time.
- The links don't work or a video fails to play.
- The energy in the room is low, and participants need re-energizing.
- The activity is confusing for participants, so they stop engaging in it.
- Participants are not connecting in groups or with one another.
- A fire drill (or equivalent) disrupts the session.
- Scheduling mishaps throw the agenda off.
- The facilitator is triggered by someone's words or actions.
- A participant is triggered by something someone said or did and has a strong reaction.
- An argument ensues between participants.
- A resistant participant or group derails the agenda.
- A participant continues to be disruptive to the learning or group dynamics.

As we shared earlier in this chapter, how we see detours, and especially the ones that cause us the most worry, depends on our context and our experience. For the more experienced PD leader, some of these detours may be relatively easy to address. For the newer PD leader, all of these situations may feel challenging. We'll focus in this section on how we can plan for the inevitable detour. Table 7.2 guides facilitators through the process of making decisions in the face of potential detours. Take a look at the steps in the process before we delve into the more detailed explanations and examples that follow.

Step 1: Slow Down

When a PD session goes off course, the first step is to slow down. When we slow things down, we are doing several things: We are calming our bodies and minds and resetting our brains; we are giving ourselves some time to weigh possible responses; and we are being intentional about how to proceed. Rather than reacting abruptly, we are identifying how to be responsive and how to consider all the factors in play.

If something occurs while you're leading a PD that triggers an emotional response in you, take a break, if possible. This break gives you space to reboot yourself. Usually when you're triggered, your body gives you cues such as physical

Table 7.2 Steps to Facilitate Adaptively When Things Go Wrong

Step		Actions
1. Slow down.	→	Take a breath. Notice and name what you're feeling. Tend to any triggers that evoke a response in you.
2. Consider the context.	→	Consider who is in the room. Determine if any harm has occurred and who was harmed. Determine participants' levels of trust in you and levels of trust with each other. Consider what you can control and influence.
3. Assess the stakes.	→	On a scale of 1–10, determine the level of urgency the situation poses to trust, psychological safety, and learning.
4. Determine how to proceed.	→	Identify what is within your spheres of control and influence. Consider what actions you can take in the moment and what will take more time. Make a plan of action. Implement your plan (while letting go of the outcome).
5. Follow up.	→	Check in with participants, organizers, co-facilitators, and any others with whom follow-up is needed.

discomfort, tension, or a slight headache. You might also notice that the thoughts going through your mind become foggy or uncomfortable. Finally, your emotions will let you know that you're triggered (after all, to be triggered is to have strong, uncomfortable emotions). Perhaps you notice a surge of irritation or fear. When this happens, do the following (a variation of this activity can also be found in *The Art of Coaching Workbook*):

- *Notice that you're triggered and name it for yourself:* "I'm triggered!"
- *Pause to acknowledge your emotions.* Take a few deep breaths.
- *Investigate and tend to the emotions that are calling for your attention.* Typically this happens after the workshop, or perhaps during a break. Identify which emotions you're feeling and investigate what they are trying to tell you.

- *Ask yourself, "Who do I want to be?"* In any situation, how you show up is firmly within your sphere of control. Repeating a mantra or message, or returning to any intentions you set, can remind yourself who you want to be.

When we tend to our own needs, even briefly, it prepares us for the next steps in the process of responding to PD detours.

Step 2: Consider the Context

Your ability to respond will vary depending on your role, on who is hosting the PD, on the size of the group, on how well you know those you're leading, and on the severity of what occurred. Take into account what you can control and influence within the context, and consider the factors out of your control. When considering context, ask the following questions:

- How well do I know this group?
- How will group size affect my ability to intervene?
- How does this detour have an impact on the group? Is this something I should address right now, or can this wait?
- What can I control and influence in this situation?

Margaret was halfway through a grading workshop she led for her department. She had developed an online quiz for participants to complete, and the rest of the session was contingent on this quiz. A few minutes into the activity, Greg shared, "The quiz isn't working."

"Yeah," Wynn said, "I keep getting an error message." When Margaret checked the site, the quiz wasn't loading. Slightly rattled, Margaret took a breath and centered herself. She considered the context:

- She knew the group well; she led this department.
- The department contained six members, and this was a weekly department meeting.
- This detour needed to be addressed in the moment because the rest of the session relied on the quiz.
- Margaret couldn't fix the technology issue, but she considered a workaround for this glitch. She gave the group a five-minute break and wrote the quiz questions on the whiteboard.

Let's consider another example. Theo was a consultant working with the Hornbeam School District, and he was presenting on writing across the curriculum.

Communication was inconsistent between him and district liaisons. As he introduced the first activity, he found out half the participants hadn't received their books and didn't complete the pre-work. As he considered this piece of the context, he reflected on the following:

- He didn't know this group well at all, outside what the district liaisons shared.
- The group was comprised of 250 participants, and Theo was the sole facilitator.
- He decided to address this situation in the moment by acknowledging the situation. He knew he couldn't control the books not arriving, so he adapted the first activity by asking the group more general reflective questions about their experiences with teaching writing in their subject areas.

If you are an external provider who is leading a one-day PD at a district, you may be able to address what happens in the moment, but opportunities for follow-up or repairing any harm will be tougher. If you are leading PD at the site where you work, you know your context well; at the same time, your heightened awareness of interpersonal dynamics, your role, and the power dynamics may also make it trickier to respond. Weigh all the contextual factors you're aware of when deciding how to proceed.

Step 3: Assess the Stakes

Every detour—and each return to the planned route—is complex in its own unique way. As we shared earlier, the stakes of a situation are also a matter of perception. Assessing the stakes from your perspective will help you to determine the level of urgency of the situation and the additional factors involved for responding. It helps to ask: On a scale of 1–10, how urgent would you rate the situation?

When a facilitator runs short on time or their pacing is off, when the caterer arrives late, when the online quiz isn't working, or when the packet is missing the last half page of a reading, the stakes tend to feel lower—we rate these situations closer to 1–3 on the scale. In lower-stake situations, the facilitator can usually make a quick decision about how to proceed. They can cut or postpone an activity, abandon a tool that's not working, thank participants for their patience with catering, or summarize the contents on the page that was missing from the packet.

The stakes are higher when individual identities are involved. Consider the stakes when one participant says something explicitly hurtful to another like, "If you weren't always hungover, you'd know what we were talking about. . . ." Or when an influential group of participants derail the PD agenda in the middle of a session and say to the facilitator, their vice principal, "Some of us have been talking, and we don't agree with the direction you're taking with this curriculum." Either of these situations might fall higher on the urgency scale, typically between 7–10, and will require more deliberation about what to do next. We'll address that in the next section.

When identity-related harm happens, the stakes are always high. You may want to bypass steps 1–3 laid out in this process and go straight to step 4, *Determine how to proceed*. You also may want to draw on the questions listed in the "When Harm Happens" section earlier in this chapter. If you have co-facilitators, you can collaborate on what the best plan of action is. Depending on the severity of the harm, you may need to address some issues in the moment and plan for follow-up as necessary.

Step 4: Determine How to Proceed

Depending on the context and the stakes, this can be straightforward or more nuanced. You can't control how your plan will land. But if you've been deliberate about what's possible and taken the previous steps into account, your actions will be intentional, and the outcomes will have a good chance of working as you intend.

In Bright Morning workshops, we present participants with role-play scenarios so they can practice coaching and leadership moves in a range of situations. These role-plays give participants an opportunity to apply their knowledge and skills so that they leave the workshop ready to respond to real-life situations in their own PDs. As you read the following scenario, think about how you would have responded.

Damon, a project-based learning expert, was hired as a vice principal. This was his first PD of the year—part of a sequence to prepare teachers for an impending schedule change. Most teachers had not taught beyond an 80-minute class and were now learning how to teach six-hour-long blocks.

Damon framed today's training by saying, "As you know, shifting our schedule to these longer blocks is a big change for many of us. We want you to be well prepared and well supported in this process. As you'll see on your planning template, we're going to be using backwards design principles to plan and sequence these long blocks for your subject areas. By the end of the week, I'll ask that you share your plans with me so I can give feedback on areas that will work well for your students and areas that need strengthening. Before we get started, any clarifying questions on the purpose or what we're doing today?"

Anna smirked across the room at Reina and then raised her hand. "It sounds like this planning process is just a way to spy on our lessons and our teaching. I don't know why I have to submit my lesson plans to you; you're the only administrator who has ever asked me to do that. Others have just trusted me to do my job."

Right as Anna finished her comment, Reina interjected, "Yeah, I think we're all expert enough here to know how to do this on our own."

"Thanks for saying something. I agree," Sandy chimed in.

Damon was dumbfounded as several teachers started clapping. Half the room sat in silence, while the other half supported Anna and the others who spoke up.

Damon said, "Let me take in what I'm hearing; I need a minute to think."

Damon decided what moves to make. He could almost feel the wheels in his brain turning as he went through a few steps of his assessment and decision-making process:

- *Pause and check in with self*: Damon was stunned. He took a couple breaths.
- *Consider the context*: Damon was new to the school but thought he had good relationships with teachers. The pushback in this moment made him wonder how much trust there was between teachers and him. *You're the only administrator who has ever asked me to do that. Others have just trusted me. . .* played over in his head. He knew this schedule initiative was moving forward, but he overestimated the buy-in he had from staff. While he heard from only a few people, the claps, and affirmations in the room indicated the grumblings he heard were shared by others.
- *Assess the stakes*: This felt like an 7/10 for him. He didn't see this moment as dire, but he did see the need to address this issue.

What would you do in this situation?

Here's what happened:

Damon was initially stunned, and he could feel his stomach tighten. He realized he didn't have a good read on levels of trust, and he worried that just plowing ahead would further erode trust. He also knew that some people in the room had sat in silence. He needed data before moving forward. He also needed to not take this situation personally. He also wanted to decentralize his positional power and share *power-with* the group; to continue to build trust, he needed to meet people where they were.

Damon took a deep breath and said, "Okay, well it looks like this day didn't start as planned. Thank you to those who spoke up. I appreciate that this is a place where people can freely share their feedback in the moment. It's also not clear to me how everyone feels about this plan. I want to be transparent and name what's not going to change but where you might have some control and influence.

"What's not going to change: the new schedule. We'll be moving to long project-based learning blocks next fall. Where you have some influence: ways we can scaffold and support your learning to get there. I'll admit, I do want to see your plans. I hope I can assure you that this is not to spy on you, but to support you. I also realize I may need to earn your trust. And maybe there are some other ways we can collaborate on this process. Please take out a sheet of paper and write the following [Damon writes on the whiteboard]. . .please include your name, so I can differentiate the kinds of support people need:

- When I think about the impending schedule change and teaching long blocks, I feel. . .
- When I think about designing lessons for six-hour sessions, my degree of confidence is: Rate on a scale of 1–10, 10 being the most confident
- To feel successful in this shift, I need. . .
  - To do myself. . .
  - From my department. . .
  - From my VP. . .

When teachers finished, Damon gave them 15 minutes to talk in small groups while he reviewed what teachers wrote. When the group came back together, Damon reported back the themes he saw: There was a lot of fear and worry about the schedule change. Teachers worried about spending such a long period of time with students and about classroom management. There was also a lot of excitement. They were excited about building relationships with students and doing deep learning in longer blocks of time.

Damon then modeled a backward design process and invited teachers to create mock plans. They were not required to submit these plans, at least not yet.

Step 4 (*Determine how to proceed*) of Table 7.2 has many possibilities. Here are some tips to get started:

- *If participants are resistant, get curious about what's happening.* Damon took a pushback and reframed it as generous feedback.
- *Reframe the situation.* Ask yourself, "What are other ways to see this situation? What other perspectives might I take?"
- *Take a break.* It's okay to say, "I need a moment to think about that."
- *In moments where trust is low, redistribute power.* Ask yourself, "What might feel empowering to this group?"
- *If harm happens, follow the questions outlined in the "When Harm Happens" section earlier in this chapter.*
- *Take responsibility for your part and apologize if necessary.*

The process is the same no matter who causes the rupture. At some point, you might mess up. If and when you do, use the tips we just gave you and do what you can to move the learning forward. If you get too flustered or are disingenuous about your apology, you may lose the group entirely. The more authentically you can show up to these detours and be sincere, the more chance there is that you'll retain trust and be able to proceed with the learning.

At other times, the rupture will be caused by a participant. Sometimes people say and do things that are inappropriate, like curse at their colleagues or make a lewd joke about the facilitator or say a racist comment to an administrator—all of which rupture psychological safety. When lines are crossed by participants, it's important for you to acknowledge the breach, especially where there's potential for psychological harm. This could sound like saying, "What was just said is harmful. My responsibility is to create a safe enough space where everyone can learn, and it can't happen if you say things like that." It's okay to acknowledge what is inappropriate or unacceptable if it spares the group from further harm.

Whether you are an external or internal facilitator, sometimes cultures are toxic and people are not receptive to PD, no matter who is leading it. If you're an external facilitator, you may be asked to fix an organization's longstanding issues. If you're internal to an organization, you might be the punching bag in an unhealthy culture. When everything you've tried and all the skills you've developed aren't creating a way forward, it can be important to set a boundary. Know when you've hit your limit. When too many factors are out of your control when you've tried to share *power-with* and to see people from their place of strengths, and when you've tried to proceed with a plan only to keep getting derailed, when all that is true, it might be time to take care of yourself and plan how you want to exit the situation.

Step 5: Follow Up

Following up can bring closure after a detour. You can do this at the end of a PD or in later emails or conversations with participants and organizers. If harm occurred, consider taking the following steps:

- Process with a colleague. Talk about what happened in the workshop and how you might follow up. If the harm was identity-related, find someone who doesn't share some of your identity markers to process with and get a different perspective on the situation.
- Either approach the person who was harmed after the workshop or send a follow-up email. Say, "I noticed what happened in that situation, and I am taking

steps to address it. I can't guarantee this won't happen again, but I'll do what I can. If there is anything I can do to support you, or you want to process further with me, reach out when you're ready."

- Follow up with those who caused harm to address what happened.
- Reflect on your facilitation. Consider what you might do differently to prevent this situation from happening again.

Even a brief message checking in with participants can go a long way in building psychological safety and creating the conditions for learning.

In Damon's situation, he followed up with Anna and Reina after his PD session. Anna apologized, "My hackles went up when you asked us to submit our plans. At my last school, we had to submit them weekly. I guess I'm still affected by that."

Damon responded, "I get it. I was a teacher not that long ago."

The following semester, Anna was one of the biggest champions for teaching long blocks. She often met with Damon to discuss ways to improve her department's approach to lesson design so they could best meet the needs of students.

The five steps to address PD detours are not an exact science, nor will they make all challenges easier to navigate. Use these steps as you see fit. For example, you might find you want to assess the stakes first before doing anything else, or if you're a more seasoned facilitator, you might quickly make a decision about how to address a detour. Or perhaps all you can do is breathe before addressing any of these steps. Do what makes the most sense to meet the needs of the moment. And slow down.

Reimagining What's Possible

Let's pull back the curtain one more time. There have been multiple times when we needed to adapt our facilitation in a workshop to address a tense moment between participants, ask a different coaching question in a role-play demonstration, or apologize for a misstep. Participants often say, "I appreciate how you handled that." More often, they ask, "How did you know how to do that?" While it might seem that we are fortresses of strength and courage when we deal with challenges, it's not magic. We know ourselves; hone our skills; share our vulnerabilities and play to our strengths; are intentional about how we address detours; take risks and hold lightly to what happens, knowing we can only control what we can control.

The strategies outlined in this chapter aren't just for hard moments in workshops. They also are for hard moments in our work and personal lives. How you respond to a grumpy teacher may be the same way you respond to a grumpy sibling. How you address harm between colleagues may be the same way you repair harm with a dear friend. You may need to remember your strengths and what you value. How you respond when a fire alarm goes off in your workshop may be the same way you respond to vacation plans that get canceled. Remember: Slow down, take care of yourself, consider context, assess the stakes, and determine a path forward. The habit of adaptive facilitation, like all the habits in this book, can be learned, practiced, and refined.

Once again, breathe.
You've got this.

Before You Go

Pause and Process:
- Recall a moment in a PD session when things took a detour. If you could go back and replay that moment, what would you do differently based on what you learned in this chapter?
- Imagine you have the best co-facilitator who writes you sticky notes with encouraging words. What would you want those notes to say to remind you that you're amazing?

Remember:
- Slow down.
- Repair harm.
- Your power as a facilitator comes from knowing yourself.

CONCLUSION

In 2016, Elena spent a week in Nairobi, Kenya, leading a workshop on coaching and learning about education in Kenya. One afternoon, she observed a PD session for school leaders. As the 20 weary educators ambled into the training room after lunch, Elena was reminded of the many teachers and administrators to whom she'd presented PD in the United States. Perhaps it was the big lunch they'd just been treated to, Elena thought, as she registered her own lack of energy.

The similarities between the two contexts abruptly ended as the Kenyan educators rose from the seats they'd momentarily rested in and began to sing and clap. As the pace of the call and response increased and the rhythm accelerated, the Kenyans began to sway their bodies. Everyone sang, and everyone moved. When the song wound down, the administrator who had led the singing said, "Let us pray," and, still standing, the educators bowed their heads.

Later, when Elena debriefed with the facilitators, she was curious about the opening. "Why did that happen? What was the reason?" she'd asked. Their response was nonchalant. "All PD starts like that in Kenya," one of the trainers explained.

In the years since that experience, Elena has often recalled those first remarkable five minutes and the harmonies that filled the classroom. And, while the content of the ensuing session was relevant and engaging, the content may not have accounted for the fact that energy was notably high throughout—despite it being a Friday afternoon after a long week and a heavy meal. Elena has wondered, many times: What would it be like if all PD sessions started with song and dance? With an opportunity for folks to connect with what's essential in us? To our life's purpose? This, of course, would look different in a country as diverse as the United States, where we don't bring religion into public schools or the workplace, and where singing or dancing at work is not a cultural norm. But what might we do that could bring us together and energize us at the outset of a learning session?

While PD sessions in the United States (or many other countries) might never begin with singing and dancing, they can start with storytelling, intention setting, a grounding meditation, or a moment to anchor in one's core values. These kinds of activities bring adults together, anchor us in purpose, and allow us to connect to our best selves. We may not share the same cultural practices as our Kenyan counterparts, but we absolutely can generate the kind of energy and connection that their melodies created in that classroom of 20 tired educators.

Audre Lorde's wisdom has long guided us, so these words of hers are the epigraph for this book: "Tomorrow belongs to those of us who conceive of it as belonging to everyone; who lend the best of ourselves to it, and with joy."

Throughout this book, we've circled around questions raised by Audre Lorde's words: What might be possible for children if adults had more opportunities to generate connection, self-awareness, and joy as part of their professional development? What might be possible if PD sessions felt inclusive? How might transformative PD enable us to come together and serve children in the way that we truly want to? And over and over, we've asked explicitly, what might be possible if PD felt more celebratory?

In addition to raising a whole lot of questions, we have given you some important answers. We've laid out seven habits that can transform PD. We've pulled back the curtain on our practice as facilitators and revealed the specific moves we make, the beliefs from which we work, and the ways of being that we embody to create transformative PD sessions. We've shown you how to create the conditions in which people learn. As you can see, there's no magic involved—just a whole lot of intentionality, presence, purpose, and a firm conviction that we can create a more just and equitable world.

That said, here's one final peek behind the curtain at a practice that Elena has never shared publicly. On mornings when Elena facilitates PD, she begins her day in meditation and contemplation. As part of this practice, she visualizes her ancestors standing in the back and on the sides of the room in which she'll present, and she imagines them cheering her on. Her mother and grandmother are in the front and center and are flanked by many ancestors whose names she doesn't know and whose faces she doesn't recognize. But they show up to witness Elena's leadership and they radiate pride. Elena also imagines the participants' ancestors in the learning space and their happiness at seeing their descendants learning. Elena believes that our ancestors wanted better lives for us and that they saw learning as a way to create those better lives; she believes they celebrate our growth.

When Elena steps into the conference room, library, or training hall, she imagines all those ancestors on the periphery of the space. This helps Elena remember that she's part of a lineage of people who have contributed to transforming the world, and it provides a sense of support. Sometimes presenting can feel lonely and scary, but this meditation helps Elena remember that she's not alone. So while Elena doesn't use magic in her workshops, maybe there is something else behind the curtain— maybe the power of her imagination, or maybe the support of the ancestors.

In this anecdote, please read our final suggestion: an invitation to access your inner sources of strength or a connection to something ineffable—and then to consider how that might manifest as a practice to prepare you for presenting or to guide you in rocky moments. Perhaps it's not necessary that we share the same beliefs; perhaps we just need to tap into the power of love and kindness and bring that energy into the PD room. What might be possible for ourselves, for participants, and for children if we could do this?

May the PD you lead be purposeful, joyful, and transformative. May the PD you facilitate contribute to creating the conditions in which adults can learn and every child gets what they need and deserve in school in every day. May your PD heal and transform the world.

Before You Go

Pause and Process:
- Flip through this book and create a list of your 10 biggest takeaways. Then narrow that list down to five, and finally, to three. Write those top-three takeaways in colored markers on a big sheet of paper and post it near your desk.
- What's an analogy for how you'd like to experience PD—both as a facilitator and as a participant? If a party resonates for you—what is it about a party that you'd want to experience? Perhaps another analogy would help you understand your

desires—maybe you want PD to feel like an adventure? Like attending a religious service? Like a dinner party? Explore symbolism to more deeply understand what you want to create as a facilitator of learning.

- What have you learned about yourself as a learner through reading this book? How has this book helped you identify the conditions in which your learning happens?
- Who do you want to be as a facilitator? How do you want people to experience you? How do you want those who attend your sessions to remember you and the learning you facilitate?

Remember:
- Less is more: we need less new content and more time for processing and practicing.
- PD can feel celebratory, energizing, and uplifting.
- The purpose of PD is for adults to learn so that we can meet the needs of the children and communities we serve.

APPENDIX A

THE CORE EMOTIONS

(Adapted from *Wise Mind Living* by Erin Olivo)

Core Emotion	Fear	Anger	Sadness	Shame
Common terms for this emotion	Agitated	Aggravated	Alienated	Besmirched
	Alarmed	Agitated	Anguished	Chagrined
	Anxious	Annoyed	Bored	Contemptuous
	Apprehensive	Antagonized	Crushed	(of self)
	Concerned	Bitter	Defeated	Contrite
	Desperate	Contemptuous	Dejected	Culpable
	Dismayed	(other than for	Depressed	Debased
	Dread	self)	Despairing	Degraded
	Fearful	Contentious	Despondent	Disapproving
	Frightened	Contrary	Disappointed	Disdainful
	Horrified	Cranky	Discouraged	Disgraced
	Hysterical	Cruel	Disheartened	Disgusted (at
	Impatient	Destructive	Dismayed	self)
	Jumpy	Displeased	Dispirited	Dishonored
	Nervous	Enraged	Displeased	Disreputable
	Panicked	Exasperated	Distraught	Embarrassed
	Scared	Explosive	Down	Guilty
	Shocked	Frustrated	Dreary	Hateful
	Shy	Furious	Forlorn	Humbled
	Tense	Hateful	Gloomy	Humiliated
	Terrified	Hostile	Grief-stricken	Improper
	Timid	Impatient	Hopeless	Infamous
	Uncertain	Indignant	Hurt	Invalidated
	Uneasy	Insulated	Insecure	Mortified
	Worried	Irate	Isolated	Regretful
		Irritable	Lonely	Remorseful
		Irritated	Melancholic	Repentant
		Mad	Miserable	Reproachful
		Mean	Mopey	Rueful
		Outraged	Morose	Scandalized
		Resentful	Neglected	Scornful
		Scornful	Oppressed	Sinful
		Spiteful	Pessimistic	Stigmatized
		Urgent	Pitiful	
		Vengeful	Rejected	
			Somber	
			Sorrowful	
			Tragic	
			Unhappy	

Core Emotion	Jealousy	Disgust	Happiness	Love
Common terms for this emotion	Competitive Covetous Deprived Distrustful Envious Greedy Grudging Jealous Overprotective Petty Possessive Resentful Rivalrous	Appalled Dislike Grossed out Insulted Intolerant Nauseated Offended Put off Repelled Repulsed Revolted Revulsion Shocked Sickened Turned off	Agreeable Amused Blissful Bubbly Cheerful Content Delighted Eager Ease Elated Engaged Enjoyment Enthusiastic Euphoric Excited Exhilarated Flow Glad Gleeful Glowing Gratified Harmonious Hopeful Interested Joyful Jubilant Lighthearted Meaningful Merry Optimistic Peaceful Pleasure Pride Proud Relieved Satisfied Thrilled Triumphant	Acceptance Admiration Adoring Affectionate Allegiance Attached Attraction Belonging Caring Compassionate Connected Dependent Desire Devoted Empathetic Faithful Friendship Interested Kind Liking Passionate Protective Respectful Sympathetic Tender Trust Vulnerable Warm

APPENDIX B

NONVIOLENT COMMUNICATION'S UNIVERSAL HUMAN NEEDS

In the nonviolent communication model, universal human needs are often grouped into four categories: subsistence and security, freedom, connection, and meaning, and each has subcategories. This is not an exhaustive or definite list.

Subsistence and Security

Physical Sustenance

Air
Food
Health
Movement
Physical safety
Rest
Shelter
Touch
Water

Security

Consistency
Emotional safety
Order/structure
Peace
Stability
Trusting

Freedom

Autonomy

Choice
Independence
Power
Responsibility

Relaxation

Humor
Joy
Play
Pleasure
Rejuvenation

Connection

Affection

Appreciation
Attention
Closeness
Companionship
Harmony

Love
Nurturing
Support
Sexual expression
Tenderness
Warmth

To Matter

Acceptance
Care
Compassion
Consideration
Empathy
Kindness
Mutual recognition
Respect
To be heard and seen
To be known and understood
To be trusted
Understanding others

Community

Belonging
Communication
Cooperation
Equality
Inclusion
Mutuality
Participation
Partnership
Self-expression
Sharing

Meaning

Sense of Self

Authenticity
Competence
Creativity
Dignity
Growth
Healing
Honesty
Integrity
Self-acceptance
Self-care
Self-connection
Self-knowledge

Understanding

Awareness
Clarity
Discovery
Learning
Sense-making

Meaning

Aliveness
Challenge
Contribution
Effectiveness
Exploration
Integration
Purpose

Transcendence

Beauty
Celebration
Flow
Hope
Inspiration
Mourning
Peace (internal)
Presence

APPENDIX C

WHAT-WHY-HOW AGENDA TEMPLATE

Title of workshop goes here.
Facilitator name(s) and their pronouns go here.

INTENDED OUTCOMES *Participants will...*
Include outcomes here. Put your verbs in all caps as a reminder of what
participants will do.
Outcome 2
Outcome 3
Outcome 4

Agreements or Norms
If you have any community agreements, include them here.

Agenda			
Time	**What**	**Why**	**How** **Materials**
Put time stamps in this space, either the literal time or how long a section might take	**Topic Headings Go Here** **For this first heading, it's helpful to have an opening segment.** Subtopics go here (stick to about 3–5 per section). Shift topics about every 30–45 minutes. Use just enough words to explain the subtopic, but be concise.	*Purpose goes here. Start each segment with the word "To…" and briefly explain why you're addressing each topic.*	List all the ways participants will learn: facilitator sharing, small-group sharing, protocols, drawing, individual writing, movement, etc.
			Include any materials participants need in this section here: readings, handouts, links, surveys, specific activities in your learning packets.
	Topic: Your first main topic goes here; include as many rows as you need for topics you'll address. Subtopic Subtopic	*To…*	How participants will learn
			Materials
	BREAK: Depending on the timing of your session, you'll want to take a break every hour to hour and a half.		
	Topic: Subtopic Subtopic	*To…*	How participants will learn
			Materials
	Closing Subtopic Subtopic	*To…*	How participants will reflect and transfer their learning
			Materials Materials Include some type of feedback form here as well

APPENDIX D

STRUCTURES FOR VIRTUAL LEARNING

Learning Structure	Technology Consideration or Application	Purpose
Opening hospitality comments (restrooms, snack breaks, nametags. . .)	• Tech check with nonverbal controls • Orientation to platform features • Opening question in the chat or on a polling tool (e.g., Poll Everywhere or Slido)	• Help people feel "at home" in the space, take care of basic needs
Icebreakers	• Sound check • "Humanizing" question on a poll or in the chat • Something real and physical as an opener (e.g., hold up something that's "alive" in your workspace, something unexpected on your desk, the drink you have on hand and drink together. . .)	• Get everyone's voice in the room, build connection

(Continued)

(Continued)

Learning Structure	Technology Consideration or Application	Purpose
Note-taking	• Blank document or table • Chat boxes • Shared collaboration board (e.g., Jamboard, Padlet) • Connect an iPad for live scribing/drawing	• Gather information from participants visually • Crowdsource information in one place
Facilitator sharing/direct instruction	• Visual cues on the screen: color, borders, icons, arrows, frames • Annotation tools • Spotlight video	• Focus attention of the group on the task at hand
Individual processing time	• Writable template to download or copy • Dedicated space in the document or on a shared whiteboard • All participants on mute • Pre-work (complete in advance)	• Individual worksheets and templates • Quiet time for internal processors
Pair or small-group conversations	• Breakout rooms • Chat boxes • Pre-work (meet or complete in advance)	• Interaction, full involvement, process thinking and learning in conversation
Large-group work	• Writable template to download or copy • Dedicated space in the document or on a shared whiteboard • Breakout rooms • Pre-work (complete in advance)	• Provide structure for group conversations
Energizers, movement, and breaks	• Bring your own fidget toy • On-screen polling questions • Karaoke, clapping, stretches, scavenger hunts, races • Stand and stretch breaks • Encourage bio breaks on your own • Take "real" breaks every two hours	• Encourages focus and attention when sitting for long periods
Attention getters and checks for understanding	• Raising hands, thumbs up, reaction buttons, shaking head, or other nonverbals	• Get attention • Provide feedback • React

APPENDIX E

CHECKLIST FOR ATTENDING TO THE DETAILS

Long-Term Planning Checklist	
Context	☐ Know your audience: understand demographics, roles, needs of the group, and larger contextual factors that can support the planning phase.
Partnership	☐ Identify all the partners necessary to execute PD: site leaders, hosts, co-facilitators, technology coordinators, custodial staff or security who might be on-site, meal service providers, or caterers. ☐ Clarify roles and responsibilities to ensure everyone is clear about what they need to accomplish and by when. ☐ If co-facilitating, build relationships through understanding core values, strengths, identities, roles, and responsibilities for planning.
Location	☐ Confirm details of the location, the size and capacity of the space, seating arrangements, technology, accessibility for those with mobility needs. ☐ Determine how you (if applicable) and participants can access the location (transportation and parking, if applicable). ☐ Determine whether signage is needed to direct participants. ☐ Identify what setup is needed to get the space ready.

Resources	☐ Prepare materials: pre-work, packets, or handouts.
	☐ Consider tools and supplies participants will need to supplement their learning.
Communication	☐ Send a message to participants with all the essential details of your PD.

Short-Term Planning Checklist

Context	☐ Check site website and local news for any events that might have an impact on participants.
Partnership	☐ Connect with host/site leaders and co-facilitators (if applicable), technology support, and meal providers.
	☐ Confirm final details and do a run-through of the PD.
Location	☐ Arrive the day before if you're traveling.
	☐ Preview the space if you are able to.
Resources	☐ Review and proofread agendas, slides, handouts, and any additional resources.
	☐ Make sure any web links work.
	☐ Get supplies you need.
	☐ Print any materials.
Communication	☐ Send a brief reminder message with key details (pre-work, accessing location).

The Day-Of Checklist: Presentation

Before	☐ Mentally prepare yourself for the day through visualization and personal getting ready rituals.
	☐ Gather your materials.
	☐ Arrive early and do one final rehearsal.
	☐ Greet participants and build relationships.
During	☐ Use opening routines to usher participants into the learning.
	☐ Project confidence and care for the group.
	☐ Foster and nurture relationships.
	☐ Circulate during small-group time.
	☐ Model leadership and learning.
After	☐ Use closing routines to transition participants out of the learning.
	☐ Share appreciations.
	☐ Ask for feedback.
	☐ Plan for next steps.

Closing Checklist	
Follow-Up	☐ Clean up and leave the space better than you found it. ☐ Celebrate and appreciate your hard work. ☐ Reflect on the experience and review feedback. ☐ Send your final message to participants to close out the experience and identify next steps.

APPENDIX F

RESOURCES FOR FURTHER LEARNING

We've decided to keep this short and provide an annotated guide for extended learning and inspiration.

Our Favorite Book on Gatherings

Parker, Priya. *The Art of Gathering: How We Meet and Why it Matters*. New York: Riverhead Books, 2018.

Dismantling Racism and Mitigating the Dominant Culture

Okun, Tema. "(divorcing) White Supremacy Culture: Coming Home to Who We Really Are." White Supremacy Culture, https://www.whitesupremacyculture.info.

For Developing Affinity Spaces

Baum, Joel, and Kim Westheimer, et al. "Making Space." Learning for Justice, https://www.learningforjustice.org/magazine/summer-2015/making-space.

Land Acknowledgments

"A Guide to Indigenous Land Acknowledgment." Native Governance Center, 27 Oct. 2021, https://nativegov.org/news/a-guide-to-indigenous-land-acknowledgment/.

For Selecting Activities in Your Design Process

Greenberg, Sarah Stein. *Creative Acts for Curious People: How to Think, Create, and Lead in Unconventional Ways.* Ten Speed Press. 2021.

"Protocols." National School Reform Faculty, 9 Mar. 2021, https://nsrfharmony.org/protocols/.

"Protocols." School Reform Initiative, https://www.schoolreforminitiative.org/protocols/.

Macanufo, James, and Sunni Brown. *Gamestorming: A Playbook for Innovators, Rulebreakers, and Changemakers.* O'Reilly Media, 2010.

"Project Zero's Thinking Routine Toolbox." PZ's Thinking Routines Toolbox | Project Zero, http://www.pz.harvard.edu/thinking-routines.

Restorative Practices: For Building Community and Repairing Harm

Costello, Bob, and Joshua Wachtel and Ted Wachtel. *The Restorative Practices Handbook: For Teachers, Disciplinarians, and Administrators, Second Edition.* Bethlehem, PA: The International Institute for Restorative Practices, 2019.

GLOSSARY

Affinity groups A group of people linked by a common interest or purpose. An affinity group is a designated "safe space," where everyone in that group shares a particular identity. This identity can be based on race, gender, sexual orientation, language, nationality, physical/mental ability, socioeconomic class, family structure, religion, etc. Affinity groups can be a place for historically marginalized or represented people in a community to come together to feel less isolated and more connected.

Agency The capacity to act autonomously and make your own choices; free will or self-determination.

Asynchronous learning A general term used to describe forms of education, instruction, and learning that is not delivered in the same place or at the same time.

BIPOC An acronym used to refer to Black, Indigenous, and people of color.

Blended learning The practice of using both online and in-person/synchronous learning experiences when teaching or delivering PD. Also called hybrid learning and mixed-mode learning.

Coaching up Engaging with a superior through a coaching stance, in which you see them as learners and you ask questions that provoke reflection.

Collaboration board An interactive discussion board that allows participants to post text and images to a shared online tool. Examples include Padlet, Nearpod, Miro, Jamboard, and other online collaboration board platforms.

Crowdsourcing The practice of obtaining information or input into a task or project by enlisting the input of a large number of people. This input is shared via survey or using poll-taking tools.

Dominant culture The cultural values, beliefs, and practices that are assumed to be the most common and influential within a given society.

Emotional intelligence The capacity to recognize our own feelings and those of others and to engage with our own feelings and those of others in a healthy way.

Equity Every child gets what they need in our schools—regardless of where they come from, what they look like, who their parents are, what their temperament is, or what they show up knowing or not knowing. Every child gets what he, she, or they need every day in order to have all the skills and tools to pursue whatever they want after leaving our schools, to live a fulfilling life. Equity is about outcomes and experiences—for *every child, every day*.

Equity check Time set aside in a meeting or a workshop to pause and consider how the meeting/learning experience is addressing issues of equity.

Ethnicity A group of people who share a common or distinct ancestry and cultural practices, generally according to a geographic region and often with psychological attachment.

Gradual Release of Responsibility Also known as "scaffolded" instruction. When a learner is in the Zone of Proximal Development, if they are provided with appropriate assistance and tools—the scaffolding—then they can accomplish the skill. Eventually the scaffolding can be removed, the responsibility can be released, and the learner can complete the task independently.

Implicit (unconscious) bias An unconsciously held set of associations about a social group. Can result in the attribution of particular qualities to all individuals from that group, also known as stereotyping. Implicit biases are the product of learned associations and social conditioning. They usually begin at a young age, and these biases do not necessarily align with personal identity. It's possible to unconsciously associate positive *or* negative traits with one's own race, gender, or another identity marker.

Latinx A person of Latin American origin or descent (used as a gender-neutral or nonbinary alternative to Latino or Latina).

Learning organization An organization in which everyone is committed to their learning, everyone is expected to learn, and everyone learns.

Mental model or mindset Our beliefs, assumptions, and ideas about how things work. Mental models are often hidden, even from ourselves, and are made up of our values and beliefs and a series of assumptions about how the world works.

Microaggressions Statements, actions, or incidents regarded as an instance of indirect, subtle, or unintentional discrimination against members of a historically marginalized group.

Normative culture/White-dominant culture Defines what is considered "normal" by creating the standard for judging values, privileging individuals over groups, and assigning a higher value to some ways of behaving and knowing than others without considering the broad social-cultural differences that exist across communities and identifying markers. For example, white-dominant culture presupposes that the thoughts, beliefs, and actions of white people are superior to people of color.

Positional power The power or authority that is assigned to a person because of their position or rank in an organization.

Privilege Refers to gaining benefits, advantages, and rights by default at the expense of others, because one belongs to the perceived "us," "normal," or "natural" state of the "mainstream" or dominant culture. Privilege allows for active, persistent exclusion and devaluation of "them," those who are "othered" or "marginalized."

Professional development (PD) A transformative process in which learners are actively engaged and for which the aim is to explore and expand behaviors, beliefs, and ways of being; a learning process that results in a change of practice.

Psychological safety A shared belief in a group or organization that people can make mistakes, ask questions, share opinions, and offer feedback without facing rejection or repercussions. Psychological safety is considered a prerequisite for true learning to occur.

Race A socially constructed phenomenon, based on the erroneous assumption that physical differences such as skin color, hair color and texture, and facial (or other physical) features are related to intellectual, moral, and cultural superiority. Although race is a socially constructed concept, it has significant impact on the lives of people of color.

Racism A system of oppression that emerges from beliefs that one race is superior to another based on biological characteristics. Racism is fueled by the ideology of white supremacy, which designates white people as superior to people of color. In racist systems, white and light-skinned people are granted unearned privileges or advantages by society just because of their race. Social attitudes, actions, and structures that oppress, exclude, limit, and discriminate against individuals and groups.

Restorative practices Restorative practices build trust and relationships proactively and repair harm when it happens.

Social capital The value of social networks; the links and bonds formed through friendships and acquaintances.

Sociopolitical identity A person's identity is constructed around a number of markers that could include race/ethnicity, gender, socioeconomic status, sexual orientation, (dis) abilities, and religion. Your sense of who you are is based on your group memberships.

Sphere of influence The idea that there are things that are out of your control, things that are within your control, and things that you can influence.

Synchronous learning All types of learning in which learner(s) and instructor(s) are in the same place, at the same time, in order for learning to take place.

White privilege Unearned, and largely unacknowledged, advantages based on race, which can be observed both systemically and individually. Peggy McIntosh coined the term and described it as "an invisible weightless knapsack of special provisions, assurances, tools, maps, guides, codebooks, passports, visas, clothes, compass, emergency gear, and blank checks." We can also have unearned privilege related to class, religion, ethnicity, sexual orientation, age, or ability.

White supremacy The belief system that underlies the concept of whiteness—a historically based, institutionally perpetuated system of exploitation and oppression of continents, nations, and individuals of color by white individuals and nations of the European continent for the purpose of maintaining and defending a system of wealth, power, and privilege.

Whiteness A social construction that has created a racial hierarchy that has shaped all the social, cultural, political, educational, and economic institutions of society. Whiteness is linked to domination and is a form of race privilege invisible to white people who are not conscious of its power.

Zone of Proximal Development The difference between what a learner can do without help and what they can do with help. It is the range of abilities that they can perform with assistance but cannot yet perform independently. A learner needs "scaffolding" in order to move out of the ZPD.

REFERENCES

Aguilar, Elena. *Coaching for Equity: Conversations that Change Practice*. San Francisco: Jossey-Bass, 2020.

Aguilar, Elena. *Onward: Cultivating Emotional Resilience in Educators*. San Francisco: Jossey-Bass, 2018.

Aguilar, Elena. *The Art of Coaching: Effective Strategies for School Transformation*. San Francisco: Jossey-Bass, 2013.

Aguilar, Elena. *The Art of Coaching Teams: Building Resilient Communities that Transform Schools*. San Francisco: Jossey Bass, 2016.

Aguilar, Elena. *The Art of Coaching Workbook: Tools to Make Every Conversation Count*. San Francisco: Jossey-Bass, 2020.

Broadwell, M. M. "Teaching for learning (XVI)" 20 February 1969. brown, adrienne maree. *Emergent Strategy: Shaping Change, Changing Worlds*. Reprint edition. AK Press, 2017.

Brown, Tim. *Change by Design, Revised and Updated: How Design Thinking Transforms Organizations and Inspires Innovation*. Harper Business, 2019.

Costello, Bob, and Joshua Wachtel and Ted Wachtel. *The Restorative Practices Handbook: For Teachers, Disciplinarians, and Administrators, Second Edition*. Bethlehem, PA: The International Institute for Restorative Practices, 2019.

Darling-Hammond, L., R. C., Wei, A. Andree, N. Richardson, and S. Orphanos. "State of the Profession: Study Measures Professional Development." *Journal of Staff Development*, 2009, 30(2), 42–50.

Duke, Nell. K., and P. David Pearson. Effective Practices for Developing Reading Comprehension. *What Research Has to Say About Reading Instruction* A. E. Farstup and S. J. Samuels, 205–242. Newark, DE: International Reading Association, 2002.

Edmondson, A. C. *Teaming. How Organizations Learn, Innovate, and Compete in the Knowledge Economy*. 2012. New Jersey: Wiley. 2012.

Foucault, M. *The History of Sexuality, Volume 1: An Introduction*. New York, NY: Vintage, 1978: 95-96.

Freire, Paolo. *We Make the Road by Walking: Conversations on Education and Social Change*. Philadelphia: Temple University Press, 1990.

Garvin, D. "Building a Learning Organization." *Harvard Business Review,* 1993, 71(4), 78–91.

Garvin, D., A. Edmondson and F. Gino. "Is Yours a Learning Organization?" *Harvard Business Review,* March 2008, 109–116.

Ginott, Haim G. *Teacher and Child: A Book for Parents and Teachers*. Harper Collins, 1976.

Greenberg, Sarah Stein. *Creative Acts for Curious People: How to Think, Create, and Lead in Unconventional Ways*. Ten Speed Press. 2021.

Guskey, Thomas R. "Does It Make a Difference? Evaluating Professional Development." *Educational Leadership*, 59(6), pp. 45–51. 2002.

Hall, E. *Beyond Culture*. New York, NY: Anchor, 2007.

Heen, Sheila, and Doug Stone. *Thanks for the Feedback: The Science and Art of Receiving Feedback Well*. Viking, 2014. *Indigenous Peacemaking Initiative*, 4 Oct. 2021, https://peacemaking.narf.org/.

Kelley, R. D. G. *Freedom Dreams: The Black Radical Imagination*. Boston: Beacon Press, 2003.

King, Ruth. *Mindful of Race: Transforming Racism from the Inside Out*. Boulder: Sounds True, 2018.

Lipmanowicz, Henri, and Keith McCandless. *The Surprising Power of Liberating Structures: Simple Rules to Unleash a Culture of Innovation*. Liberating Structures Press, 2014.

Macanufo, James, and Sunni Brown. *Gamestorming: A Playbook for Innovators, Rulebreakers, and Changemakers*. O'Reilly Media, 2010.

New York Times. Google Study on Teams. Retrieved from https://www.nytimes.com/2016/02/28/magazine/what-google-learned-from-its-quest-to-build-the-perfect-team.html

Oakley, Barbara, and Terrence Sejnowski. *Learning How to Learn*. New York, Penguin, 2018.

Palmer, Parker J. *The Courage to Teach: Exploring the Inner Landscape of a Teacher's Life*, 20th Anniversary Edition. Jossey-Bass, 2017.

"Project Zero's Thinking Routine Toolbox." *PZ's Thinking Routines Toolbox | Project Zero*, http://www.pz.harvard.edu/thinking-routines.

Selassie, Sebene. *You Belong: A Call for Connection*. HarperOne, 2020.

Sims Bishop, R. (1990). Mirrors, windows, and sliding glass doors. Perspectives, 1(3), ix–xi.

Sue, Derald Wing, and Lisa Spanierman. *Microaggressions in Everyday Life (2nd Ed.)*. Wiley: 2020.

Vella, J. *Learning to Listen, Learning to Teach: The Power of Dialogue in Educating Adults*. Jossey-Bass: New Jersey, 2002.

Zak, P. "Why Your Brain Loves Good Storytelling." *Harvard Business Review,* October 2014. Retrieved from https://hbr.org/2014/10/why-your-brain-loves-good-storytelling

INDEX

surveys
  categories, 173
  feedback surveys, design, 149
  learner survey, 147, 148t
  participant data, 146–149
  usage, 33
synchronous learning, 265

T

takeaways, usage, 160
teacher expertise, honoring, 37
Teaching Fundamentals workshop, 172–173
Team Strategy Sprint (Bright Morning), 173
technology strengths, knowledge, 220–221
time, assessment/allocation, 154–158, 155t–158t
title slide, sample, 189f
Tolle, Eckhart, 43
topics, prioritization, 34–35
training
  framing, 232
  goal, 9
transcendence (Universal Human Need), 251
transformation, 240
  conditions, support, 181
  definition, 10
  engagement, 26–27
  individual/collective transformation, 39
  timeline, 181–182
transformational leadership workshop, design, 159
transformative learning
  experience, recall, 2–3
  occurrence, teacher creation, 18

transformative professional development (transformative PD), 9–11
  delivery, emotions (impact), 51–59
  design/delivery, 97
  facilitation, 58
  principles, 18, 141
transparency, modeling, 6
Triangle, Circle, Square process, 44
triggers, 59–64
  identification, 60–61
trust
  building, 211
  levels, 215

U

unconscious bias, 77, 222, 264
unconscious competence, 13, 138
unconscious incompetence, 137
understanding (Universal Human Need), 250
unhealed trauma, 74
Universal Human Needs, 122–123, 247–251
unmet needs, 114–115, 116

V

value, communication, 59
virtual design, considerations, 170
virtual learning
  considerations, 191
  preparation, 202–203
  structures, 255–256
virtual PD, adult learning, 139–141
virtual professional development (virtual PD), self-awareness, 220–221
virtual settings, power (navigation), 116

visualization, usage, 2–3, 43
volunteering, enjoyment, 40
vulnerability, 57
    modeling, 6

W

What-Why-How agenda, 151–154,
        253–254
    facilitator sharing, 39
    template, usage, 143
White-dominant culture, 264
White fragility, 77–78
Whiteness, 215, 265, 266
White privilege, 265
White supremacy, 265–266
    culture, 78
whole-group discussions, invitation,
        59

Why, sharing, 64–65
will, addressing, 37
Wise Mind Living (Olivo), 244
workshop
    feedback, 219
    handouts, usage, 188
    highlights, sharing, 206
    opening, 203

Y

you, 15. *See also* Purpose, Audience,
        Routines, Technique, You
    defining, 18–20
You Belong (Selassie), 145, 172

Z

Zone of Proximal
        Development, 264, 266